Financial Times

PERSONAL FINANCE LIBRARY

UNDERSTANDING

MUTUAL FUNDS

YOUR NO NONSENSE

EVERYDAY GUIDE

BY STEVEN G. KELMAN

D0466028

Canadian Cataloguing in Publication Data

Kelman, Steven G. (Steven Gershon), 1945
    Understanding Mutual Funds
(Personal finance library) Canadian ed.
Earlier ed. published under title: Mutual fund advisor.

ISBN 0-14-010605-7

    1. Mutual funds - Canada.   I. Title.
    II. Title: Mutual fund advisor   III. Series.

HG5154.5.K45 1988   332.63'27   C88-095023-4

Printed and bound in Canada

CONTENTS

INTRODUCTION

INVESTOR INTEREST IN MUTUAL FUNDS HAS SOARED IN RECENT YEARS as more Canadians have discovered the potential for profit in funds. Between the summer of 1982 and October 1987, the value of funds held by Canadians jumped sevenfold to about $35 billion and the number of Canadians investing in funds has climbed from a few hundred thousand to about 1.5 million. The October stock-market crash cooled the investor ardor somewhat and, indeed, the value of mutual fund sales in the eight months since the decline is running at less than half its pre-crash level with sales barely exceeding redemptions. At the end of June the value of funds held by Canadians was about $30 billion. Many investors in growth funds have suffered minor declines on paper from the 1987 highs. Yet they have excellent longer-term returns, which in general exceed significantly what they would have earned holding guaranteed investments. (Of course those investors who had the courage to buy at the October bottoms were up more than 20% in some cases by the end of June.)

As well, the future looks bright for the fund industry and fund investors. The number of funds offered over the past year has climbed from about 350 to more than 460. More financial service companies, including banks and trust companies, are entering the fund business. And people who have never considered anything other than bank or trust company guaranteed investments are looking at funds.

The reasons are simple. Mutual funds offer professional investment management at an affordable price. They offer safety through diversified portfolios. There is a broad choice of funds to meet virtually every investment objective. Finally, funds have given investors excellent returns, better than most individuals would have been able to achieve on their own.

But choosing the right fund or funds from the more than 460 offered by fund dealers, stockbrokers, banks, trust companies, insurance companies, or by fund managers directly, can be confusing. First, buyers must consider the objectives of a fund and whether those objectives are compatible with their own investment goals. Second, they must determine how a fund has performed in recent years.

Understanding Mutual Funds explains, in detail, the aspects of the fund business that you need to understand to make a wise buying decision. Understanding Mutual Funds, for instance, shows you how fund managers manage their funds, how you can match funds to your specific investment objectives and your age, even how to evaluate a fund salesperson.

It also contains essential information on the top 100 mutual funds in Canada to help you determine exactly which funds might best meet your personal investment objectives. A lot has happened in the world of Canadian mutual funds since Mutual Fund Advisor, the predecessor to Understanding Mutual Funds, was published in September 1987.

First and foremost in the minds of investors is the October stock-market crash. During that month, the Toronto Stock Exchange total return index, which is a broad measure of stock-market performance, fell more than 22%. (From the August peak to the October trough the decline was 31%.) Its impact is discussed in greater detail elsewhere in this book. However, many funds which invest in Canadian stocks did a lot better than the general market. Indeed, some funds which held bonds made gains during October as interest rates fell. And even after the biggest market drop in a generation, most funds invested in stocks could still report positive returns on a one-year basis. What the October crash did was put the market back to where it was less than a year earlier. The October disruption also gave some investors a buying opportunity. Those investors who bought at the October bottom – there were a few who had the courage – were up about 20% by the end of June 1988, depending on what they bought.

Nevertheless the October crash had some major negative effects on the mutual fund industry. Many people selling funds had never experienced a market decline and had difficulty comprehending it, never mind explaining it to clients. As well, the drop made many investors rethink their strategy of investing everything they own for growth.

It also cooled mutual fund sales drastically, to the point that many people who sold funds left the industry rather than face incomes which were at least 50% lower than pre-crash levels. Indeed, several fund distributors went out of business because of the decline in sales volume.

Most notable was British Columbia-based Stenner Financial Services Ltd. A key point, however, was that other than for some inconveniences, clients did not suffer. Money paid to firms for purchase of funds is held in trust and is not part of a distributor's assets. In the case of Stenner, clients' accounts generally moved with their brokers.

Western Canadian investors had more than their share of crises in 1987. The collapse of Principal Group Ltd. was a disaster for investors in British Columbia, Alberta, Saskatchewan and the Atlantic provinces. Some 67,000 people who bought investment contracts issued by two Principal subsidiaries, First Investors Corp. Ltd. and Associate Investors of Canada Ltd., face losses of more than $100 million.

Principal also had a mutual fund subsidiary, Principal Securities Management Ltd. It was sold to Metropolitan Life Holdings Ltd. Investors in Principal mutual funds suffered inconvenience. But the assets in the funds, like the assets in all mutual funds, belonged to the investors in the funds and were not at risk.

Another major development during the past year was the introduction of National Policy No. 39. Securities regulation is a provincial responsibility. The various provincial securities regulators have adopted a series of policies which are regulations that apply in all jurisdictions. Policy No. 39 includes regulations covering advertising. Unfortunately for the public, these regulations prohibit fund companies from providing shareholders and prospective buyers with comparative performance statistics. One regulation states:

> *Performance figures respecting related mutual funds or respecting stock or bond market indices or respecting other similar types of mutual funds or other accounts managed by the same manager or portfolio advisor may not be referred to in sales literature.*

This regulation appears to favor fund groups that sell their products directly to the public using captive sales forces and sales strategies which don't acknowledge a competitive environment. Fund groups that sell through independent sales organizations or directly to the public are placed at a disadvantage because they cannot market their funds on the basis of their performance relative to widely accepted benchmarks or, for that matter, the performance of their fund managers in other funds.

Moreover, any independent fund salesperson would be derelict if he or she failed to include comparative performance as a basis for recommending specific funds for specific client needs.

Fund companies are also prohibited by another regulation from promoting or advertising individual mutual funds on radio and television. This is a carryover from old CRTC rules which prevented promotion of securities over the airwaves.

The various securities commissions could easily meet their objectives by setting rules that require all statements about and comparisons of performance used in promoting a specific fund to be valid. These overly restrictive policies may be modified in the months ahead.

About the author

Steven G. Kelman is an investment counsellor and one of Canada's foremost experts on mutual funds. He has hands-on experience as a consultant in the fund industry and as a financial planner for individuals. Mr. Kelman is Vice-President of Dynamic Capital Corporation, which is involved in mutual funds, tax shelters and merchant banking.

As well, he is a Financial Times contributing editor responsible for the monthly survey of investment funds, the most widely used mutual fund and RRSP performance table in Canada, and editor of the Financial Times Mutual Fund Sourcebook, the mutual fund information guide used by fund professionals in Canada. In addition he is an advisor to the Financial Times on its Mutual Fund Sourcedisk.

One of Canada's most widely read business writers, he is author of RRSPs 1989 and co-author of Investment Strategies, both produced by Financial Times. His articles have appeared in the Financial Times, in several magazines and on the business pages of dailies from coast to coast. He has lectured on financial planning, RRSPs and mutual funds across the country. For several years he taught a course on applied investments to MBA students at York University's Faculty of Administrative Studies.

Mr. Kelman is a chartered financial analyst and a member of the Toronto Society of Financial Analysts. After graduating in 1969 from York University with his MBA, Mr. Kelman worked as an analyst, then portfolio manager, for a major insurance company before becoming a senior analyst with an investment dealer. In 1975 he joined Financial Times as a staff writer. He became investment editor in 1977. In April 1985, he joined the Dynamic Group of companies.

About the editor

David Toole, Financial Times Personal Finance Library Editor, is a Toronto-based freelance writer and editor who specializes in business and personal finance. His journalism experience spans 15 years and includes senior editorial positions with Financial Times of Canada, The Toronto Star and several other major Canadian publications.

Acknowledgements

As I noted in the previous edition, there are literally dozens of people in the fund and investment business whose views and advice are reflected in Understanding Mutual Funds. Some sections of the current edition have been expanded at the suggestion of a number of fund sales representatives. In particular, in the chapter entitled Strategies and Gimmicks, I've added more illustrations of "leverage," or the use of borrowed money to buy growth mutual funds. I would like to thank my colleagues at Dynamic Capital Corporation for their support and advice, especially my assistant Leslie Murray for keeping track of my research notes; and David Groskind, Nadine Kostiuk and Rudy Luukko of Financial Times.

In particular I would like to thank Ron Blunn, business development manager of Financial Times, who was responsible for producing and editing Understanding Mutual Funds.

And finally, I'd like to thank David Tafler, publisher of Financial Times, for making this book possible.

CHAPTER ONE

HOW IT STARTED

NINETEEN-THIRTY-TWO WAS AN UNLIKELY TIME TO ESTABLISH CANADA'S first open-end mutual fund. Unemployment in the depression-ravaged economy was running at about 40%. Canadian share prices as measured by the Financial Times of Canada were off about 80% from their 1929 highs.

Yet it was in 1932 that 31-year-old Alan Chippindale of the New York-based Calvin Bullock organization travelled to Montreal. His assignment: to start and manage Canada's first open-end mutual fund, Canadian Investment Fund (CIF).

It was not an easy task. First, tax regulations had to be changed to accommodate the mutual fund corporation concept. Second, he faced the problem of selling a new investment concept to a public that was gun-shy, to say the least.

The only experience most people had with funds of any type involved investment trust shares. These were closed-end funds whose shares were bought and sold on stock exchanges. Most had leveraged, unpublished portfolios and there were few restrictions on what they could buy and hold in their portfolios. Chippindale's open-end fund was different in that the fund issued and redeemed shares on an ongoing basis at a price reflecting the full value of the assets the fund held.

The closed-end investment pools had performed exceedingly well during the roaring '20s. But when the market crashed, the value of their underlying assets plunged as well. Those investors who wanted to sell couldn't, as the market for the shares had dried up.

CIF offered shares through dealers and brokers in the United States and Britain as well as in Canada. Chippindale spent $50,000 on newspaper advertising in Canada in the three months after launching the fund in

December, 1932. Gross sales during that period were disappointing – only about $50,000. It was years before the fund turned a profit.

But Chippindale had pioneered the concepts that mutual fund investors today take for granted: regular reports to investors; redemptions at net asset value; diversification; no borrowing; and generally no conflicts of interest.

The concept of open-end funds caught on slowly. In 1934, Commonwealth International (now Viking Commonwealth Fund Ltd.) changed to an open-end fund from a closed-end fund. In the same year, a new fund, United Gold Equities, was established. (It later was wound up as investor interest in gold declined.) In 1938, Corporate Investors Ltd. converted to an open-end fund from a closed-end fund.

But funds really didn't take off until the 1950s. It was at this time that Investors Syndicate of Canada formed Investors Mutual of Canada. This group, with an expanding sales force, increased investor awareness in funds by selling through instalment accumulation plans.

Statistics on mutual funds covering that period are sketchy. The Investment Funds Institute of Canada (IFIC) – the umbrella organization of the Canadian mutual fund industry – estimates that the market value of funds offered by its members in 1951 was about $57 million, held in 22,000 accounts.

But through the 1950s the industry grew quickly. By 1960 IFIC members had assets of about $540 million in 179,000 accounts; in 1963 the figure broke $1 billion in 324,000 accounts.

It was during 1962 that IFIC's predecessor organization, the Canadian Mutual Fund Association, was founded, with the objective of becoming a self-governing and self-disciplining association of mutual fund companies. The name was changed to the Investment Funds Institute of Canada in 1976.

IFIC membership includes funds representing about three-quarters of fund assets held by Canadians. Its Canadian Investment Funds Course is recognized by provincial regulators as a requirement for registration of mutual fund salespeople. Its views are sought by provincial securities commissions. And its various committees – which consider everything from advertising ethics to education – have a major influence on the funds business in Canada.

As the stock market soared in the 1960s, the industry expanded. A number of "private" funds were established during this period. Tradex Investment Fund Ltd. was set up for federal government employees posted overseas. MD Growth Investments was established by the Canadian Medical Association for its members.

At the end of 1968, IFIC-member funds controlled $2.8 billion in assets in 702,000 shareholder accounts. Sales continued at a hefty pace until 1969. But the stock market peaked in May and by year-end total assets for the industry were down marginally. More important, redemptions began to exceed sales.

For the next nine years, the industry's shareholder base shrunk as redemptions outpaced sales. Several U.S.-based fund companies left Canada because of declining sales and because of new regulations that required Canadian ownership of investment companies. Many fund salespeople who jumped in during the boom years also left the industry, leaving their clients to fend for themselves.

Most important, it was in the early 1970s that the mutual fund business suffered through a scandal that shattered investor confidence.

In the late 1950s, Bernard Cornfeld, an American, established Investors Overseas Services (IOS) to manage and distribute mutual funds. By the late 1960s he was the undisputed king of the fund business, with more than one million investors and more than $2 billion in assets under management. His organization, which was registered in Panama, operated primarily in Europe, Central and South America and the Middle East. It was not registered with the U.S. Securities and Exchange Commission (SEC) so it could not operate in the U.S. Similarly, these offshore funds were not cleared in Canada. IOS, however, did purchase a Canadian group of funds. These were operated under Canadian law and were not involved in the subsequent IOS offshore funds scandal and the collapse of IOS.

Cornfeld and his colleagues, as controlling shareholders of IOS, were paper multimillionaires. To convert some of this paper wealth to cash they decided to go public. Their first step was to change IOS from a Panamanian company to a Canadian one, registering the head office in Saint John, N.B. Its base of operations, however, was Switzerland. The share issue in 1969 was a roaring success, with the opening price more than double the $10 issue price.

But when IOS released its annual report in April 1970, its financial results were dismal. Moreover, its auditors questioned the value of some of the company's assets, including 22 million acres of Arctic oil leases. By the summer, IOS shares were trading at $2.

Concerns about IOS caused massive redemptions of its fund shares and as a result bailout proposals were made by a number of parties. In the summer of 1970 control of IOS passed to Robert Vesco, an American financier. Vesco obtained control as part of a deal that included a $5-million rescue loan to IOS. He then allegedly diverted assets of the offshore

IOS funds into investments which provided indirect benefits to him. In November 1972, the SEC and other regulators in Canada, Luxembourg, the Netherlands Antilles and the United Kingdom forced IOS and its related funds into liquidation.

When the Canadian operations of IOS were liquidated by a trustee, the Eaton group of funds bought the contracts to manage the Canadian IOS funds, and integrated them into the Eaton group – now the Viking group.

It took a long time for the industry to recover. By 1978 fund sales began to exceed redemptions once again and the industry began its major growth from a base of about 150 funds and an asset base of about $2 billion. By 1985 there were about 200 funds with assets exceeding $10 billion. Two years later there were more than 350 funds with assets exceeding $35 billion.

The surge reflected the growing recognition by both investors and the investment industry that funds are the best way for many people to participate in the stock and bond markets. Billions of dollars of RRSP money flows into mutual funds each year from people seeking better long-term returns than are available from guaranteed plans. And many stockbrokers who previously ignored funds or discouraged their clients from investing in funds now see them as an important source of business. Indeed, a number of investment dealers offer their own families of funds. Similarly, many insurance companies are offering or plan to offer mutual funds to their clients. Banks and trust companies are expanding their fund operations or are entering the business for the first time. These newcomers have increased general investor awareness about mutual funds.

As well, the industry has expanded its product line to include a wider range of funds. Besides the traditional stock and bond funds, investors have a choice of ethical funds, precious metals funds, and funds that specialize in foreign government bonds, health-care product companies and investments in the food industry.

The October crash had a short-term negative impact on fund sales,which plunged in the months following the crash. However the industry is still growing, albeit marginally.

Companies continue to introduce new funds to meet investor needs. During the first half of 1988 a number of fund companies introduced global bond funds which invest in fixed income securities on a global basis. The banking and trust industries have applied to the regulatory authorities to set up their own educational courses which meet registration requirements for selling funds.

The fund industry will continue to grow as more and more Canadians discover how funds can be used to meet virtually any type of investment objective and bring returns that are superior to the guaranteed investments that they traditionally have chosen.

CHAPTER TWO

THE IMPACT OF OCTOBER 1987

THE FACT THAT THE STOCK MARKET FELL SHARPLY IN OCTOBER 1987 WAS no surprise to most professional investors. In fact most fund managers had been building cash positions in the months prior to the decline because they felt that stocks were expensive or that the market was ahead of itself. As well, the markets had become exceptionally volatile, with the major indexes moving sharply up and down on a day-to-day basis as investor confidence rose and fell.

What caught virtually every manager off guard was the magnitude of the decline: In the six sessions to October 23, the Toronto Stock Exchange 300 composite index – a widely used measure of stock market performance – fell almost more than 16%.

The biggest drop was on Black Monday, October 19, when the TSE 300 fell 407 points, its largest drop, losing 11% of its value. However, the bloodbath really began on the previous Friday when the TSE 300, taking its lead from the New York market, fell 76 points, or 2%. By the time the month ended, the TSE was more than 22% below its September closing level. In effect, investors who bought near the top of the market in August saw the value of their investment, assuming they had a broadly based portfolio, plunge by one-quarter. (If they bought the day the market peaked and sold the day the market bottomed, they would have lost about 31% of their capital before commissions.)

And while some investors bought at the peak, hundreds of thousands of investors have been in funds for years, holding them as long-term investments. What they saw was the crash eliminating most of the gains they had made over the previous 12 months. Even then, many funds tied to the stock market showed significant one-year gains after October. Several funds tied to natural resource stocks had gains of more than 25%. Some funds with substantial cash positions and broadly based portfolios showed small but positive returns.

Surprisingly at the time, the industry was not hit with a flood of redemptions. While there was a substantial amount of switching from growth funds to more stable bond and money market funds, few fund companies reported large amounts of redemptions. In total about 2% of mutual fund assets were redeemed the week of the crash.

There are several explanations for this. Many fund salespeople claim that most of their clients are long-term investors and decided to continue holding. Indeed with 10-year rates of return for many funds in excess of 16%, long-term investors could still smile. But the lack of redemptions might also reflect the fact that many investors got busy signals when they tried to call their brokers to redeem. By the time they got through, the market had levelled and they decided to hold, particularly when they realized that the damage wasn't as great as they thought.

There was concern in the industry that some investors who bought their holdings in part with borrowed money would be forced to sell by banks and trust companies which had financed the purchases. However, this did not become a major problem because the crash, at least for investors who had held funds for some time, only trimmed profits and did not eliminate them.

As to the cause of the crash, a simple explanation is that the number of people who wanted to sell exceeded the number of people who wanted to buy. There are many more complex explanations. One points to sales of stocks by major U.S. fund companies. Mutual fund investors can redeem at any time. Apparently on Friday, October 16, fund companies were hit by an extraordinary number of redemptions when the New York Stock Exchange fell 108 points as measured by the Dow Jones industrial average. To raise cash to meet these redemptions, some funds became major sellers of stocks on October 19. This helped drive the market down further because many potential buyers were on the sidelines.

Those investors who bought stocks or funds which invest in stocks on October 19 did quite well. By early July 1988 they were showing gains of about 24% using the Toronto index as a bench-mark.

The crash has had some major effects on fund investing. For one thing, many investors started taking a more cautious approach. Rather than putting everything in funds that invest in growth stocks, more and more investors are taking a balanced approach, spreading their money among different classes of assets such as bond funds, precious metal funds and money market funds.

However, new sales dried up and the incomes of people who sold funds plunged. At least one company which had planned to enter the fund business, New York Life Insurance Co., changed its mind. As well, a number of Canadian fund companies or fund-management contracts were sold to other management companies. Fund groups absorbed by larger companies included the Sentinel group of funds, the Walwyn funds, the Rabin-Budden funds and the Hume funds.

The drop in sales hurt fund sales organizations, which quickly discovered that revenues were not enough to cover overheads. In the West, Canadian Equity Planners, a major distributor, decided to close its doors. Two other firms – Stenner Financial Services Ltd. and the Herman Group – had their doors closed for them by regulatory bodies. In the East, several firms talked merger. Salespeople at various firms jockeyed for position within their own firms or other firms that offered them a better deal.

Clients of the firms that ceased operations suffered inconvenience but no financial losses. Money held by a fund-company on behalf of a client is kept in a trust account that is separate from company funds. Also, any securities held by the firm are held in trust.

CHAPTER THREE

WHAT IS A MUTUAL FUND?

A MUTUAL FUND IS A POOL OF SAVINGS THAT BELONGS TO MANY INVESTors. This pool is invested by a professional manager or managers in a broad portfolio of investments. Depending on the objectives of the fund, these can be Canadian common stocks, foreign common stocks, bonds, mortgages, preferred shares, precious metals, specialty investments, treasury bills or combinations of several groups. Some funds are designed for specific purposes, such as RRSPs; others are multi-purpose.

Funds that issue and redeem shares or units on a continuous basis are called open-end funds. There are more than 400 open-end funds offered in Canada. The value of their shares or units changes with the underlying value of the securities in the fund. But each share or unit represents a portion of the underlying portfolio. Most funds are valued daily, although some are valued weekly and a few monthly or quarterly. The fund company determines the value of the underlying portfolio at the close of the stock and bond markets, then divides that value by the number of shares or units outstanding to determine the net asset value of each share or unit. The number of shares or units outstanding varies on a day-to-day basis, depending on sales and redemptions.

Bolton Tremblay International Fund is a typical open-end fund that invests primarily in foreign common stocks. Its portfolio, as of March 31, 1988, was valued at $444 million. At that date it had about 65.88 million units outstanding. So the value per unit was $6.74. That is the amount you would pay for a share on December 31. (Your order would have to reach the fund before the close of business that day.) It is also the price you would have received for your shares if you redeemed them on that date.

In addition to open-end funds, there are a handful of closed-end funds. Unlike open-end funds, closed-end funds have a fixed number of shares. These are traded on stock exchanges. The market value of their shares may be greater or less than the underlying value of their securities. For example, BGR Precious Metals shares trade on the Toronto Stock Exchange. On August 5, 1988, BGR shares closed at $10.88. But the underlying value was $13.54 a share. Closed-end funds can be useful for some investors. They will be discussed in detail elsewhere.

At least one fund, Global Strategy Corp., is a hybrid. It was originally offered to the public as a unique fund that invested its assets entirely in foreign property but at the same time was eligible for RRSPs. The fund was able to do this because its managers discovered a way around the law that limits RRSP-eligible funds to 10% foreign property. The federal government soon plugged that loophole but allowed the fund to continue to operate, provided no new shares were issued. Shareholders can redeem their shares at net asset value, just like every other open-end fund. However, the shares trade on the Vancouver Stock Exchange and investors who want to sell find they are better off doing so on the exchange because they get a price that exceeds the net asset value. Apparently, some investors are willing to pay a premium for the fund's shares so they can hold an RRSP investment whose assets are not tied to the Canadian market.

The majority of investors in funds hold open-end funds. With the exception of the chapter on closed-end funds, all examples and comments in this book refer to open-end funds.

The advantages of funds

A mutual fund offers several important advantages to you as an investor which you might have difficulty getting on your own:

1. **Diversification**. Funds generally hold a large number of securities. It is common for a fund invested in Canadian common stocks to hold shares of 40 or more companies. By holding such a large number of securities your risk is spread. So if one company flounders, it will have little impact on the performance of the overall portfolio. Few individuals have enough assets to build a diversified portfolio on their own. But with a mutual fund you can get diversification with a small amount of money.

How small? The minimum contribution allowed to most funds is between $500 and $1,000. However, most funds also have monthly contribution plans that allow you to start with as little as $100 a month. Holdings of mutual fund investors range from $1,000 to $1 million or more. According to the Investment Funds Institute of Canada, the average holding in 1986 was about $10,200. But many investors hold several funds.

2. **Liquidity.** A key benefit of mutual funds is that they are liquid. You can purchase or redeem shares and units on short notice, generally locking in a purchase or sale price on the day you make your decision to buy or redeem (in the case of funds valued daily). This is an advantage to individuals who want to be able to cash in their investments at any time. In this way, holding a mutual fund can be more advantageous than holding stocks, particularly if the stocks held rarely trade in large volumes and therefore may be harder to sell at any one time at a good price.

Orders to buy mutual fund shares or units received by the fund before the close of business on a day when shares are valued will be purchased at that price (less any sales fee, if applicable). Orders received to redeem shares will be redeemed at that price (less any redemption fee, if applicable) and your money will be available within a few days, generally in five. The trend in the industry is toward daily pricing and virtually all major fund groups now price daily. (In the U.S., some funds are priced hourly.)

A handful of funds, mainly real estate funds, are valued monthly or quarterly and as a result are somewhat less liquid.

3. **Professional Management.** Mutual fund investors benefit from having investment professionals decide what securities should be held and at what prices they should be bought or sold. Most fund managers have substantial experience in the investment field and have taken specialized investment courses leading to the designation of chartered financial analyst. The cost of professional management is low to mutual fund holders because the cost is spread so widely. Generally, you can expect to pay about 2% a year for portfolio management and other fund expenses (excluding trading costs of the underlying securities). This management fee is usually charged to the fund rather than to your account.

Mutual funds are the only cost-effective way for individuals with limited funds to get a diversified, professionally managed portfolio. No stockbroker or other investment professional can afford to service a small account, except through using mutual funds. Unless you are able to generate several thousands of dollars of trading commissions a year, you are unlikely to get timely advice and top-quality service on a stock portfolio from a stockbroker.

But small investors aren't the only investors who use mutual funds. Many wealthy individuals who don't want to be bothered making decisions about the stock market also use funds. Similarly, some people use funds for specific purposes in their investment portfolios. For instance, if you decide you want to invest part of your assets in Japanese securities, the easiest way is through a fund that specializes in this market.

The funds in Canada can be divided into two broad categories: those that invest in growth securities such as common stocks and whose objective is to provide long-term growth, and those that invest in income securities and whose objective is to provide current income or stable growth.

Types of funds

Growth funds historically give the highest rates of return measured over a period of, say, 10 years. While the returns of all mutual funds are a combination of capital gain and income, the major portion of return from growth funds is from capital appreciation. It is impossible to predict what a growth fund's future rate of return will be. The assumption is that it will be higher than the rate of return of a fund that invests for income. That has been the case historically. But annual rates of return for growth funds vary widely. In some years, the returns will be large. But in other years, the returns will be mediocre. And there will be years when fund values drop.

Fixed income funds give somewhat lower long-term rates of return than growth funds. However, their annual returns are more stable because the major portion is income. This income comes in the form of interest in the case of bond and mortgage funds, and dividends in the case of preferred-dividend income funds.

Growth funds

Growth funds include common stock and real estate funds as well as balanced funds whose portfolios may include both stocks and bonds.

The largest group of growth funds is Canadian common stock funds. Because they concentrate in the Canadian market, holding no more than 10% of their assets in foreign securities, they can be held in RRSPs.

Most Canadian common stock funds invest across the spectrum of the market, generally sticking to issues traded on the Toronto Stock Exchange and the Montreal Exchange. A few funds, however, specialize in specific segments of the market. For example, Royal Trust Energy Fund and Dynamic Precious Metals Fund invest, respectively, in Canadian energy issues and shares of precious metal producers and precious metals.

There is also a wide choice of growth funds that invest in American stock-markets. While most of these funds stick to senior blue-chip issues, others concentrate on specific areas. For example, the Putnam Health Sciences Trust invests primarily in the U.S. health-sciences industry. Still others focus on junior stock issues or resources.

If international diversification is what interests you, there are a number of funds that invest outside North America. Some, such as AGF Japan

Fund, concentrate on a specific market. Others, such as Bolton Tremblay International Fund, invest in a variety of overseas markets. A few, such as Cundill Value Fund, will invest in whatever markets, including Canada and the U.S., are perceived to offer the best values. There are also a number of international bond funds which may provide growth through changes in currency values.

Foreign Property

Mutual funds that invest primarily outside Canada are considered "foreign property" by the federal government for purposes of the Income Tax Act and cannot be registered as RRSPs. However, they can be held in self-directed RRSPs as part of the foreign property component provided the total foreign property holding does not exceed 10% of the plan.

Appendix A contains the statement of investment assets of Bolton Tremblay International Fund, managed by Bolton Tremblay Funds Inc., which invests in a broad spectrum of common stocks on a worldwide basis.

Balanced funds

A number of funds call themselves balanced funds. Historically, a balanced fund was one that invested a portion of its assets in bonds and a portion in stocks. Such funds aimed to have long-term rates of return that were larger than those offered by pure bond funds and that were more stable than pure stock funds.

Lately, however, the term balanced has been used by a number of new funds which have the traditional balanced fund objectives but whose portfolios are primarily equities. Depending on their holdings, some balanced funds are eligible for RRSPs, while others are not.

Real estate funds

There are a handful of funds that invest in real estate. These differ from other mutual funds in several major respects. First, they use borrowed capital in addition to shareholder capital; virtually all other funds use just shareholder capital.

Second, their unit or share values are based on appraisals rather than actual market transactions. The net asset value per unit or share in an equity fund is determined by the value of the portfolio as measured by the closing trades in each stock divided by the number of shares outstanding. With a real estate fund, the value of the fund is based on annual appraisals of each property the fund owns. An appraisal is simply the opinion of a real estate expert as to the market value of a particular property.

Third, real estate funds are less liquid than other funds. Most are valued quarterly, which means you can buy or sell only four times a year (some are valued monthly).

Income funds

The second major category of funds is income funds, whose investment objective is to produce income. These funds invest in bonds, mortgages or preferred shares of Canadian companies. As the income from these is fairly predictable and relatively stable, the rates of return of income funds are less uncertain than the rates of return from growth funds.

Income funds can be divided into two broad categories: those that invest primarily in preferred shares of Canadian corporations and those that invest in bonds, mortgages or both.

To understand the differences you have to consider how the federal government taxes individuals on the interest and dividends they receive from Canadian corporations. Interest is taxable at the marginal tax rate – the rate of tax paid on an individual's last dollar of income earned. A person with taxable income of, say, $40,000 has a marginal tax rate of about 39%. So, on $1,000 in interest income, this person would have to pay $390 in taxes (assuming the investment-income deduction was already used). The actual rate depends on the province. (The federal tax rate in this case is 26% with the provincial tax rate at half that, or 13%.)

To encourage Canadians to invest in dividend-producing shares, the government devised the federal dividend tax credit. It works like this: Instead of simply adding dividend income to other sources of income, dividends are grossed up by 125%. Then, after you have determined how much tax you owe, you can subtract a tax credit equal to 13.33% of 125% of your dividends. It works out that you end up paying less tax than if you'd simply added the dividends to income in the normal way.

For example, let's say you have $1,000 of dividend income. For tax-calculation purposes this would be grossed up to $1,250. Assuming your federal tax rate is 26%, the federal tax payable on the dividend would be $362.50. From this, subtract the dividend tax credit of 13.33% of $1,250, or $167, so net federal tax payable on the dividend would be $196. Add on provincial tax at 50% of federal tax ($98) and the total tax bill on $1,000 in dividends ends up being $294, or about 29% of the actual dividend received. That would compare with $390, or 39%, on interest received by the same person. The rule of thumb is that on an after-tax basis, $1 of dividend income has the same after-tax value as $1.26 of interest income. So an 8% dividend yield is about equal to a 10% interest yield.

Now, back to the two categories of income funds. Funds that invest primarily in preferred shares are usually called preferred-dividend income funds. Their purpose is to maximize after-tax income. They are popular with people who want current income and the highest after-tax return possible without taking significant risk.

Bond and mortgage funds may have slightly lower after-tax rates of return than preferred-dividend income funds. But many people prefer the security of having debt instruments and are willing to give up some income as a tradeoff for more security.

For RRSP purposes, bond and mortgage funds make more sense because all income goes untaxed inside an RRSP, so RRSP investors cannot take advantage of the tax break that comes with the preferred-dividend income.

There are a number of types of non-dividend fixed income funds. There are the funds that invest only in bonds, funds that invest only in mortgages, funds that mix bonds and mortgages, and, finally, there are money market funds and savings funds.

Bond funds generally invest in government or government-guaranteed bonds and bonds and debentures issued by the strongest banks and corporations.

There are other factors that can affect performance, such as the maturities of the various bonds held and whether a major portion of the fund is invested in bonds that are denominated in currencies other than the Canadian dollar.

Mortgage funds are designed to provide maximum current income to investors by investing in mortgages. Mortgage rates are generally at least a point higher than bond yields. They are less likely to provide capital appreciation than bond funds because mortgage funds rarely trade their mortgages.

Money market and savings funds have similar objectives: to provide current income with no fluctuation in the value of an investor's capital. Money market funds invest in short-term debt securities with maturities of less than a year. Typically, a money market fund's portfolio will be concentrated in treasury bills, bank-guaranteed debt and short-term issues of strong corporations.

The unit value of most money market funds is fixed at either $10 or $1, so the unit value of the fund is always constant. Income earned on capital accrues to your account daily, weekly or monthly, depending on how often the fund is valued, and is generally used to purchase additional units of the fund. Money market funds are by far the least risky of mutual funds.

A savings fund has the same objective as a money market fund. But rather than investing in a portfolio of short-term securities, it keeps the fund's assets on deposit with major financial institutions, earning wholesale deposit rates which can be a couple of percentage points more than the rate paid individuals on premium savings accounts.

How funds can be used

Mutual funds can be used for virtually any type of savings program. But the fund or funds you use should be matched to your specific investment objective. And you should also develop an understanding of what we'll call fund volatility or rate-of-return variability.

Unlike a guaranteed investment, you do not know what your rate of return will be from a mutual fund because the rate you earn will depend on the rates of return of the underlying investments. You expect to get back more than you put in. And that's the reason you would buy a fund rather than a guaranteed investment certificate or hold money in the bank. However, the rates of return from some types of mutual funds are a lot more stable or, conversely, less volatile than rates of return of some other types of funds.

Since money market and savings funds invest only in short-term securities, you can predict fairly accurately your rate of return over a relatively short period.

In contrast, there are some funds whose rates of return over short periods are virtually impossible to predict. These funds may give very high rates of return over long periods. But over the short term their rates will vary widely.

For example, funds that invest in the Japanese stock market are very volatile. Much of this volatility is caused by the exchange rate of the Canadian dollar against the Japanese yen. Exchange rate fluctuations can be as much as several percentage points up or down in a month. Similarly, funds that invest in gold and other precious metals have historically been volatile.

Money market funds as a group are the least volatile, followed by mortgage funds, bond funds and preferred-dividend income funds. Common stock funds are more volatile than fixed income funds. Equity funds that invest in senior stocks and balanced funds are generally much less volatile than equity funds that concentrate on specific groups of stocks such as energy shares, junior companies or gold.

So if your savings objective is rather short-term, like saving for a vacation or a down payment on a home, the fund that would best suit your needs is a money market or savings fund. Your money would not be at risk and you would likely earn a rate of return that is a couple of points above what you would get in a bank account.

If you don't need your money for a couple of years, a mortgage or bond fund might suffice. Similarly, you could consider a preferred-dividend income fund. In this case you would have to consider the individual portfolios of the funds and your tax situation. Fixed income funds that have securities maturing in a few years are likely to be less volatile than fixed income funds whose portfolios have securities that mature in, say, 15 to 20 years. This will be discussed in more detail elsewhere in the book.

If you are saving for the long term, you would likely consider funds invested primarily in equities. You would expect to do better with these funds than you would with income funds. But on a month-to-month or year-to-year basis such growth funds would have more volatile rates of return than fixed income funds.

Historically, investors who are willing to accept some fluctuation in their rates of return have done better over the long haul than investors who want guaranteed returns.

The Financial Times of Canada has been publishing its comprehensive mutual fund survey for more than a decade. On a 10-year basis, funds that invest primarily in equities have annual average returns approaching 15%. Fixed income funds have returns averaging just over 11%, while money market funds have returns averaging just under 11%.

Table I shows the year-by-year performance of the Toronto Stock Exchange total return index beside the rate of return you would have earned if you held treasury bills. The TSE index is a good representation of what you would have earned holding an "average" mutual fund investing in Canadian stocks. The treasury bill returns parallel what you would have earned holding a money market fund. The point to note is that annual returns of the stock market vary widely compared with treasury bills.

Table I

**Annual returns of
TSE versus treasury bill yields
for periods ending June 30th**

	TSE	T-bills
1974	-9.3%	6.8%
1975	9.7%	7.5%
1976	4.7%	8.5%
1977	2.6%	8.2%
1978	14.6%	7.5%
1979	49.9%	10.2%
1980	32.6%	12.9%
1981	18.8%	14.8%
1982	-39.1%	16.5%
1983	86.6%	10.0%
1984	-6.1%	10.0%
1985	26.6%	10.7%
1986	17.4%	9.3%
1987	24.6%	8.0%
1988	-5.2%	8.7%

CHAPTER FOUR

ALL ABOUT GROWTH FUNDS

IF YOUR INVESTMENT OBJECTIVE IS LONG-TERM CAPITAL GROWTH, CON-
sider equity funds, which invest primarily in common stocks. These are the
most popular type of fund. More than 250 are included in the Financial
Times of Canada monthly survey of investment funds.

There are several major groups of equity funds that are designed to
meet particular objectives by investing in specific markets or certain areas
of specific markets.

Regardless of their type, all equity funds have the common thread of a
diversified portfolio of shares, and performance that reflects individual
funds' objectives and the skills of their managers.

A key point to consider when choosing an equity fund is its volatility
or the stability of its monthly rate of return. The Financial Times ranks
mutual funds by variations in its monthly rate of return using a statistical
measure called standard deviation. It indicates the amount a return is likely to diverge from its average monthly rate of return. Sixty months of data
is used where available, or a minimum of 36 months, to determine standard deviation.

Volatility is useful in comparing two funds with similar rates of return.
For investors who buy and hold for the long term, a fund with a high historical return and a low volatility ranking would be preferable to a fund
with the same return but a high volatility rating. Conversely, if you're
trying to catch the swings in a market cycle, you might want to choose a
fund with a high volatility rating over one with a low ranking.

For example, Growth Equity Fund Ltd. and Canadian Security
Growth Ltd., both part of the AGF Group, were among the top 10-year
performers among Canadian equity funds for the period ended June 30,

1988, with rates of 16.3% and 17.8% respectively. However, Growth Equity is much more volatile than Canadian Security Growth.

A fund's volatility will change from time to time. But usually the changes are not significant because the fund objectives and investment philosophy are generally stable.

Certain groups of funds tend to be more volatile than others. Gold funds, for instance, are among the most volatile groups, reflecting the volatility of precious metals prices and gold mining stocks. Similarly, Japanese funds are fairly volatile as a result of swings in the exchange rates of the Japanese yen and Canadian dollar. Generally, funds that invest in a narrow segment of the market are more volatile than funds that draw their portfolios from a broad spectrum of industries.

Equity funds that have relatively low volatility tend to invest in securities that are more stable in price than the general market. For example, a fund holding stocks with substantial dividend yields would have below-average volatility. One such fund is Corporate Investors Ltd., which invests in shares that pay, or are expected to pay, above-average dividends.

Here is a summary of the major types of growth funds:

1. **Canadian equity funds.** The largest group of investment funds are those that invest primarily in Canadian stocks and are eligible for RRSPs. Most invest in a broad spectrum of industries and have rates of return that are similar to that of the Toronto Stock Exchange total return index. Others, however, have somewhat different objectives. For instance, several invest primarily in dividend-paying common shares of mature companies giving rates of return that are somewhat more stable than the market. Others specialize in specific areas of the market such as natural resources.

2. **American equity funds.** Funds that invest in the U.S. are also very popular among Canadian investors. These funds appeal to individuals who expect the U.S. markets to outperform their Canadian counterparts or who want a hedge against the Canadian dollar. Within this group there is a wide variety of choices. Some invest primarily in blue chips. Others base their portfolios on companies that offer above-average growth potential or in specialty areas of the marketplace.

3. **International funds.** International funds take advantage of investment opportunities in different countries. Some will invest in any country, including Canada. Others will exclude Canada or concentrate on overseas markets. International funds have performed quite well in recent years as the Canadian dollar has fallen against overseas currencies and Canada's natural resource-based stock markets underperformed other markets.

4. **Specialty equity funds.** A number of funds specialize in specific industries, specific markets or follow hedged investment strategies. For in-

stance, AGF Hitech Fund Ltd. invests in high-technology stocks in Canada, the U.S., Japan and certain European countries. Several funds specialize in Japanese securities, while a number concentrate on precious metals. In addition, some funds attempt to give their investors stable rates of return through hedging strategies such as writing call options against positions.

5. **Balanced funds.** Balanced funds try to stabilize returns by combining equities with fixed income securities. Some, however, have rates-of-return patterns more typical of equity funds.

Lured by promises of returns far above those available from guaranteed investments, individuals poured billions of dollars in recent years into mutual funds that invest primarily in Canadian equities. Indeed, many funds have given their holders rates of return averaging better than 15% over the past 10 years, using a June 30, 1988, ending date.

But it's important to realize that 15% is an average and that year-to-year rates vary widely. Over the 10 years ended June 1988, the annual returns of the Toronto Stock Exchange total return index ranged from a low of minus 39.1% to a high of plus 86.6% as shown in Table I.

And because stock markets move in cycles, annual rates don't tell the whole story. So the returns depend a lot on when stocks are bought and when they are sold. Over the past 60 years, the Toronto market has gone through nine cycles consisting of declining markets followed by rising markets.

Toronto statistician Richard Anstett has compiled some of the most comprehensive statistics available on the performance of the TSE. Looking at some of the more recent cycles, Anstett notes that the Toronto market rose 193% in the 72 months ended November 1980, then proceeded to slide 44% over the next 20 months to June 1982. Between June 1982, and August 1987, the market rose 202%. Then it started its slide, which ended in late October, down 31% from its peak. From October 1987 to early July 1988 it rose 24%.

Table II on the next page shows major cyclical market patterns of the TSE 300 composite index since 1921. (Changes in market sentiment reflect gains or declines of 20% or more.)

The return that a broadly based fund earns in any period or cycle depends on what happens in the market and on the skills of the fund's investment advisor. But, generally speaking, it is difficult for a fund manager to consistently outperform the market. It can be done for short periods or with smaller funds. But on a long-term basis it is unrealistic to expect mutual funds as a whole to generate returns significantly greater than the general market. Superior returns do occur. They are generally due to the

Table II

Market Cycles on the Toronto Stock Exchange

Bullish Periods	no. of months	% gain	Bearish Periods	no. of months	% loss
August 1921, to			September 1929, to		
September 1929	97	300	June 1932	33	80
June 1932, to			March 1937, to		
March 1937	57	201	April 1942	61	56
April 1942 to			May 1946, to		
May 1946	49	159	February 1948	21	25
February 1948, to			July 1956, to		
July 1956	101	273	December 1957	17	30
December 1957, to			May 1969, to		
May 1969	137	162	June 1970	13	28
June 1970, to			October 1973, to		
October 1973	40	64	December 1974	14	38
December 1974, to			November 1980, to		
November 1980	72	193	July 1982	20	44
July 1982, to			August 1987, to		
August 1987	61	202	October 1987	2	31
October 1987, to					
July 1988	9	24	(Changes in market sentiment reflect gains or declines of 20% or more.)		

decisions of a single manager or handful of individuals working together. Most managers, however, parrot the general market or follow the crowd.

To understand why, you have to look at the environment in which managers of broadly based Canadian equity funds have to work. You also have to consider a fund manager's objectives and management style.

Most fund managers try to outperform the market. So a manager of a broadly based Canadian equity fund would gauge his or her performance against the TSE 300 composite index, the index which includes the 300 stocks with the largest market capitalizations traded on the exchange, or against the TSE total return index, which includes dividends paid by the stocks included in the TSE 300.

There are several ways fund managers can construct portfolios. One way is to structure portfolios along the lines of the general index, over-weighting or underweighting specific industry groups.

As Table III on page 26 shows, the index is divided into 13 major industry groups: metals and minerals, gold and silver, oil and gas, paper and forest, consumer products, industrial products, real estate and construction, transportation, pipelines, utilities, communications, merchandising, financial services and management companies. At the end of June 1988, metals and minerals were about 11% of the index, while financial services were 17%. A portfolio manager who was positive on the outlook for metals and minerals but negative on banks might have put a heavier weighting than 11% in metals shares and a lower weighting in financial services.

A variation of this is to adjust the cash component of the portfolio. All mutual funds hold cash. But the percentage held in cash reflects the fund manager's view on the direction of the market. A manager who expects a sharp rise in the market soon might hold only enough cash to cover normal redemptions. A manager who expects the market to pull back or who believes that prices of individual stocks are expensive, might have 30% or more of the fund's assets in cash.

Alternatively, fund managers can build portfolios choosing individual securities while ignoring what is in the general index. Many fund managers, however, end up with portfolios that arc similar to the general index.

The major problem they face is finding stocks that can be bought and sold in volume. There are several thousand public companies listed on Canadian exchanges. But only a relatively small number trade in large enough volume or have enough shares outstanding to be considered by fund managers. A fund with assets of $5 million could have a portfolio of smaller companies. But a fund of $150 million would have to have the bulk of its assets in larger companies. Otherwise its manager would be faced with a portfolio containing too many companies to be manageable.

You can figure out a stock's capitalization by multiplying its share price by the number of shares outstanding. A company with 10 million shares outstanding and a stock price of $25 would have a market capitalization of $250 million.

The heaviest weighting among the 300 stocks in the TSE composite index belongs to BCE Inc., with 6.97% of the index at June 30, 1988. Next is Canadian Pacific Ltd. with 4.61%, followed by Alcan Aluminium Ltd. at 4.04% and Toronto Dominion Bank with 3.13%. These four stocks are almost 19% of the total value of the TSE 300. The top 10 stocks in the index represent almost 34% of the index; the top 100 represent almost 84% of the index; the top 200 represent more than 95% of the index. In contrast, the smallest 50 stocks in the index represent less than 2% of the index; each is one-twentieth of 1% or less.

Virtually all funds have rules that limit their holdings of individual stocks. For example, concerns about liquidity would prevent a fund (and

Table III

TSE index and subindex weights as of June 30, 1988

Integrated Mines	10.32%	Property Management	0.96%
Metal Mines	0.34%	REAL EST. & CONSTR.	1.36%
Unanium & Coal	0.45%	TRANSPORTATION	2.07%
METALS & MINERALS	11.12%	Oil Pipelines	0.43%
Gold and Silver Mines	9.02%	Gas Pipelines	3.15%
Precious Metals Funds	0.21%	PIPELINES	3.58%
GOLD & SILVER	9.23%	Gas Utilities	0.68%
Integrated Oils	3.85%	Electrical Utilities	1.78%
Oil & Gas Producers	5.99%	Telephone Utilities	8.00%
OIL & GAS	8.85%	UTILITIES	10.45%
PAPER & FOREST	3.42%	Broadcasting	0.48%
Food Processing	0.80%	Cable & Entertainment	0.60%
Tobacco	1.25%	Publishing/Printing	4.08%
Distilleries	2.67%	COMMUNICATIONS	5.16%
Breweries	1.28%	Wholesale Distributors	0.29%
Household Goods	0.29%	Food Stores	1.57%
Autos & Parts	0.38%	Department Stores	0.37%
Packaging Products	0.48%	Clothing Stores	0.41%
CONSUMER PRODUCTS	7.15%	Specialty Stores	1.13%
Steels	2.14%	Lodging, Food & Health	0.91%
Metal Fabricators	0.31%	Services	
Machinery	0.70%	MERCHANDISING	4.68%
Transportation Equipment	0.38%	Banks	12.79%
Electrical/Electronic	2.91%	Trust, Savings & Loan	1.47%
Cement/Concrete	0.30%	Investment Companies	0.52%
Chemicals	0.44%	Insurance	0.49%
Business Forms &	1.99%	Financial Management	1.59%
Equipment		FINANCIAL SERVICES	16.86%
INDUSTRIAL PRODUCTS	9.18%	MANAGEMENT COMPANIES	6.91%
Developers & Contractors	0.39%		

other funds managed by the same advisor) from holding more than 5% of the outstanding shares of a specific stock.

Consequently, Canadian equity funds, particularly medium and larger funds, end up having larger companies as a major portion of their portfolios, and these are generally the stocks that are found in the TSE 300.

Since the federal government allows RRSP-eligible mutual funds to hold up to 10% of their assets in foreign stocks, many Canadian equity funds have a U.S. or overseas component that may contribute to results that differ from the Canadian market.

Some managers try to beat the market by catching the swings. They build up cash when they believe the market is near the top and they spend their cash when the market is near the bottom. These managers are called market timers and they often base their decisions on technical analysis – the analysis of market cycles and graphs. Market timers face some major difficulties. First, it is very difficult to call a market top or bottom. Second, it is even more difficult to move out of or into a stock if you have a large portfolio. The manager will simply be unable to sell as much as he or she wants at peak prices, or buy at the bottom.

The third problem faced by market timers is that if they are wrong in their timing, they will drastically underperform their competitors.

The funds that do seem to outperform the market have three things in common: The decisions are made by a single person or a small group of individuals; the decisions are made quickly; and they are not afraid to act differently from the crowd.

Moreover, their methods of choosing stocks are based on finding undervalued situations. They seek out companies whose shares trade in the market at levels below the values of the assets, less liabilities, and which offer good potential for earnings growth. Such managers will spend cash when they find plenty of stocks that meet their criteria and will build cash when shares become overvalued and they cannot find undervalued stocks to purchase.

In most cases the stocks held may not represent the largest companies. Moreover such funds' monthly performance may differ from the general market's performance.

In contrast, many funds have their decisions made by ponderous committees that are unable to act quickly. By the time they act on the data available – which is most likely the same information available to other institutional investors – the information has been fully reflected in share prices. Consequently, such funds are unlikely to do better than the market, nor much worse.

U.S. equity funds

If you're interested in investing in U.S. markets, you can choose from among about 30 U.S. equity funds. These are very popular among investors who believe that the U.S. market offers investment opportunities not available in Canada and who expect the U.S. economy to outperform Canada's.

As well, the funds appeal to people who have U.S. dollar savings (most U.S. funds accept subscriptions in either Canadian or U.S. dollars) and who wish to keep this money in U.S. dollar-denominated growth securities. Similarly, individuals who plan to retire in the U.S. often invest a portion of their assets in U.S. securities.

U.S. equity funds should be considered as an alternative to U.S. stock portfolios for estate-planning purposes. If you own substantial U.S. assets, such as stocks, and you die, your estate could be subject to U.S. probate. However, holding mutual funds invested in U.S. assets avoids this potential problem because the funds are a Canadian asset.

Like Canadian equity funds, there is a wide variety of funds that invest in the U.S. Many try to parrot the major U.S. stock market indexes. For example, AMD American Blue Chip Growth Fund invests primarily in companies included in the Standard & Poor's 500 composite stock index and which "best represent the investment characteristics of blue-chip securities." Similarly, Green Line U.S. Index Fund tracks the performance of the S & P 500.

Other funds have investment policies that are a variation of this theme. Century DJ Fund seeks above-average rates of return by investing in major blue-chip companies with above-average earnings and dividend records.

Others attempt to beat the averages by choosing investments from a broader range of stocks. AGF Special Fund Ltd. looks for companies that are expected to grow at above-average rates of return. American Growth Fund Ltd., also managed by AGF, has a similar objective but puts the greatest portion of its assets in stocks listed on the New York Stock Exchange.

United American Fund seeks long-term capital growth by investing its assets in U.S. common stocks that its managers consider undervalued in relation to earnings, dividends and assets.

In terms of performance, U.S. funds as a group have not fared better than Canadian funds. Comparing the top 10 performers for one and three years, Canadian funds have performed better; on a five- and 10-year basis, there is significant overlap.

International equity funds

Virtually every industrialized country and many Third World nations have stock markets that trade shares of local companies. The performance of any given market reflects local and international economic conditions. And while all important markets move somewhat in concert because of the shrinking global marketplace, there can be large differences in performance. This reflects the fact that at any given time certain markets might be in an earlier or later stage of the economic cycle than North American markets. A nimble portfolio manager can take advantage of these differences. The result is that an international fund might show gains in a year in which U.S. and Canadian markets head lower.

But the performance also reflects the fact that some markets performed better than others. For example, in 1986 virtually all major world stock markets had positive returns. These ranged from Switzerland, with an increase of 0.1% in Swiss franc terms, to 108% for Spain. Canada was at the bottom end of the range with a 5% gain for the TSE 300. The Tokyo Stock Exchange, the world's largest market, was up 44%. During 1986 the Canadian dollar fell against most overseas currencies. In fact, in Canadian dollar terms the Toronto market was the worst performer. Adjusting for exchange rates, the Swiss market was up 25%; the Spanish market was up 138%; and the Tokyo market was up 79%.

The graph on the next page shows how world markets fared in 1987 in local currency and in Canadian dollar terms. Many exchanges showed negative returns and the Canadian dollar made gains against some currencies.

While there are several dozen countries with stock markets, most international funds stick with the major European, Far East and Australian markets as well as Canadian and U.S. markets. So, a typical fund might restrict the bulk of its portfolio to shares traded in the United Kingdom, West Germany, France, Switzerland, Australia, Japan, Canada and the U.S.

Occasionally it will invest in shares traded in other markets such as Italy, Austria, Singapore, Hong Kong or the Scandinavian countries. But equity investments in these markets usually reflect a view of the outlook for a specific company rather than an economy or currency. Trading volumes in many overseas markets are simply too light to allow a portfolio manager to invest with reasonable diversification. So while a specific overseas market may rise 138%, as Spain's did in 1986, it is unrealistic to expect a fund manager to have a heavy position of Spanish stocks in a portfolio.

Managers of international funds must consider the relative values of assets in different countries, currency trends, and, of course, stock market movements.

Managing an international fund can be more complicated than managing a single-market fund. Some firms have developed the expertise and have Canadian managers who base their decisions on their own research or on information supplied from abroad. Others retain overseas advisors to make recommendations. For instance, Global Strategy Fund uses N.M. Rothschild International Asset Management Ltd.; National Trust Global Fund uses Hill Samuel Investment Management Ltd.; Dynamic

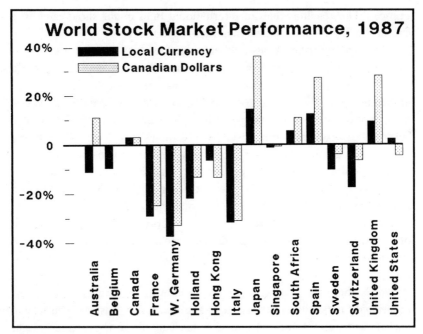

World Stock Market Performance, 1987

Global Fund has Beutel Goodman International PLC as its advisor. All are based in London.

The rates of return of the top-performing international funds suggest that location of the manager should not be a concern for investors.

Specialty funds

For investors who want a hefty weighting in a specific market or industry there are a number of specialty funds. They can be useful for investors who want to speculate on one industry or who want a heavie weighting in their portfolio of a specific type of investment than they can get by holding a broadly based fund.

Specialty funds can be divided into several categories: Japan funds, energy funds, gold funds, technology funds, small-company funds, health funds and natural resource funds.

Specialty funds include some of the best performers. For example, the four top-performing mutual funds in Canada in 1986 were Japanese funds: Universal Savings Japan Fund (up 68%); Royal Trust Japan Fund (up 63.5%); Investors Japanese Growth Fund (up 61.2%); and AGF Japan Fund Ltd. (up 54.7%).

But often this kind of performance goes hand in hand with volatility. Three of the four Japanese funds have been in existence long enough to be ranked by volatility. The three ranked fifth, six and seventh out of 172 funds ranked by volatility. Indeed, looking at the 12 months ended June 30, 1988, their returns were very moderate.

The 10-year average annual compound rates of return for Japanese funds are superior to the rates for Canadian funds over the same period. However, to understand these rates you have to look at year-by-year performance. An investment made in the Japanese market in 1976 and held until 1983 or 1984 would have performed about the same as an investment in the Canadian market (although year-by-year performance would have varied widely). But 1985 and 1986 were banner years for Japanese funds because stock prices and the yen soared.

Gold funds are the most volatile mutual funds, reflecting the volatility of bullion prices and gold mining shares. In 1979, Goldfund jumped 161.5%; in 1980 it added 89.7%. The following year it was off 38.7%.

Energy funds have also had their ups and downs. They rose spectacularly during the late 1970s as world energy prices soared. But the federal government's national energy program and the oil glut made them dismal performers from 1981 to 1986, underperforming the general market. In 1987 they did well because of rising energy prices and increased investor interest in energy-related stocks. Their fortunes have reversed again and have been showing average and below-average returns.

The specialty group includes what are called "small-cap" funds. These invest in companies with smaller capitalizations. Small can mean capitalizations of less than $150 million or less than $50 million, depending on the fund.

Several studies of market performance suggest that small-cap companies outperform the general market during bull markets and don't fall as much as the general market during bear markets. Small-cap funds reflect this view.

Balanced funds

Balanced, or variable-asset-mix funds, have as their objective maximizing growth and income while preserving capital. They do this by changing the asset-mix ratio of stocks to bonds to reflect anticipated market conditions. Some funds restrict their investments to Canadian stocks and debt securities. Others will include a wider range of instruments.

The funds that are truly balanced should be less volatile than pure equity funds because of the revenue from the fixed income portion of the portfolio. Some balanced funds, however, have investment policies that allow them to hold a mixture of fixed income securities and equities. Because they do not have to be diversified among asset classes, they may prove more volatile than funds that are always diversified.

While equity funds are the largest group, balanced funds are likely to attract new investors at a faster pace. The toughest investment decision for many people centres around asset mix – the percentage they should hold in Canadian stocks, bonds, short-term deposits, foreign securities and gold. For investors who don't want to get involved in this type of investment decision, a good balanced fund might make the most sense.

Real estate funds

Real estate funds invest primarily in income-producing commercial real estate properties. The return from a real estate fund includes income as well as capital gains from the change in value of the underlying properties.

But real estate funds differ in three important ways from other mutual funds. First, real estate funds use borrowed capital as well as investors' capital to purchase properties. Virtually every equity, bond, mortgage and money market fund has a prohibition against borrowing for investment purposes. Second, real estate mutual funds are valued differently. Their values are based on appraisals. Third, real estate funds are much less liquid than other funds. Where most other funds are valued daily or weekly, real estate funds are generally valued quarterly, and in some cases monthly. Investors can only redeem on specific dates and may have to give prior notice. And over the past three years two real estate funds have suspended redemptions while their portfolios were reappraised. So don't buy a real estate fund if you need liquidity.

The net asset values per share of equity, bond and mortgage funds are based on market values of underlying assets. These reflect actual prices of trades that took place in the market at the close of trading on the day when the fund shares or units were valued.

But a real estate holding is very different from a position in BCE common shares. While BCE shares held in a mutual fund are identical to shares traded on the TSE, no two pieces of real estate are exactly alike. They may be similar to other properties. But there are likely to be significant differences that will affect the value of one compared with the other.

The value of a real estate fund is based on appraisals of the properties held by a fund. And appraisals are only educated guesses or estimates – what a qualified appraiser believes the market value of a specific property to be on a given date.

In January 1987, the Ontario Securities Commission introduced new regulations for real estate mutual funds, including guidelines for appraisals. The new rules removed a cloud hanging over real estate funds as a group. During 1985, Real Property Trust of Canada suspended redemptions after its trustees changed managers and the appraised values of its properties were questioned.

In 1986, Halifax-based Canadian Property Investors Trust suspended redemptions after the OSC expressed concerns about appraisals on two of its properties.

The new regulations set general investment standards as well as standards for appraisals and valuation of shares.

Appraisals of each property in a real estate fund are generally performed annually. So in a rising real estate market the selling and buying price of a fund unit might be less than the actual value of the underlying assets.

As well, an appraisal is an estimate. There is no way of knowing whether the appraisal accurately reflects the amount that would be received if the property were sold. Moreover, if the fund were liquidated, the amount shareholders receive might be less than the net asset value of the fund.

If the assets of a real estate fund were put on the block, some of its holdings might go at fire-sale prices.

While the minimum capital for an equity fund is $100,000 and for a mortgage fund $350,000, the OSC set minimum capital requirements for a real estate mutual fund of $10 million. So a new fund has to raise that amount before it can invest in real estate.

These subscriptions have to be in cash. The fund cannot issue shares in return for a property or on the condition that the seller of the property buy units of the fund. The purpose of this is to avoid a potential conflict of interest.

The appraiser cannot be affiliated with the fund, its manager or the property being appraised. The fee charged can't be based on the valuation or on the appraisal reaching a specified value. The OSC requires that the independent appraiser, whose name must be included in the prospectus, be a member of the Appraisal Institute of Canada and have the Accredited Appraiser Canadian Institute designation. The appraiser must have five years' experience in appraising the type of property being appraised in the province where the property is located.

Each property in the fund must be reappraised annually on the anniversary of its acquisition or last appraisal. However, the trustees of the fund are required to obtain an appraisal more frequently, if in their opinion, there is a development that may materially change the value of the property. For instance, an arm's-length bid for the property could be made at a price substantially different from the appraised value.

Equity-based mutual funds can have sharp jumps or declines in value reflecting changes in the marketplace. Values of real estate funds, however, are less volatile because their values are in effect "managed." To prevent sharp fluctuations in a fund's unit value, no more than 50% of the fund's properties can be reappraised in the same calendar quarter.

So not only may values be out of date and too high or too low, but real estate funds will be shown as having relatively low volatility on the Financial Times monthly fund survey. As a result, comparing the volatility of real estate funds with other mutual funds is not valid.

Because real estate funds appraise their properties so infrequently, they cannot price their shares more than once every quarter. The exceptions are funds that update their annual appraisals monthly on the basis of the income stream generated by those properties.

Real estate isn't as liquid as a stock portfolio. So a fund may require 30 days' notice to redeem shares. A fund must pay for the shares it redeems within 15 days of the day on which the net asset value is calculated. If it doesn't have the cash to redeem all shares submitted, it must redeem on a pro rata, or proportional, basis.

No delay in payment can exceed six months unless approved by a two-thirds vote of investors. The suspension can't exceed 12 months unless 80% of investors agree.

A defeat of such a motion would likely mean a fund would be forced to sell off all or part of its property portfolio to raise funds to meet redemptions.

Real estate funds are allowed to pay the fund manager an incentive fee of up to one-quarter of the capital appreciation on the sale of a building, in excess of 8% a year, not compounded.

Commodity funds

It's possible to have a mutual fund that speculates in the futures markets.

Futures are contracts calling for the delivery of a specified commodity, security or currency at a specific price on a specific date. Futures contracts cover major food commodities, precious metals, trading currencies, bonds and even the stock market. Trading in futures is very risky because investors have to put up only a fraction of the value of the underlying contract as a "down payment." You either make a lot or lose a lot.

Because of the risks involved in futures trading, anyone who wants to offer a mutual fund that invests in commodity futures must meet some stringent criteria.

And while commodity funds have been brought to market from time to time in Canada, they have failed to generate lasting investor interest. Currently it appears that none is being offered nationally, although one, Mustard Seed Fund, is available in British Columbia. (This fund is unique in that its manager earns an incentive fee based on profits.)

The lack of interest in commodity funds largely reflects the regulatory environment. First, the OSC, whose rules must be followed by anyone who wants to sell securities to the public in Ontario (most other provinces have regulations borrowed from or patterned after those of the OSC), must be satisfied that an investor's liability is limited to the amount invested. If you speculate in commodities on your own, your liability is unlimited.

Second, the people selling such a fund generally have to be registered under the Commodity Futures Act as well as the Securities Act.

This dual registration reflects the OSC's recognition that someone selling a commodities fund should have expertise both in trading commodities futures and mutual funds.

Third, to be a potential investor, you have to be wealthier and more experienced in investing than the average person. The OSC says that dealers offering such an investment must determine that the potential investor understands the nature of the investment through work experience, educational level, independent advisors or prior experience.

As well, the OSC sets minimum suitability standards based on income and assets:

Investors must have a minimum annual gross income of $30,000 and a net worth of $30,000. Alternatively, a net worth of $75,000 is required.

The maximum annual management fee can't exceed 6% of net assets of the fund. Incentive fees can't exceed 25% of the profits calculated no more than quarterly.

The minimum capital for a commodity fund is $500,000.

The prospectus must state on the front page that a participant in the fund must be able and prepared to lose his or her entire investment; that the fund is highly speculative; and that there are substantial management and advisory fees and brokerage commissions before an investor is entitled to a return on investment.

Investors in a commodity fund must be notified within seven days of any decline in net asset value of 50% or more from the beginning of the year or the last valuation date.

Potential investors must be informed in the prospectus whether the fund will wind up automatically if the fund's net asset value per share falls below a certain level. As well, the manager of the fund must disclose his or her track record in managing comparable pools.

Because of the volatile nature of commodities futures, disclosure requirements are more stringent than for other mutual funds. Investors get
monthly reports on performance, commissions paid, and the like.

CHAPTER FIVE

ALL ABOUT INCOME FUNDS

FIXED INCOME MUTUAL FUNDS ARE PRIMARILY DESIGNED TO PROVIDE maximum income rather than growth, while preserving capital. These types of funds invest in income-producing securities – bonds, mortgages, treasury bills, and in some cases common stocks and preferred shares that have high yields. By investing for income rather than growth, fixed income fund returns are more stable than equity fund returns.

Depending on the specific fund, capital appreciation or depreciation can be a significant portion of total return, particularly during periods of volatile interest rates. But, generally, capital appreciation is a secondary objective for most bond funds, mortgage funds and preferred dividend funds.

Managers of fixed income funds are concerned primarily with the quality of the issuers of the securities they purchase, interest-rate trends and, depending on the fund, currency exchange rates.

Because preservation of capital is a primary objective, most fixed income funds have similar policies regarding the quality of the investments they make. For example, all mortgage funds invest primarily in first mortgages. These are the most secure type of mortgage. If a borrower defaults, the holder of the first mortgage has first call on the assets.

Similarly, most bond funds have a major portion of their assets in government bonds and government-guaranteed obligations. Debentures in their portfolios are generally of large companies whose assets are significantly greater than their debt loads and whose earnings have historically exceeded interest expense by a broad margin.

Preferred income funds have the vast majority of their assets invested in preferred shares of blue-chip Canadian companies whose securities are rated highly by the widely used rating services, Canadian Bond Rating Service Ltd. and Dominion Bond Rating Service. In order to assign ratings, the rating services examine the income statements and balance sheets of major companies that issue preferred shares, and consider industry trends. Most preferred income funds have some common shares but the portion is generally limited to a maximum of 20% to 25%.

Returns from fixed income funds have two components. First, of course, there is the income which reflects interest and dividends paid by the underlying securities. Second is capital appreciation, which reflects the impact of the market on the value of the underlying securities.

In periods of rising interest rates, the market values of fixed income securities decline. For example, in December 1980, Government of Canada bonds with 13% coupons maturing May 1, 2001, were trading at about $1,000. Seven months later, interest rates were at record levels and long-term Government of Canada bonds were yielding about 17.5%. At that point the bonds with 13% coupons were changing hands at about $750. The decline from $1,000 reflects the price that investors were willing to pay for that bond when new bonds were available at substantially higher yields.

This is an extreme example because the period noted was exceptional. As well, the volatility of a specific bond depends on the number of years to maturity – the date when the issuer will redeem the bond at face value. Bonds with only a few years to maturity are much less volatile.

Bond fund and preferred share fund managers have some control over performance in the way they structure their portfolios. Managers who expect a jump in rates sell their longer-term securities and move into shorter-term securities. Mortgage fund managers have less control because they have few, if any, opportunities to trade their portfolio to shorten or lengthen the terms of mortgages they hold. Also, the terms of the mortgages they hold largely reflect what was available in the marketplace at the time they made their purchases. More on this later.

Some fixed income fund managers try to increase their returns by holding debt instruments issued in foreign currencies. Several provinces, some Crown corporations and many major banks and corporations borrow abroad by issuing bonds and debentures denominated in U. S. dollars, Japanese yen, Australian dollars and some European currencies. Funds that hold these benefit if the foreign currencies appreciate against the Canadian dollar. However, performance suffers if the Canadian dollar does better.

Table IV

Taxation of Interest and Dividends

	Interest	Dividend
Interest received	$100.00	
Dividend received	-	$100.00
Dividend "gross up"	-	$25.00
Taxable Dividend	-	$125.00
Federal Tax (29%)	$29.00	$36.25
Less: Dividend Tax Credit	-	$16.67
Net federal tax + surtax	$29.87	$20.17
Add: Provincial Tax*	$14.50	$9.79
Total Tax	$44.37	$29.96
Net: After Tax	$55.63	$70.04

*50% of basic federal tax. Provincial tax rates vary from province to province.

Preferred-Dividend income funds

If your investment objective is current income, and the capital you want to invest is outside your RRSP, consider a preferred-dividend income fund. Your after-tax rate of return will generally be higher than the after-tax return from an interest-income mutual fund.

The federal government taxes various types of investment income differently. Interest income beyond the first $1,000 covered by the investment-income deduction is fully taxed. In contrast, the first $100,000 of capital gains is tax free, as a lifetime exemption.

Dividend income from Canadian corporations is treated in yet another way. To encourage Canadians to invest in shares and to help companies raise capital, the government invented the federal dividend tax credit to reduce the effective tax rate on dividend income from Canadian corporations. In effect, your after-tax rate of return from investing for dividends should exceed the after-tax return from interest vehicles.

Table IV compares the taxation of interest and dividends.

The impact of the dividend tax credit is to reduce the tax you pay on dividends from Canadian corporations so that on a pre-tax basis $1 of dividends is equal to about $1.26 of interest. So, on an after-tax basis a 6.4% dividend yield is equal to an 8% interest yield; an 8% dividend yield is equal to a 10% interest yield; and a 12% dividend yield is equal to a 15% interest yield.

Quebec sets its own tax rates independent of federal rates. A Quebec resident paying the top federal and provincial tax rates would net about $49 after-tax on $100 of interest income and about $62 on $100 of dividend income.

If you invest for dividends rather than interest, it's reasonable to expect an additional half a percentage point return after tax.

Managing a preferred share fund is a complicated task. First, there are several different types of preferred shares. Straight preferred shares pay a fixed dividend in perpetuity. They can be very volatile in periods of rapidly changing interest rates and, as a result, many investors are reluctant to buy them. So the investment community has developed other types of preferred shares in response to changing market conditions.

Floating-rate preferred shares, for instance, offer a dividend rate that is a certain percentage of the prime rate, say 70%. And there are floating-rate preferreds that have a fixed-minimum dividend rate.

Retractable preferreds give investors the right to return their shares to the issuer at full face value at a specific date.

Sinking-fund preferreds require the issuer to purchase or redeem a specific number of shares each year so that the total issue is retired after a certain number of years.

Convertible preferred shares give the holder the right to convert the shares into common stock. Investors buy convertible preferred shares because they provide more income than common shares. Then they can convert if the common dividend grows to a point where it exceeds the preferred.

A few companies have issued preferred shares denominated in U.S. dollars. A fund manager might also hold some common shares in a preferred fund if the yield on the shares was attractive.

Most fund managers use a similar universe of preferred shares, basing their investment decisions on quality, yield, liquidity and specific features of a preferred share, such as whether it is floating or retractable.

Quality considerations don't vary much from fund to fund. All invest the majority of their assets in high-quality preferred shares. By high quality, most Canadian fund managers mean preferred shares that carry P1 and P2 ratings issued by Canadian Bond Rating Service and Dominion Bond Rating Service. A portion of a fund may be invested in preferred shares that aren't rated or that have a lower rating, if the expected returns are superior. Similarly, a portion of the portfolio may be invested in high-yielding common shares.

A small portion of a fund may be invested in preferreds of smaller companies or of companies that have lower ratings, provided that the manager is satisfied about the safety of the dividend and the return is superior.

Depending on interest-rate spreads, a portion of the fund might also be invested in treasury bills. Because fund expenses, such as the management fee, can be charged against interest income, a fund manager will include some interest-paying investments such as treasury bills if the interest rate is higher than the rate available from preferreds.

Interest income funds

If interest income or a stable return is your major investment objective, as it is for many investors in RRSPs or registered retirement income funds, you have your choice of four different types of mutual funds: bond funds, mortgage funds, funds that invest in both bonds and mortgages, and money market and savings funds.

All four are backed by assets that carry little or no risk. Bond funds, for example, include bonds and debentures that are guaranteed by governments, Crown corporations, major banks, or the credit-worthiness of major corporations. Mortgage funds have as their underlying securities mortgages that are secured by specific properties. In some cases these mortgages are insured against default, guaranteed by a government agency or guaranteed by the manager of the fund. Money market funds generally hold either: treasury bills that are guaranteed by the federal government, provincial treasury bills that are guaranteed by the issuing province, securities issued or guaranteed by major financial institutions, or top-quality short-term notes issued by major corporations.

So with an interest income mutual fund you don't have to worry much about losing your money. That can, of course, happen. But the quality of the overall portfolios as well as the various guarantees make the impact of any such defaults insignificant to the value of an interest income fund.

There are, however, some differences among the four different types of funds, and these affect the returns you may receive. These differances reflect the types of securities they hold. To understand how this works you have to look at the underlying securities in which such funds invest.

Let's assume you have a choice of three funds. The first invests only in Government of Canada treasury bills, the second in Government of Canada bonds and the third in mortgages guaranteed by the federal government under the National Housing Act. So, in all three cases, we have Ottawa guaranteeing the underlying securities.

Even so, the returns you can earn from these funds may differ widely. For instance, during the 12 months ended June 30, 1988, the top 10 bond funds gave rates of return that ranged from 7.8% to 12.1%; the top 10 mortgage funds gave returns between 7.9% and 9.7%; and money market and savings funds had returns clustered around 9%.

Interest rates were volatile, rising until October, then falling sharply when the Bank of Canada eased the money supply following the stock-market crash. During the first half of 1988, interest rates generally moved higher. This differed dramatically from 1986, when interest rates generally were in a downward trend. Consequently, bond funds with large portions of their assets in long-term bonds showed significant capital appreciation; mortgage funds showed some capital appreciation; and money market funds showed virtually no capital appreciation, with income coming almost entirely from interest.

Of course, the reverse can happen, too – periods when interest rates rise and money market and savings funds perform better than mortgage or bond funds. In those periods mortgage and bond funds showed capital depreciation or declines in the value of their underlying portfolios.

Money market and savings funds have the most stable rates of return. That's because the securities they hold are very short-term and will be redeemed at full face value by the issuer within one year. So the rates of return on money market funds are almost entirely income, with little that can be attributed to changing market values of the underlying securities.

A mortgage fund is more volatile than a money market fund. A mortgage fund holds securities that may mature in as little as six months or as long as five years. Its rate of return includes the interest paid on the mortgages it holds, plus or minus an adjustment to the market value of the mortgages in its portfolio. The market values change with changes in mortgage rates. If rates go up, the values of mortgages in the portfolio decline, with longer-term mortgages declining more than shorter-term mortgages.

A $50,000 five-year mortgage issued at 12.5%, for example, would have a market value of about $40,000 if new five-year mortgages were available at 19%.

But mortgage funds are not as volatile as this example seems to indicate because fund holdings include both shorter- and longer-term mortgages. Also, new money coming into the fund or mortgages coming up for renewal will enter at prevailing rates. This serves to stabilize returns.

Bond funds are generally more volatile than mortgage funds because they hold securities that may not mature for 20 years or more. A manager expecting rates to fall will trade the portfolio to increase the percentage of bonds which mature in, say, 20 years. That way the portfolio "locks" in a high rate of return. Conversely, a manager expecting higher rates will move into the shorter end of the market.

To sum up, money market and savings funds have the most stable rates of return. But over the long haul that stability has a cost. The cost comes in the lower rates of return that money market funds earn over the longer term, compared with bond or mortgage funds. Bond funds have given higher long-term total returns than mortgage funds. But they have been more volatile and in some years have underperformed mortgage funds. For current income, however, mortgage funds often have an edge over bond funds because mortgage rates are generally higher than bond yields.

Funds that invest in bonds and mortgages combine the characteristics of both types of funds.

Bond funds

The primary objective of most bond funds is to earn the maximum interest income possible without taking significant risk. But an important part of a bond fund's total return can include capital gains that stem from trading. Still, earning income is more important. The fund manager meets this objective by investing in quality bonds. Virtually all bond funds offered in Canada hold a major portion of their assets in government and government-guaranteed bonds, issues guaranteed by the major chartered banks and debt issues of the most credit-worthy corporations.

Canadian Trusteed Income Fund, for example, restricts its holdings to Government of Canada bonds; Hallmark Bond Fund restricts its investments to Government of Canada securities and debt instruments issued or guaranteed by chartered banks.

The investment policies of bond funds generally reflect the investment objectives of the conservative investors who use them for their RRSPs, RRIFs and for income.

But even though virtually all funds invest in the same quality of issuers, performance can vary widely. These variations reflect the expertise of the fund manager as well as the fund's investment policy.

There are many ways that bond fund managers can increase returns. But most involve structuring a portfolio to reflect anticipated moves in interest rates. A fund manager who expects long-term rates to fall might increase the fund's holdings of long-term bonds. This would lock in high-yielding coupons of bonds which mature in, say, 20 years. Conversely, a manager who expects interest rates to rise will move into shorter-term bonds.

The actual management of the bond portfolio can be quite complicated. Not only does the manager have to consider the direction of interest rates, but also the relative yields of short-term and long-term bonds. In some periods long-term bonds yield significantly more than short-term bonds. Other times their yields will be about the same. There have been some occasions when short-term rates have actually been higher than long-term rates.

Managers will trade bonds to improve yields. Each trade may improve the yield of a small portion of the portfolio by only a fraction of a percentage point. But done often enough, this can have a significant impact on overall performance.

Bond funds can also generate significant capital gains. This can happen when a manager sells bonds at a profit. For instance, a fund manager expecting an imminent drop in rates might buy discount bonds – bonds that sell at a discount to their face value because their coupons offer lower yields than new bonds.

Fund managers can also boost yields by increasing the portion of their portfolios invested in corporate bonds. Corporate bonds generally have higher coupon rates than government bonds of the same maturity. The higher yields, of course, reflect the fact that corporate bonds don't have the backing of a government. In addition, corporate bonds aren't as liquid as government bonds so the spread between the buy and sell prices can be significantly wider. As a result, the trading costs of a fund that has a heavy corporate component may be higher.

Another way of potentially boosting return is to invest in bonds denominated in foreign currencies. Crown corporations, provinces, banks and companies have raised money outside Canada by issuing bonds and debentures in foreign currencies. The U.S. dollar is the most common currency used. But Canadian governments and companies also commonly raise money in Australian dollars, New Zealand dollars, Japanese yen, Swiss francs and West German marks.

Even though these bonds are denominated in foreign currencies, their issuers are Canadian so they are eligible for inclusion in RRSPs and pension funds.

A fund manager might hold foreign currency bonds if the interest rate paid were substantially higher than the rate paid on Canadian dollar bonds of the same issuer and same maturity and there appeared to be no foreign exchange risk. Or the manager might want to hold foreign currency bonds because he or she expected a sharp decline in the value of the Canadian dollar.

The statement of investments held by Dynamic Income Fund in Appendix B includes Canadian bonds denominated in foreign currencies as well as Canadian dollar bonds.

Specialty bond funds

Most of the bond funds offered by investment counsellors, investment dealers, banks and trust and insurance companies are designed to appeal to investors seeking income rather than capital appreciation. These funds are eligible for RRSPs and pension funds.

There are several exceptions, such as AGF Global Government Bond Fund. It invests in bonds issued by central governments of countries with developed capital markets. Its objective is high income and capital appreciation.

Some years ago, one company launched a "junk-bond" fund that invested in lower-quality bonds of U.S. corporate issuers. The fund provided a yield much higher than other bond funds offered in Canada. The fund failed to attract investor attention and was dropped. Apparently, few investors understood how the manager selected securities for the portfolio.

One equity fund that has done well with lower-quality bonds is Vancouver-based Cundill Value Fund. Its manager, Peter Cundill, looks for debentures of companies in financial difficulty. He purchases these at a fraction of face value, anticipating corporate reorganizations that will make the debentures much more valuable.

Mortgage funds

Mortgage funds are designed to provide maximum interest income for investors. Because mortgage rates are generally at least a point higher than bond yields, mortgage funds pay more current income per dollar invested than bond funds.

Unlike bond funds, mortgage funds rarely trade what they buy. Consequently, capital gains are unlikely to be part of a mortgage fund investor's income. And because few mortgages are available with interest rates fixed beyond five years, mortgage funds as a group are less volatile than bond funds.

A mortgage is a loan secured by property. A residential mortgage is on a home; a commercial or industrial loan is on a commercial or industrial property. Commercial and industrial loans often have longer terms than residential mortgages and higher yields. A property can have several mortgages on it representing several loans. A second mortgage is less secure than a first mortgage; a third mortgage is less secure than a second mortgage. Virtually all the major bank, trust-company, investment counsellor and insurance company mortgage funds hold first mortgages only. The amount of the loan is generally no more than 75% of the value of the property. Lenders can go higher than the 75% ceiling but in these cases they usually insure the mortgage against default.

Some funds, such as London Life Mortgage Fund, invest in residential, commercial and industrial mortgages. But most restrict their investments to residential mortgages.

Because the funds invest in first mortgages, investors needn't worry much about losses. For example, First Canadian Mortgage Fund, offered by Bank of Montreal, invests only in mortgages that amount to no more than 75% of the value of the property or are guaranteed under the National Housing Act or insured by the Mortgage Insurance Co. of Canada. If a mortgage goes into default, the bank guarantees to buy it at no penalty to the fund.

The bank has had its fund reviewed by Canadian Bond Rating Service and Dominion Bond Rating Service. Both gave it an "AAA" rating. The rating demonstrates minimum risk and good returns. The fund was the first to be rated by the two agencies. Generally, ratings are used for institutional investment products rather than investments aimed primarily at smaller investors.

Unlike bonds, mortgages – especially residential mortgages – are not traded actively. Consequently, mortgage fund managers are somewhat restricted relative to bond fund managers in their ability to change the structure of their portfolios in anticipation of changes in interest rates.

Mortgage fund managers, particularly of bank and trust company funds, have little choice in the terms of mortgages purchased by the funds. The mix of, say, six-month, one-year, three-year and five-year mortgages is dependent largely on market conditions rather than on what the managers want. For instance, if most mortgage customers of the sponsoring bank or trust company choose four- and five-year terms – as happens in periods of rising interest rates – then that's where new money in the fund will be invested. Conversely, in periods of falling rates, when managers would like to increase the portion of four- and five-year mortgages, more borrowers will opt for shorter-term mortgages.

How this affects a fund depends on the portion of mortgages up for renewal in a given period and the growth rate of fund sales.

Of course, if demand for longer-term mortgages drops drastically, then the spread between longer-term and shorter-term mortgages will narrow, shifting some of the demand.

The rate-of-return differences between two mortgage funds reflects the manager's ability to keep the portfolio balanced to minimize interest rate risk and keep the unit value relatively steady. Funds offered by the larger financial institutions probably have more flexibility in that the funds are often a minute fraction of the total mortgage portfolio offered by the institution, in some cases less than 1% of the total. This gives fund managers some discretion as to which mortgages with which terms will be acquired by the fund.

Bond - and - mortgage funds

There are a number of funds that invest in both bonds and mortgages. Some have rigid asset-mix ratios. For example, Canada Life Fixed Income S-19 fund invests 75% of its assets in liquid, fixed income securities and the balance in securities "which provide a premium return in exchange for a lower level of liquidity." Others don't follow fixed ratios. Several, such as Mackenzie Mortgage and Income Fund, may include common and preferred shares with attractive yields and the opportunity for capital appreciation.

Rates of return of these funds, as a group, are more volatile than simple mortgage funds but less volatile than pure bond funds.

Money market and savings funds

Money market and savings funds provide interest income with virtually no risk to capital. In fact most money market and savings funds price their units at a constant value. Values of $1 and $10 are the most common. Yields on these funds move in concert with short-term yields such as on treasury bills. Interest earned on the fund is used to purchase additional units on investors' behalf. Income is credited to clients' accounts daily in the case of funds that price their units daily and weekly in the case of funds that price weekly.

Money market funds invest in a portfolio of highly liquid short-term debt instruments which generally mature within one year. These include federal and provincial government treasury bills, chartered bank certificates of deposit and instruments guaranteed by chartered banks, such as bankers' acceptances, and short-term notes issued by the most credit-worthy major corporations.

Savings funds keep their money on deposit with financial institutions, earning wholesale rates of interest that are generally at least a couple of points higher than retail rates paid on premium savings accounts.

The rates of return on savings funds are tied to the prime rate. And changes in the yields on money market funds may lag or precede changes in the prime rate, depending on the holdings of the portfolio and the moves in the "short end" of the market.

Returns vary moderately among money market funds, with the differences reflecting the aggressiveness of the manager. Some funds will restrict their holdings to instruments that mature within 90 days and keep them until maturity. Even a sharp jump in interest rates would have only a moderate impact on such funds' performance. Other funds might hold instruments with longer maturities to pick up a slightly higher return. Generally, the longer the term to maturity the higher the rates. Managers of these funds would trade their holdings to increase yields, too.

CHAPTER SIX

ALL ABOUT CLOSED-END FUNDS

NOT ALL FUNDS AUTOMATICALLY ISSUE NEW SHARES WHEN INVESTORS want to buy. A handful of funds called closed-end funds have a fixed number of shares or units. These are traded on a stock exchange such as the Toronto Stock Exchange. If you want shares of a closed-end fund, you have to buy them from someone who already owns them by placing an order with your stockbroker. (Closed-end precious metals funds have their own TSE sub-index.)

Closed-end funds, like other funds, invest in a portfolio. Most closed-end funds are specialty funds that invest in particular areas such as precious metals, global investments or bonds. These funds are closed-end investment holding companies.

In addition there is a small group of funds called income trusts. They use investors' and borrowed capital to invest in a portfolio of fixed-income investments that pass on the interest income to investors.

The closed-end investment holding companies that invest in gold and in international portfolios are corporations, just like other companies listed on stock exchanges. Instead of, say, making or selling something, they invest capital. They have the same powers and responsibilities as other corporations. In fact, they can have a lot more leeway as to investment policies than open-end funds.

In addition, their profits are taxable like those of other corporations. So any income earned or capital gains realized by a closed-end investment holding company are taxable in the corporation's hands. This differs from the case of open-end funds where income and gains are generally flowed through.

Closed-end funds have been around for more than half a century. But their numbers increased in the early 1980s. The surge in popularity of

Table V

TSE Net Asset Value & Share Prices

Fund	Share price	Net asset value
BGR Precious Metals Inc.	$10.88	$13.54
Central Fund of Canada Ltd.	7.00	7.60
MVP Capital Corp.	0.81	1.24

closed-end funds coincided with the push by brokerage houses to promote self-directed RRSPs. At the time, shares listed on Canadian stock exchanges could be held in self-directed RRSPs without any restrictions. Closed-end funds qualified, even if their portfolios held investments such as gold bullion that would be ineligible if held directly in an RRSP or if their portfolios exceeded the 10% limit on foreign property that applies generally to RRSPs. So closed-end funds were promoted by investment dealers partly as a way of getting around the intent of the rules restricting RRSP investments. During this period Central Fund of Canada, one of the older closed-end funds, became a gold fund and had a share issue. Three new closed-end gold funds – Goldcorp Investments Ltd., Guardian-Morton Shulman Precious Metals Inc. and BGR Precious Metals Inc. – were also established. Shortly after, several global funds were underwritten: Guardian Pacific Rim, Guardian International Income and Worldwide Equities.

Ottawa revised its rules in 1986 so that closed-end funds that were primarily invested in foreign securities would be considered foreign property and limited to 10% of an RRSP. Closed-end funds that were already primarily invested in foreign property were "grandfathered" provided they did not arrange to issue additional shares after December 4, 1985, the date when Ottawa proposed the change.

But even under the new rules, a closed-end fund could have up to 50% of its income from foreign property in its portfolio and still not be considered foreign property for RRSP purposes. A closed-end fund could be 100% of the assets in a self-directed RRSP.

Closed-end funds have a limited following compared with open-end funds. That's largely because closed-end funds have tended to trade at a significant discount to the value of their underlying assets. Table V shows several funds and their share prices on the TSE as well as the value of the underlying assets per share as of August 5, 1988.

The discounts apparently reflect the relative lack of liquidity of closed-end funds. Shareholders of open-end funds can redeem their shares at full net asset value on any valuation day. But holders of closed-end funds can sell their investments only if other investors are buyers. In a falling market, potential buyers of a closed-end fund might be scarce. The discount from underlying asset value will increase accordingly, reducing the market value of the fund units.

In a rising market the discount may shrink or even disappear. If, for instance, foreign investors become heavy buyers of closed-end gold funds as a means of buying a portfolio of Canadian gold shares, their prices might rise sharply.

The discount might also shrink on speculation that a closed-end fund might convert to an open-end fund. In mid-1987, Guardian Pacific Rim announced it was asking shareholders to approve a proposal to convert the closed-end fund to an open-end fund. Its shares were trading at about a 17% discount to asset value before the announcement. Two months later the discount had shrunk to about 12%.

But there are also advantages to the fact that shares of a closed-end fund cannot be redeemed on demand. For instance, managers could be allowed more leeway in making investments.

A manager of a closed-end fund might decide to invest in shares with restricted marketability. Because shareholders can't redeem shares on demand, the manager could afford to have a portion of the portfolio in illiquid securities. About 90% of the portfolio of open-end funds must be in liquid investments.

Similarly, a closed-end fund might invest in part with borrowed funds. (The investment policies of closed-end funds are generally included in their annual reports.) For investment-income trusts, the Ontario Securities Commission restricts debt to a maximum of 25% of the assets of the fund. In contrast, open-end funds may not borrow other than temporarily (up to 5% of assets) to meet redemptions.

The minimum equity capital for an investment-income trust closed-end fund is $1 million. The minimum for an equity mutual fund is $100,000.

Income and realized capital gains made by a closed-end fund are taxable at corporate rates. And corporations aren't eligible for the lifetime capital-gains exemption. Consequently, the rate of return to an investor holding a closed-end fund might be lower than the rate of return earned on an open-end fund with a similar investment program.

There are several closed-end funds that were issued as flow-through limited partnership tax shelters. These funds purchased what are called flow-through shares from mining companies and obtained certain writeoffs which their investors were able to use to reduce taxes. After the minimum holding period required by regulatory authorities, these closed-end funds could roll their holdings tax free into open-end funds in exchange for shares in the open-end funds. At this point the limited partnerships would dissolve and the holdings of open-end fund shares would be distributed to their investors.

Among the better known flow-through limited partnerships that follow this route are the CMP partnerships, which roll into funds in the Dynamic Group.

CHAPTER SEVEN

WHAT
TO DO
FIRST

MUTUAL FUNDS CAN BE USED SUCCESSFULLY TO MEET BOTH YOUR short-term and long-term objectives, either inside RRSPs or outside of them. The trick, of course, is to make sure the funds you choose meet your objectives and are compatible with your financial picture.

Assuming you've taken care of the basics, such as making sure you have adequate life and disability insurance, an up-to-date will and a cash cushion equivalent to several months' salary, the first thing you should do is make a list of your investments (including your home) and your debts.

Interest paid on personal debts such as outstanding credit card balances and mortgages is generally not deductible from income for tax purposes. The rule to follow is this: pay off all personal debt before starting any long-term investment program outside your RRSP.

Look at it this way. Paying off your debt is like making a risk-free investment that pays premium rates of return. Bank credit card charges are around 16% – higher in some cases. And while many mutual funds have given moderately higher long-term rates of return, you wouldn't run out to borrow money at 16% in the hope of earning 18%, particularly if the 18% rate wasn't guaranteed and the 16% wasn't deductible from tax. Yet that is exactly what you would be doing if you invested in mutual funds while carrying unpaid balances on your credit cards.

Paying off your mortgage isn't as cut-and-dried as paying off your credit card debts because mortgage rates are generally a lot lower than the historical rates earned on equity-based mutual funds. Even so, you should still pay off your mortgage as quickly as possible. You always have the option of borrowing against the equity in your home and using the proceeds to buy mutual funds. You'll still owe money on your home. But this way the interest on the loan will be tax deductible. Whether you should borrow against your home is another story. More on this later.

Once you've got your balance sheet in order, you should develop a basic understanding of how the federal government taxes different types of investment income. Knowing this will help you structure your portfolio so that you'll pay the least amount of income tax possible on your investment income.

There are four basic types of investment income to consider: interest from Canadian sources, dividends from Canadian corporations, interest and dividends from foreign sources, and capital gains.

Interest income from Canadian sources, such as interest earned on bank and trust company deposits, Canada Savings Bonds and mortgages, is fully taxable at marginal tax rates. (Remember, your marginal tax rate is the rate of tax you pay on the last dollar you earn. As income increases, so does your tax rate in most cases. So your marginal rate is the highest rate of tax you pay.)

Interest income and dividends from foreign corporations are fully taxable at your marginal tax rate. This includes interest earned on foreign bank deposits, such as a trust company account in Florida or income from a U.S.-based money market fund. It also includes dividends from U.S. corporations such as General Motors Corp. and International Business Machines Corp., even if the shares are listed on Canadian exchanges or flowed through to you through a Canadian mutual fund.

Dividends from Canadian corporations, whether paid directly or flowed to you through a mutual fund, are eligible for the dividend tax credit, which effectively reduces the rate of tax paid. .

Capital gains are the gains made on the sale of capital property. This includes real estate, stocks, mutual funds and precious metals. The property can be Canadian or foreign. Gains on the sale of your principal residence are tax free and excluded from capital gains, but gains on the sale of a second property, such as a cottage, are considered capital gains for tax purposes.

The Mulroney government originally allowed each individual a lifetime capital-gains exemption of $500,000. Under tax reform this has been capped at $100,000, other than for farms and small business corporations, where the $500,000 limit still applies. Capital gains stemming from the sale of a principal residence are exempt from tax.

In 1987, half of capital gains were taxable. So if you realized $100,000 of capital gains in 1987 and had not previously claimed any of your exemption you would have payed no tax. If, say, you realized $150,000 in capital gains and had not yet claimed any of your exemption, the first $100,000 would have been tax free and one-half of the remaining $50,000 would have been taxed.

The rules changed dramatically for 1988 and beyond. First, the portion of capital gains that will be taxable increased from 50% in 1987 to 66.7% in 1988, and to 75% in 1990.

Moreover, you can apply capital gains to your lifetime exemption only after subtracting any cumulative net investment losses. For 1987, you were able to claim a capital-gains exemption on cumulative capital gains less cumulative capital losses and cumulative allowable business losses. Simply put, if you have realized gains of $60,000 and realized losses of $20,000, you could have claimed $40,000 against your exemption.

For 1988 and beyond it becomes a lot more complicated: Only those gains that exceed your cumulative net investment losses (investment losses less investment income) can be applied against the lifetime exemption.

Suffice to say that for 1988 and 1989, 66.7% of your capital gains are taxable. So if you realize capital gains of $150,000, have no cumulative net investment losses and have not previously claimed any of your lifetime deduction, the first $100,000 will be tax free and you will pay tax on two-thirds of the remainder, or on $33,333. If however, you have $10,000 of interest expense net of dividends and interest received, you will pay tax on $43,333. You'll be able to claim the remaining $10,000 of your exemption in a subsequent year.

For 1990 and beyond, 75% of capital gains will be taxable. Using our example of $150,000 realized capital gains, 75% of the amount exceeding the lifetime exemption will be taxable, in this case $37,500.

It is important to note that inside RRSPs – the largest if not the only major savings program for many people – investment income compounds untaxed. However, when money is withdrawn from an RRSP either directly or in payments from an annuity or registered retirement income fund, the money is fully taxable whether it reflects interest income, dividends or capital gains.

Consequently, you should structure your total savings and investment package to reflect this tax treatment of investment income.

In fact, many people don't do this and end up paying more tax than they should. For example, many people hold interest-paying investments such as CSBs and guaranteed investment certificates outside their RRSPs and growth mutual funds inside their plans. They pay tax on the interest earned outside their RRSPs. And while capital gains inside their RRSPs grow untaxed, they will eventually be fully taxed.

If these people restructured their holdings so that their growth assets were outside their RRSPs and their interest-paying assets were inside their RRSPs they would reduce their taxes. They would still own the same assets. But now their interest would compound untaxed inside their RRSPs while any capital gains earned would be eligible for the lifetime capital-gains exemption.

If you currently hold interest-paying assets outside your RRSP and growth assets inside your RRSP you can switch them around on a dollar-for-dollar basis using a self-directed RRSP available through virtually all investment dealers and most trust companies.

CHAPTER EIGHT

HOW TO MEET YOUR OBJECTIVES

ONCE YOU HAVE STRUCTURED YOUR SAVINGS AND INVESTMENTS, THE next step is to list your specific investment objectives. They could include saving for the down payment on a house, saving for retirement, saving for your children's education, investing for current income or simply investing for long-term growth.

Investment objectives can generally be categorized as short-term, medium-term or long-term. For our purposes, short-term means up to a couple of years, medium-term means three to 10 years, and long-term is anything longer than that.

Generally, short-term savings objectives are best met with money market funds simply because they are virtually risk free. If you know that you will need the money fairly soon for a specific purpose, then a money market fund is for you.

If you won't need the money for three years or more, you have a lot more leeway. You can use fixed income funds without too much worry. Even in years with sharp increases in interest rates, most fixed income funds show positive returns. Over a three-year period, virtually all fixed income funds show positive returns.

Whether you use equity funds really depends on how much risk you are willing to take. There is nothing wrong with using equity funds for medium-term investment objectives, provided you can accept the risk. It depends largely on whether you may find yourself forced to sell your holdings in a period when prices are down.

For long-term objectives, consider equity funds, which have traditionally outperformed fixed income and money market funds over periods of a decade or more.

Your investment objectives should be considered very loose guidelines. There will be times when even long-term investors may want a heavy portion of assets invested in income and money market funds because of nervousness about the stock market. And there will be times when stocks seem very inexpensive, and conservative investors who would normally invest for income may move into growth funds. Saving for the down payment on a home or to pay down mortgage principal is usually considered a short-term objective. Saving for children's education can be a short-, medium- or long-term objective, depending on the children's ages. If you start the program when the child is born it's a long-term program. If you wait until the child is in his or her early teens, it's a short- or medium-term program. Similarly, a 20-year-old's RRSP is a long-term savings program while a 63-year-old's RRSP is a short-term program.

The rule of thumb is that the shorter the term of the savings program, the more conservative you should be and the less risk you should take.

Meeting short-term objectives

If you're going to need your money soon, say within a year or so, it is probably best to play it safe and invest in a money market or savings fund. You'll pay tax on any interest earned. But the tradeoff for what is a relatively low return is the knowledge that you are not taking any risk and that you'll be getting all your money back, plus interest.

Alternatively, you may want to look closely at preferred dividend funds. Many have had relatively stable returns. Depending on your income and tax bracket, the difference in rate of return between a money market fund and dividend fund can be significant. But remember: dividend funds, while relatively stable, are still more volatile than money market funds.

Generally, equity funds, and to a lesser extent bond funds, are too volatile to meet short-term savings objectives, particularly if a decline in capital will affect your lifestyle. So if you're saving for the down payment on a home, don't invest in equity funds if a decline in the value of your investment will keep you out of that home. If you do invest in equity funds, particularly a specialty fund, in the hope of significant short-term performance, realize that you are a speculator – possibly even a gambler – betting that the market will perform as you expect.

Meeting medium-term objectives

If you are a conservative investor your best bet is probably a fixed income fund, either a bond or mortgage fund for an RRSP, or a preferred dividend fund if you are trying to maximize your after-tax return.

You can, of course, go into growth funds, too. It all depends on where the market is. A lot can happen in relatively short periods of time. During the first quarter of 1987 the Toronto Stock Exchange 300 total return index gained 22.8%. But it doesn't always move up, as many investors learned when the index plunged 31% between its August peak and October trough. Unless you've got a crystal ball or more than enough financial assets to meet your medium-term objectives, you should look at fixed income funds rather than equities.

Meeting long-term objectives

If you won't need the money for more than a decade, go for growth using equity-based funds. Even if you measure performance using a market bottom as an ending date, such as the summer of 1982, almost all equity funds show positive returns over a 10-year period.

Of course, it makes little sense to jump into equity funds at a market top. So if you are a bit nervous about the near-term direction of the market, take a conservative stance by putting only part of your money into equity funds and place the rest in money market funds.

Alternatively, look for funds that have heavy cash components, indicating that the manager has the same concerns as you. You should also consider balanced funds because managers of these funds change asset mixes to reflect market conditions, increasing or decreasing equities according to market outlook.

Personal objectives

The following pages outline some of the more common savings and investment objectives and how mutual funds can be used to meet them.

1. **Saving for the down payment on a home.** If you're saving for a home, you are probably looking to buy within a year or two. This makes your program relatively short-term, which means you can't risk having to redeem your holdings when the market is down. Consequently, your investments should be confined to low-risk funds – funds whose investment policies virtually guarantee your principal and interest.

Money market and savings funds are the only funds that meet these requirements. They should be used exclusively if you expect to need your money within a year or so.

If you don't intend to buy a house for several years, you can accept more risk in the expectation of earning a higher rate of return. Look at dividend income funds or bond funds. Both, while more volatile than money market funds, are substantially less volatile than equity funds. Over most one-year periods, bond funds have done better than money market funds. In periods of sharply rising interest rates, a bond fund could do worse than a money market fund, even declining in value. Nevertheless, over a three-year period or longer you will almost certainly do better in dividend income or bond funds than in money market funds, if what has happened historically holds true for the future.

You may be tempted to use equity funds to save for the down payment on a home. Indeed, the gains of recent years may make this a tempting option. Just remember that equity funds are volatile and that there will be some periods when prices will drop dramatically. If you can't afford to see the value of your holdings drop, then don't go near equity funds.

2. **Paying down your mortgage.** Most banks and trust companies allow you to prepay the principal outstanding on your mortgage. The limit is generally 10% of the principal annually on the anniversary of the mortgages. (Some institutions set the limit at 15%.) As well, you can pay off any portion at the renewal date.

Paying off your mortgage should be a priority before starting any long-term savings program other than your RRSP. You pay interest on your mortgage using after-tax dollars. This means that you have to earn $1.63 to pay off every $1 of interest, assuming your taxable income is between $27,501 and $55,000. If it's higher, you have to earn $1.78 to pay $1 of interest after tax.

So if your mortgage rate is 12%, you would have to earn more than 19% on your investments – before tax – to break even. And remember, paying down your mortgage is a risk-free investment.

You can, of course, have your cake and eat it too by paying down your mortgage, borrowing against the equity in your home, then investing the capital. That way your mortgage interest is deductible. This strategy will be covered in detail in the next chapter.

3. **Saving for your children's education.** Since, for most families, saving for children's education is a medium- to long-term objective, mutual funds fit the bill. What you have to remember is that any interest or dividends earned on the capital you provide is taxable in your hands. However, any capital gains earned are attributed to the child or children.

You should also keep in mind that if you invest family allowance cheques directly in your children's names, any interest or dividends earned are taxable in their hands, not yours. In effect, each child can earn several thousand dollars of interest and dividends tax free, so it makes sense to use family allowance as the cornerstone of any education savings program.

If you prefer to be on the conservative side when it comes to investing your children's money, use a bond or a mortgage fund. Alternatively, choose a balanced fund.

If university or college is a decade or more away, consider growth funds to give you a higher expected rate of return.

What many families do is use a combination of income and growth funds. Family allowance cheques are invested in bond and mortgage funds while other capital is invested for growth. Just remember: When the children are a few years away from university, educational savings becomes a short-term objective. You may want to lock in your profits from growth funds and move into income funds or money market funds.

If you or a grandparent wants to invest a lump sum for children's education you might want to consider a mutual fund registered education savings plan (RESP). The capital contributed to a RESP is not deductible for tax purposes. However, any income earned grows untaxed. The income is taxable in the child's hands when withdrawn to finance post-secondary education but the capital is withdrawn tax free. However, the child's total income is likely to be low, so little or no tax will likely be paid. The money must be used to finance post-secondary education. If the child who is named as beneficiary does not continue his or her education, you can name another beneficiary.

A number of mutual fund companies, including Bolton Tremblay Funds Inc. and Mackenzie Financial Corp., offer RESPs through mutual fund dealers and brokers.

4. **RRSPs.** By far, the largest single use of mutual funds is in RRSPs. Some estimates indicate that more than half the $30 billion that Canadians have invested in mutual funds is in RRSPs. Because of the federal government's requirement that 90% of assets be invested in Canadian securities, RRSPs are concentrated in Canadian equity and balanced funds, bond funds and mortgage funds.

However, investors are allowed 10% foreign content in their RRSPs, so many people have funds in their RRSPs that invest outside of Canada. They do this by holding their funds in self-directed RRSPs. These are available from virtually every organization involved in marketing mutual funds.

An RRSP is a way of saving tax-deferred dollars for retirement. Your contribution is deductible from income for tax purposes. In effect, you are saving untaxed dollars. Income within an RRSP grows untaxed as well. However, when you withdraw money from an RRSP, either by cashing in your plan or by using one of the retirement options allowed, such as a registered retirement income fund (RRIF) or annuity, the proceeds are taxed.

If you are a member of a company pension plan, your contribution limit for 1988 and 1989 is a maximum contribution of 20% of your earned income (this excludes investment income) up to $3,500, less whatever you contribute to the company plan.

If you are not a member of a company plan your contribution limit for 1988 and 1989 is 20% of earned income up to a maximum contribution of $7,500. Contributions must be made during the taxation year or within 60 days of year end.

The federal government has been proposing major revisions of the pension system that will allow greater contributions to RRSPs. But in August 1989, white paper the government announced it would introduce these higher contribution limits at a slower pace than originally proposed. This was the third time it announced delays in implementing higher contribution limits.

The proposed contribution limits will be based on 18% of the previous year's income up to a maximum contribution of $10,500 for 1990, $11,500 for 1991, $12,500 for 1992, $13,500 for 1993, $14,500 for 1994, and $15,500 for 1995. From these contribution limits you must subtract any contributions made to a pension plan by you or on your behalf by your employer.

There are a couple of major points you should consider when using mutual funds for your RRSP. How does your RRSP fit in with your other savings? How much risk are you willing to take?

As noted earlier in this chapter, when you withdraw money from an RRSP, proceeds are fully taxable whether your gains are interest, dividends or capital gains. So if you are saving both inside and outside an RRSP and you have both growth and interest-paying investments, you should structure your holdings so that as much of the interest-paying portion as possible is inside your RRSP. Keeping the growth portion outside your RRSP allows you to take advantage of the $100,000 capital gains exemption, or if it is already used up, have your capital gains taxed only partially.

As far as risk is concerned, you have two basic strategies from which to choose, one that is active and one that is passive. The active strategy is to constantly change the mix of mutual funds within your RRSP, moving into growth funds when they offer the best values and into income funds and money market funds when the outlook for equities is cloudy. This strategy, if successful, will give you the best returns from growth and income while preserving capital.

The passive strategy reflects the view that the closer to retirement you are, the more conservative you should be. The following are some guidelines based on age for structuring your retirement savings between interest-paying and growth investments. They apply to your total retirement savings, including those outside your RRSP.

If you are in your 20s, you have at least three decades before retirement. You can accept volatility in your RRSP and should invest the bulk of your RRSP for growth. Over the years you'll experience some ups and downs. But over the long haul you will probably come out significantly ahead of what you would have earned by playing it safe.

If you're in your 30s, you still have many years to go before retirement, so you can still put the bulk of your assets into equity funds, say, 80%, and invest the remaining 20% for income.

If you're in your 40s, you should become a bit more conservative and move to, say, 60% growth funds and 40% in bond funds, mortgage funds or both.

Once you're in your 50s, retirement is in sight. Consider moving to 40% growth and 60% income.

When you're within a decade of retirement, your main objective should be preservation of capital rather than growth. Move to 80% income and 20% growth funds as a longer-term hedge against inflation.

But remember, these are only guidelines. People approaching retirement who have substantial investment assets – more than enough to comfortably finance their retirements – may decide to keep most of their assets invested for growth. Indeed, someone who started investing in his or her 20s might well decide to remain in equities because of the wealth he or she would likely accumulate. Similarly, if you have an adequate pension plan you might opt to keep the bulk of your retirement assets invested for growth.

You also have to consider market conditions. It doesn't make much sense to plunge into equity funds if it looks like the markets are due for a sharp correction, even if you won't be retiring for 30 years or more. Similarly, people approaching retirement may want to put more of their money in growth funds if the market has been declining and prices seem relatively cheap.

You should also consider the portfolio components of the funds you hold. For example, balanced funds hold a blend of growth and income investments. You may want to consider this in structuring your RRSP. So a 50-year-old might hold 50% to 60% in a balanced fund and the remainder in bond funds, rather than 40% in growth funds.

Just remember that the objective of retirement savings is to finance retirement. Therefore, it should be the most conservative portion of your portfolio.

5. **Registered retirement income funds.** You can't have an RRSP beyond December 31 of the year in which you turn 71. You have to roll your RRSP into an annuity or registered retirement income fund (RRIF) or cash it in and pay tax on the proceeds.

The RRIF option meets the needs of most investors. With an RRIF you can hold the same investments as in an RRSP. Moving from an RRSP to an RRIF is a simple matter which involves filling out a form provided by your fund broker or the mutual fund company with which you have your RRSP.

You can withdraw as much from your RRIF as you want each year. The least you are allowed to withdraw is determined by the following formula: divide the amount in your plan by 90 minus your age. For example, a 70-year-old with $100,000 in an RRIF must withdraw a minimum of $5,000 a year.

So the income you draw from an RRIF can be very flexible. You can convert your RRSP to an RRIF at any age. But because you have to withdraw some capital from an RRIF each year, you should postpone rolling into an RRIF until you retire and need income from your plan. (The first payment may be received in the year in which you open your plan, but you have the option of starting payments in the following year. In fact you can postpone receiving your first payment, if you want annual payments, to December 31 of the year in which you turn 72.)

Your RRIF should be invested conservatively with the objective of providing income, rather than growth. Consequently, it should be invested primarily in bond and mortgage funds. A portion, however, can be invested in equity or balanced funds to give you a longer-term hedge against inflation.

Overall preservation of capital is of the utmost importance because you will be withdrawing money from your plan each year. If you had a significant portion invested in growth funds and the market turned down, you could find yourself redeeming fund units while prices are falling or have fallen.

Again, this is a general guideline. If you retire with substantial assets you may decide you can afford to accept the volatility associated with growth funds and keep a major portion of your assets in growth funds.

6. **Financing retirement outside an RRIF.** Circumstances sometimes offer the option of a unique solution. Someone with limited assets and income would generally opt for a safe solution such as investing in bond mutual funds. However, sometimes the safe solution isn't always the best. Take, for instance, a widow with $50,000 in capital and no income other than government benefits. If she invested for interest income she would

get her basic government benefit. But if she invested for growth and cashed in a portion of her units each month her income would largely be a return of her own capital; she might qualify for the guaranteed income supplement because her "income" doesn't fit the government definition.

CHAPTER NINE

STRATEGIES
AND
GIMMICKS

MAKING $1 MILLION THROUGH MUTUAL FUNDS ISN'T DIFFICULT. ALL IT takes is the ability to set aside money each year and a long time to do it. If you can set aside $4,000 a year and earn an average annual return of 12% you'll have $1 million in less than 30 years. If you could earn an average 16%, you would have $1 million in less than 25 years.

Saving can be difficult because of the temptations to spend. So virtually every mutual fund company has a program to make saving less painful. Depending on the fund company or the salesperson, such accumulation plans are called dollar-averaging plans, automatic-purchase plans or pre-authorized purchase plans. You decide how much you want to invest each month or quarter and in which funds, fill out a bank authorization form and supply a sample cheque marked "void." The fund company will do the rest. Each month on the same date, the amount you chose will come out of your bank or trust company account and be invested in the fund or funds you pick. The plans are available for RRSPs and non-sheltered savings.

A key advantage of such plans is that if the market declines, your purchases will buy you more mutual fund units, lowering your average cost. Conversely, you'll raise your average cost in rising markets. But with these programs you're in funds for the long-term, so in the end you'll do well. Depending on the fund company, the minimum monthly purchase is generally $50 to $100.

A plan that involves monthly purchases of $100 is a money loser for the first few years for the fund company offering it and for a fund salesperson in the case of a fund sold with an acquisition fee. As a result some funds have introduced a contractual monthly accumulation plan. In effect, an investor puts up a lump sum, of say, three months' contributions, which is used to finance the sales fee. However, the investor is repaid a portion of this amount each month that he or she remains in the plan. The total amount is repaid after, say, five years.

The table in Appendix C at the back of this book shows how your investment would have grown if you had contributed $100 a month to a typical equity fund invested in the Canadian market during the 10 years ended June 30, 1988, paying a 5% front-end load or sales commission. The table is based on monthly returns of a Canadian equity fund and assumes contributions are made at the end of the month. Different funds use different dates for investing contributions.

Withdrawal plans

A second type of plan is called a withdrawal plan. These plans allow you to invest a lump sum and withdraw a constant amount each month. In the following example $100,000 is invested, less 3% commission, in a typical equity fund. Monthly withdrawals are $1,000. Only a small portion of the $1,000 is regarded as realized capital gain by the federal government in the early years of the plan – most is seen as a return of capital. Your capital gain is the increased value of the shares that were sold to provide your monthly withdrawals.

The table in Appendix D at the back of this book simulates the results over 10 years of a $1,000 monthly withdrawal plan from a Canadian equity fund started with $100,000, less 3% acquisition fee, on June 30, 1978. Different funds have different dates for withdrawals from such plans. Of note is how the value of the plan declined during the bear market that lasted from November 1980 to July 1982, the subsequent gains in the value of the plan, the decline that climaxed in the October crash, and the post-crash recovery.

Leverage programs

Be very cautious about borrowing money to buy mutual funds. Proposed tax reform changes make leverage – as the use of borrowed money to invest is called – a marginally profitable exercise in some cases and unprofitable in others. It can, however, be very profitable if used wisely. The key is to examine any proposal thoroughly and work out your projections on an after-tax basis. Compare how you would fare with leverage and without.

Investing in growth funds with borrowed money is big business. In fact, some industry estimates place the volume of sales based on borrowed money as a third of the total.

The reason for using borrowed money is, of course, to make more money quicker. If you can put $100,000 of the bank's money to work in addition to $100,000 of your own you'll make double the profit before interest expense and tax. Your interest is deductible. If the bank charges you 12% and your marginal tax rate is 39%, your after-tax cost of funds is 7.3%. So if you have $7,300 a year available for investment you could use the money to finance a loan of $100,000.

Leverage has been extremely popular in the fund industry as a means of building business. Several major fund groups made arrangements with trust companies to finance leverage programs. Many individual salespeople made their own arrangements to bring clients to banks. One trust company, First City Trust, even produced a video on leverage designed to encourage investors to use borrowed money to buy mutual funds.

Leverage sounds like a good idea. But tax reform changes regarding the lifetime capital gains exemption, the lower deductibility of interest because of lower marginal tax rates, and increased taxes on capital gains have made leverage less attractive than it was before tax reform. It is still profitable in some situations, however. But in many cases it is unlikely you will be compensated for the risk involved.

Even before the white paper on tax reform, many people involved in the fund industry issued warnings about the dangers in the event of a market decline. These included Peter Cundill, manager of the Cundill Value Fund, and Robert B. Stewart, former president of Dynamic Funds Management Ltd. and a past chairman of the Investment Funds Institute of Canada. In 1986, IFIC and the Ontario Securities Commission issued a joint statement cautioning investors about leverage. The OSC added the requirement that mutual fund dealers who recommend leverage programs give clients a written statement warning them of the risks.

The following six examples look at the results of leverage under certain circumstances and under specific assumptions. In each case the amount borrowed is $100,000. The annual interest expense is $12,000, which has an after-tax cost of $7,320. The key assumption is that if the investor does not borrow $100,000, the $12,000 that would otherwise be available to pay interest will be taxable and its after-tax value of $7,320 will be available for investment.

The following two examples look at the results of leverage in which an investor with $100,000 borrows an additional $100,000, a relatively common strategy. Table VI on the next page, covers a holding period of one year; Table VII on page 72, covers the more realistic holding period of five years. Table VII assumes that 75% of the gain is taxable (the case beyond

Table VI

**A leverage program with a one-year
holding period and 15% return**

	Without Leverage	With Leverage
Investment	$100,000	$100,000
Loan	-	100,000
Cash flow at yearend	7,320	-
Interest (Pre-tax)	-	12,000
Capital gain (15%)	15,000	30,000
WITH LIFETIME EXEMPTION		
Equity after one year	122,320	130,000
Capital gain	15,000	30,000
Taxable gain (66.7%)	10,000	20,000
Taxable portion (equal to interest expense)	-	12,000
Tax (39% of $12,000)	-	4,680
After-tax profit	15,000	25,320
Add: cash flow	7,320	-
INCREASE IN NET WORTH	22,320	25,320
WITHOUT LIFETIME EXEMPTION		
Equity after one-year	122,320	130,000
Capital gain	15,000	30,000
Taxable gain (66.7%)	10,000	20,000
Tax (39%)	3,900	7,800
After-tax profit	11,100	22,200
Add: cash flow	7,320	-
INCREASE IN NET WORTH	$18,420	$22,200

1989) and ignores the transition year in which only 66.7% of the gain would be taxable. It also assumes that profits made would increase the investor's marginal tax rate from 39% to 43.5%. All six examples ignore federal and provincial surtaxes.

The first two examples clearly show that on an after-tax basis, the benefit of using leverage is, at best, marginal, and, at worst, negative. Moreover, the additional profit stemming from leverage doesn't appear to compensate for the increased risk.

Example 1: One-year holding period

Consider two scenarios. In the first you invest $100,000 of your own capital and get a 15% return over 12 months. In addition you have cash flow available for saving or servicing of debt of $7,320, an amount equal to your after-tax cost of servicing a loan of $100,000 (assuming your marginal tax rate is 39%).

Depending on your own situation and whether you have unused lifetime capital gains exemption, your after-tax profit can be as much as $15,000. If your capital gains are taxable and your marginal tax rate is 39%, the maximum tax (assuming 66.7% of your gains are taxable) is $3,900. Thus, your after-tax profit is $11,100.

To review the situation, if you cash in at the end of one year, you'll have your $100,000 principal, your profit of up to $15,000 and your cash flow of $7,320 – for a total of $122,320 if your capital gains are tax free, or $118,420 if your gains are taxable.

Now let's look at the same time period and returns except that you invest $100,000 of your own money, plus $100,000 borrowed from your bank at a rate of 12%. Your interest expense of $12,000 is deductible from income. Using your 39% marginal tax rate, your after-tax cost of borrowing is $7,320. After 12 months you cash in with a gross profit of $30,000.

Tax must be paid

You won't escape paying tax on a portion of your capital gains, even if you haven't used any of your lifetime exemption, because the federal government requires you to pay tax on a portion of your taxable gain (the taxable capital gain for 1988 and 1989 is 66.7% of your gross capital gain) equal to your "investment loss", which in this case is your $12,000 interest expense.

It works like this: Your taxable capital gain is 66.7% of $30,000, or $20,000. From this, you must subtract your interest expense of $12,000. Therefore, only $8,000 ($12,000 gross) may be applied to your lifetime exemption from the $20,000 taxable capital gain ($30,000 gross) earned on your $200,000 investment.

The tax paid on your capital gain will be $4,680. Your profit will be $30,000, less $4,680 tax. This leaves you with $25,320. If you've already used your lifetime exemption you'll pay $7,800 tax, leaving you with $22,200.

Comparing the two cases, if you haven't used your lifetime exemption, you'll have earned $22,320 without leverage and $25,320 with leverage. In other words, the earnings on your own $100,000 plus the cash flow invested give you $22,320 at the end of one year. If you had borrowed $100,000, in addition to your own capital, you would be $3,000 ahead.

Table VII

A leverage program with a five-year
holding period and 15% return

	Without Leverage	With Leverage
Investment	100,000	100,000
Loan	-	100,000
Annual cash flow	7,320	-
Annual interest (Pre-tax)	-	12,000
Total cash flow	36,600	-
FV of cash flow (15%)	49,354	-
Gain on cash flow	12,754	-
Capital gain on investment	101,136	101,136
Capital gain on borrowed funds	-	101,136
TOTAL CAPITAL GAIN	113,890	202,271
WITH LIFETIME EXEMPTION		
Taxable capital gain (75%)	85,418	151,703
Interest expense	-	60,000
Exemption	75,000	15,000
Taxable portion	10,418	136,703
Tax (43.5%)	4,532	59,466
After-tax profit	109,358	142,805
Add back cash flow	36,600	-
INCREASE IN NET WORTH	145,958	142,805
WITHOUT LIFETIME EXEMPTION		
Taxable capital gain (75%)	85,418	151,703
Interest expense	-	n/a
Exemption	-	-
Taxable portion	85,418	151,703
Tax (43.5%)	37,157	65,991
After-tax profit	76,733	136,280
Add back cash flow	36,600	-
INCREASE IN NET WORTH	113,333	136,280

Hardly worth the risk

If you have used your lifetime exemption, you'll be ahead $18,420 without leverage and $22,200 with leverage.

In effect, by leveraging you have doubled your risk in order to increase your profit by 13% (if you haven't used your lifetime exemption) or by 20% (if you have used your exemption).

Let's look at what happens if the market declines 15%. If you're using your own capital, you'll be down $15,000 on paper at the end of the year. So your equity will have dropped to $85,000 ($92,320 if we add back the cash flow you have available for savings). Using leverage you'll be down $30,000 on paper, leaving you with $70,000.

You'll likely make the money back and more in subsequent years. But tax reform makes leverage a marginal proposition in this case.

Example 2: Five-year holding period

Consider two other scenarios. In the first you invest $100,000 and get an average annual appreciation of 15% over five years. At the end of five years you gain $101,135.

In addition, you have annual cash flow of $7,320 available for investing. We'll assume it is invested at the end of the year. Therefore, at the end of five years you have an additional $49,354, assuming a 15% annual earnings rate.

Depending on your situation and whether you have unused lifetime capital-gains exemption, your after-tax profit can be as much as $100,000 tax free plus $13,890 of additional gains, of which 75% are subject to tax. (The white paper on tax reform proposed that 75% of gains be taxable beginning in 1990.) Your tax on $13,990 would be $4,532 using a 43.5% tax rate, so your profit would be $109,358. Adding back your $100,000 capital plus $36,600 additional investment ($7,320 times 5 years) you would have $245,958, for an increase in net worth of $145,958.

If your capital gains are taxable, your maximum tax will be $37,157. So your after-tax profit is $76,733. At the end of five years you'll have $213,333, for an increase of $113,333.

In Table VII on the previous page, you invest $100,000 of your own money plus $100,000 in funds borrowed at a rate of 12%. After five years you cash in with a gross profit of $202,271.

Your annual interest expense of $12,000 is deductible from income. Using your 39% marginal tax rate, your after-tax cost of borrowing is $7,320 each year. (Depending on your circumstances, your after-tax cost might be lower, at $6,700, if you were in a higher tax bracket.)

You won't escape paying tax on a portion of your capital gains, even if you haven't used any of your lifetime exemption, because the federal government would require you to pay tax on a portion of your taxable gain equal to your investment loss, which in this case is your $60,000 interest expense. Working through the example, your taxable capital gain is 75% of $202,271, or $151,703. From this, you must subtract your interest expense of $12,000 a year, or $60,000. Your lifetime exemption is $100,000, or $75,000 of taxable gains. So of the taxable gain, only $15,000 ($20,000 gross) may be applied to your lifetime exemption from the $151,703 taxable capital gain ($202,271 gross) earned on your $200,000 investment.

Table VIII

**A leverage program with a
five-year holding period and 12% return**

	Without Leverage	With Leverage
Investment	$100,000	$100,000
Loan	-	100,000
Annual cash flow	7,320	-
Annual interest (Pre-tax)	-	12,000
Total cash flow	36,600	-
FV of cash flow (12%)	46,503	-
Gain on cash flow	9,903	-
Capital gain on investment	76,234	76,234
Capital gain on borrowed funds	-	76,234
TOTAL CAPITAL GAIN	86,137	152,468
WITH LIFETIME EXEMPTION		
Taxable capital gain (75%)	64,603	114,351
Interest expense	-	60,000
Exemption	75,000	15,000
Taxable portion	-	99,351
Tax (43.5%)	0	43,218
After-tax profit	86,137	109,251
Add back cash flow	36,600	-
INCREASE IN NET WORTH	122,737	109,251
WITHOUT LIFETIME EXEMPTION		
Taxable capital gain (75%)	86,137	152,468
Interest expense	-	n/a
Exemption	-	-
Taxable portion	86,137	152,468
Tax (43.5%)	37,470	66,324
After-tax profit	48,667	86,145
Add back cash flow	36,600	-
INCREASE IN NET WORTH	85,267	86,145

Your profit will be $142,805 – $202,271 capital gain less $59,466 tax. So at the end of five years you'll have capital of $242,805. If you've already used your lifetime exemption you'll pay $65,990 tax. In that case, at the end of five years your profit would be $136,281, leaving you capital of $236,281.

The figures speak for themselves. If you haven't used your lifetime exemption you may be worse off using leverage in some circumstances. In others the gains may prove marginal.

Table IX

**A leverage program with a
one-year holding period and 30% return**

	Without Leverage	With Leverage
Investment	$100,000	$100,000
Loan	-	100,000
Cash flow at yearend	7,320	-
Interest (Pre-tax)	-	12,000
Capital gain (30%)	30,000	60,000
WITH LIFETIME EXEMPTION		
Equity after one year	137,320	160,000
Capital gain	30,000	60,000
Taxable gain (66.7%)	20,000	40,000
Taxable portion (equal to interest expense)		
Tax (39% of $12,000)	-	4,680
After-tax profit	30,000	55,320
Add: cash flow	7,320	-
INCREASE IN NET WORTH	37,320	55,320
WITHOUT LIFETIME EXEMPTION		
Equity after one-year	137,320	160,000
Capital gain	30,000	60,000
Taxable gain (66.7%)	20,000	40,000
Tax (39%)	7,800	15,600
After-tax profit	22,200	44,400
Add: cash flow	7,320	-
INCREASE IN NET WORTH	29,520	44,400

The previous two examples assume a rate of return of 15%, which is three percentage points higher than the assumed interest costs. But what happens if the rate earned over five years only matches the interest rate. Table VIII on the previous page, assumes a compound annual return of 12% over five years and an interest expense of 12%. It demonstrates that leverage will result in a minor gain if you have used your lifetime exemption and a lower return of you have not used your lifetime exemption.

A more positive use of leverage is when you expect to earn a significantly above-average return over a short time period. Assume that your favorite fund manager has suddenly reduced the cash portion of his portfolio from, say, 40% to 10%. That signals to you that he expects a jump in the market. As a result you go out and borrow $100,000 to buy units of his fund, matching the $100,000 worth you already own. Your intention is to hold for one year. Table IX shows what happens if the fund

Table X

**A leverage/mortgage program with a
five-year holding period and 15% return**

	Without Leverage	With Leverage
Loan	-	$100,000
Annual cash flow	$7,320	-
Annual interest (Pre-tax)	-	12,000
Total cash flow	36,600	-
FV of cash flow (15%)	49,354	-
Gain on cash flow	12,754	-
Capital gain on investment	-	101,136
TOTAL CAPITAL GAIN	12,754	101,136
WITH LIFETIME EXEMPTION		
Taxable capital gain (75%)	9,566	75,852
Interest expense	-	60,000
Exemption	9,566	75,000
Taxable portion	-	60,852
Tax (43.5%)	-	26,471
After-tax profit	12,754	74,665
Add back cash flow	36,600	-
INCREASE IN NET WORTH	49,354	74,665
WITHOUT LIFETIME EXEMPTION		
Taxable capital gain (75%)	9,566	75,852
Interest expense	-	n/a
Exemption	-	-
Tax (43.5%)	4,161	32,996
After-tax profit	8,593	68,140
Add back cash flow	36,600	-
INCREASE IN NET WORTH	45,193	68,140

appreciates by 30% over that one-year period. If you haven't used your lifetime exemption your net worth with leverage would increase by $55,320, about 48% more than the $37,320 you would show without leverage. If you had used your lifetime exemption your increase in net worth with leverage would be $44,400, about 30% more than the $29,520 without leverage.

Borrowing against your home

Many Canadians are house-rich but cash-poor. They have a substantial net worth, but it's tied up in a single asset.

Some mutual fund salespeople see this as an opportunity, both for the homeowner and for themselves. They might recommend, for instance, that a homeowner borrow $100,000 using the home as collateral to invest in funds. A withdrawal plan would be used to finance the interest costs.

This type of program can be profitable, as the earlier example on withdrawal plans shows. But what happens if interest rates skyrocket and the stock market plunges? This was the case several years ago when the prime lending rate reached a record 22.75% and the stock market fell by 43% over about 18 months. The hapless homeowner could find his equity dissipating because of the market drop and because he might have to liquidate part of his fund investment to pay the higher interest charges.

Unless you can handle the interest payments out of cash flow, you shouldn't really be in a leverage program that uses your home as security. The risks are simply too great.

Alternatively, you could borrow $100,000 and finance the interest out of cash flow as shown in Table X on the previous page. Here's how you would fare over five years, assuming a 15% rate of return.

At the end of five years your gain would be $101,135. The taxable capital gain would be 75% of this, or $75,851. Your lifetime capital-gains exemption is $100,000, or $75,000 of taxable capital gains. But from that $75,000 you must subtract your accumulated investment loss, which in this case is five years of interest at $12,000 a year, or $60,000. So only $15,000 of your taxable capital gain is exempt from tax in the year you take your profit. (You can claim the rest in subsequent years.) In other words, you'll be paying tax on $60,851 of your gain, which will cost you $26,470. Therefore, your after-tax profit after five years is $74,665.

Invest cash flow

Your alternative to borrowing to invest is investing the cash flow that would otherwise have been used to service your debt. Annual cash flow of $7,320 invested at year end and earning a rate of 15% annually would be worth $49,354 at the end of five years. The loan option gives you the higher return. But only because you've exposed yourself to a lot more risk.

Leverage is sometimes used to reduce taxes because the interest expense is deductible. However, it should be compared with not using leverage and investing the cash flow that would otherwise be available for investment. You may, however, have some "locked-in" interest-paying investments such as guaranteed investment certificates. Assuming this is your circumstance, you could consider borrowing against them and using your loan to buy funds. Because your interest expense is offset by interest income, you will not have a cumulative net investment loss. Consequently, you will be able to use your lifetime exemption against your profits. An example of this strategy is shown in Table XI on the next page.

A gimmick promoted by some fund salespeople – and one you should avoid – is the so-called "tax-free" withdrawal from RRSPs. It is a misnomer. Any money withdrawn from an RRSP is taxable.

No "tax-free" withdrawals

What these salespeople really propose is a loan to purchase mutual funds. It is sometimes secured by a mortgage; demand loans are also common. And interest payments are financed by withdrawals from the client's RRSP. Because interest for investment purposes is deductible, the interest deduction offsets the taxable income that stems from the RRSP withdrawal. So, in effect, the client's tax bill remains the same because the deduction of interest expense equals the increase in income from pulling money out of the RRSP. But the withdrawal from the RRSP is definitely taxable.

Table XI	
A leverage program where interest expense is offset by interest income	
	With Leverage
Loan	$100,000
Annual cash flow	-
Annual interest (Pre-tax)	12,000
Total cash flow	-
FV of cash flow (15%)	-
Gain on cash flow	-
Capital gain on investment	101,136
TOTAL CAPITAL GAIN	101,136
WITH LIFETIME EXEMPTION	
Taxable capital gain (75%)	75,852
Interest expense	60,000
Exemption	75,000
Taxable portion	852
Tax (43.5%)	371
After-tax profit	100,765
INCREASE IN NET WORTH	100,765

The idea behind the "tax-free" withdrawal (other than boosting sales commissions) is to convert a portfolio that will be fully taxed on withdrawal to one that will be taxed at capital gains rates or partially untaxed because of the capital gains exemption.

This type of program is far too risky for most people, especially those approaching retirement and whose major investment assets are their RRSPs. It converts a conservative investment program which is designed to finance retirement to one that leaves the investor exposed to unpredictable results if interest rates move higher.

When to use leverage

Leverage can be used successfully in some circumstances to meet specific objectives. For example, you might decide that you want to take a portion of your investment assets for speculation, perhaps 10% of the total. You could earmark these for specialty funds, such as gold funds, which you expect to do much better than broad-based funds in the short term. Alternatively, you might decide to borrow an amount equal to 10% of your investment assets and use the loan to buy a specialty fund in the hope of making a substantial gain of 50% or more within a year.

Just remember that the funds that are top performers in one period may turn out to be among the worst performers in a subsequent period. As a result, be prepared to be nimble. And don't invest with borrowed funds for speculation unless you can afford to take a loss.

Also, don't second guess your fund manager. It makes little sense to borrow money to buy a fund that is, say, 40% cash because its manager believes the market is vulnerable. The time to use leverage is when your fund manager is bullish.

Trading mutual funds

You can make a lot of money by simply buying funds and holding them for a long time. As the ads for Templeton Growth Fund indicate, a single investment of $10,000 made when the fund was established in 1954 was worth $1.2 million in late 1986; $2,000 a year invested for 30 years at an average return of 16% would be worth $1.7 million. In fact, most fund-management companies recommend a buy-and-hold strategy.

Their argument is that the fund manager makes the decisions necessary to maximize gains and preserve capital, moving into those industry groups that offer the most potential at any given time and building cash when the market looks like it is going to move lower.

Some investors take a different tack. Rather than buying and holding, they trade funds. They try to buy in at the beginning of a trend and to sell at the top, to lock in profits. People who invest this way are called market timers.

They may trade their whole fund portfolio. Or they may trade the portion they have invested in specialty funds such as gold funds, energy funds or Japanese funds – groups that tend to have wide swings in rates of return over relatively short periods.

The success of market timers depends on their own skills or those of their advisors. If you are going to trade funds, however, don't ignore your costs. The time to investigate trading costs is before you start your program.

As a general rule, there is no charge to switch within a no-load group of funds. Among the groups selling load funds, the commission varies from group to group. The Guardian Group of funds has no charge for switching. The AGF Group has a maximum charge of 2%. Some other fund management companies state that the maximum commission applies when switching. However, most commissions are negotiable and, in practice, most switching within groups can be done for commissions of 2% or less.

If your fund portfolio includes funds of a number of management groups, your trading costs could be higher. Even so, you are unlikely to pay full commissions. Again, commissions are negotiable and you should be able to establish a rate with your dealer that reflects the volume of turnover in your portfolio.

A bit of advice: If you are going to trade funds, become familiar with the portfolios of the funds you plan to trade. You wouldn't want to cash in a specific fund because of worries about market direction, only to find out later that the manager had similar concerns and had moved to a heavy cash position to preserve capital. In the same vein, you wouldn't want to sell, say, 20% of a Canadian equity fund to buy a gold fund, only to find out later that your manager had taken a 20% position in gold stocks. You can get the portfolio information from the latest fund quarterlies or your fund sales representative.

Diversification

Diversification is a very important investment concept. By diversifying your investments, you spread your risk. If one investment goes sour, it is more than offset by the other investments you hold. Mutual funds are diversified portfolios. As noted earlier, a mutual fund that invests in stocks must have a minimum of 20 different stocks.

Even so, you may want to diversify your fund holdings because you're concerned about tying your fortunes to a single manager, one market or one class of assets.

You can diversify a portfolio of mutual funds in two ways. The first is by asset mix, using different types of funds such as Canadian equity, American equity, fixed income and global investments. The second is by using two or more funds of the same type, so that if one manager does poorly the others will carry the day.

Diversification by asset mix is fairly common and makes sense. Many people will hold a Canadian equity fund and a fixed income fund in their RRSP and hold a global fund and an American fund outside their RRSP. The actual mix depends largely on their age, the capital available and how much exposure they want in a given class of assets or a specific market.

Diversification within a specific type of fund also makes sense. However, many investors who diversify within a specific type of fund fail to meet their objective. They neglect (or their advisors neglect) to look at the portfolios of the funds they propose to buy and at the managers. Consequently, they end up with two or more funds with similar portfolios. An extreme example would be an investor who purchases two Canadian equity funds offered by competing fund organizations but which, in fact, have the same fund manager.

CHAPTER TEN

UNDERSTANDING COSTS

IT'S IMPORTANT TO DEVELOP AN UNDERSTANDING OF ALL THE FEES AND costs connected with mutual fund investment. First, they vary widely. Second, they can have a significant impact on the rate of return earned.

Fees and charges can be broken down into two broad categories: sales commissions, and administrative and management fees. In some cases they overlap so that part of the administrative fee is, in effect, on-going compensation to a salesperson for either selling you a fund or for giving you continuing service. At the same time, virtually all major fund groups withhold a portion of the commission paid when you purchase a fund. This is used to finance incentive programs and advertising. But whether costs are included as sales commissions or administrative fees, they affect your net returns from holding mutual funds.

Rates of return published in the Financial Times of Canada do not take sales fees into consideration but do account for all administrative and management fees charged to the fund. So if the published rate of return for a fund is 15% and its management fee is 2%, the fund actually returned 17%. The return that investors realize is 15%.

Sales fees have become more complex in recent years. In addition to the traditional no-load funds, which don't charge any commission, and the front-end load funds, which can be bought only on payment of an acquisition fee, there are funds that have flat redemption fees, funds that have declining sales charges and funds that have ongoing sales charges. Some funds even combine two types of sales fees so you'll pay a fee when you buy and when you redeem. A few funds have registration fees. For example, London Life Equity Fund has a new-account fee of $20. MONY Canadian Growth Fund has a $75 annual administration fee.

Management fees range from about 0.75% to more than 3%, depending on the fund. They include the fees paid to the portfolio manager and they may also include the expenses of operating the fund. In some cases they reflect compensation paid to the salesperson. Funds must disclose all compensation and incentive arrangements in their prospectuses, a requirement introduced by the Ontario Securities Commission in 1987. This means that all incentives be disclosed in detail, including reciprocal commissions; goods or services such as trips, TVs, microwave ovens or clock radios; contests to win "prizes"; and cash payments. The fund must disclose who is giving the compensation and on what basis.

With reciprocal commissions, or "recip," an investment dealer is given orders to purchase or sell stock for the fund with the commission on the order equal to, say, 5% of the dollar value of mutual fund orders placed.

For example, on a $30,000 purchase of a no-load fund, the broker might be entitled to a $600 commission. Instead of paying cash, the fund management company would give the broker enough orders to buy and sell stocks for the mutual fund portfolio to generate $600 of commissions.

No-load funds

Some funds do not carry any up-front sales fee or back-end redemption fee. Funds offered or sponsored by banks and trust companies generally (but not always) fall into this category. A few fund management companies offer these no-load funds through investment dealers as well as directly to investors. The fund companies compensate the dealer by paying them reciprocal commissions.

Alternatively, a fund company may compensate a seller of its no-load fund by paying a portion of the management fee for as long as the client holds the fund. This payment, which ranges from 0.25% to 0.5% of the value of the client's holding, is called a "trailer." (Many load funds pay trailers too.)

Some funds have resorted to gimmicks, such as giving away small appliances to brokers who sell their no-load funds. But recip and trailers are the most common forms of compensation for no-load sales.

Load funds

No-load funds are a minority in Canada, but their numbers are growing as more banks and trust companies jump into the fund business. Still, the vast majority of fund business written each year is in load funds – funds that pay a commission to the dealer or broker who places the order.

The most common form of load funds is the front-end load fund, which requires payment of a commission of up to 9%. The 9% is a maxi-

Table XII

Dynamic Equity Funds
Commission Schedule

Total Amount Paid	Maximum sales charge
Up to $14,999	9%
$15,000 to $24,999	8%
$25,000 to $49,999	7%
$50,000 to $99,999	5%
$100,000 to $249,999	4%
$250,000 to $499,999	3%
$500,000 to $999,999	2%
$1 million and over	1%

mum. Virtually all front-end load funds have tapered commission schedules, with the maximum commission charged declining according to the size of the purchase. Table XII shows the commission schedule of Dynamic Funds Management Ltd.'s equity funds.

The points at which commission rates change vary among fund companies and even among types of fund. For example, Trimark Canadian Fund has a maximum commission of 9% on purchases of up to $24,999 and 7% on purchases of $25,000 to $50,000. Several preferred dividend funds have maximum commission rates of 5%. Some dealers will add up the purchases made within a year for commission-calculating purposes to give clients the commission rate that would be paid if all the purchases had been made at once. Mutual Diversico Ltd. calculates sales charges on lifetime purchases of all funds in the Mutual group of funds.

Commissions often negotiable

Commissions charged on front-end load funds are generally negotiable. The phrase in the prospectus is "maximum sales charge" or "not to exceed." This phraseology allows a salesperson to discount commission to reflect a client's purchase of several funds so that the commission charged would be the same as if the client put all of his or her money in one fund. As well, it creates a competitive environment in which some brokers and salespeople are more willing to cut commissions than others. They might, for instance, accept a 3% commission on a $5,000 order rather than the maximum 9%. Of course, a broker who accepts 3% on a small order is unlikely to provide any service other than filling the forms and accepting your cheque.

Discount stockbrokers generally will place an order for half the maximum commission noted in a fund prospectus, provided the fund management company allows them to sell the fund. But most dealers will cut commissions drastically if they aren't expected to provide any advice or service. As a group, stockbrokers are more likely to cut commissions than independent fund salespeople. But there are no hard and fast rules. And many salespeople won't cut commissions under any circumstances (other than to reflect the total dollar value of a client's purchases spread among two or more funds). These salespeople generally provide detailed financial planning and feel they are compensated for their efforts only if they charge full commissions.

Fixed commissions

One major fund that does not allow commissions to be discounted is Templeton Growth Fund. This appears to be a carryover from the days when the fund's prospectus was filed both in Canada and the United States. U.S. securities regulations prohibit discounting of fund commissions. In contrast, Templeton Canadian Fund has negotiable commissions. Funds sold through insurance companies often have fixed commission rates. So do funds which have "captive" sales forces that sell only a specific family of funds.

Not all the commission paid when you buy a fund finds its way into the hands of the selling dealer. Most major fund management companies that distribute through independent fund sales organizations and investment dealers have what is called a "holdback." It is a portion of the sales commission that is retained by the fund management company to finance promotional activities. These include advertising campaigns jointly sponsored by a fund company and a broker, and educational seminars held in exotic locations for salespeople who sell a specific amount of a fund. Some funds use holdbacks to pay bonuses to brokers whose sales exceed specific targets.

The holdback varies among fund groups. In some cases it will be a flat percentage amount, such as one percentage point, so that if a salesperson sells a fund with a 9% commission, 8% is returned to the broker and 1% is held back for promotion. If a salesperson sells a fund with a 4% commission, 3% is returned to the broker and 1% is held back. In other cases, the holdback is a constant fraction of the commission charged, say, 10%, so that the smaller the commission, the smaller the holdback. Not surprisingly, salespeople are likely to be less generous about discounting a fund that has a flat percentage of the amount you invest as its holdback.

A handful of funds charge a flat fee when you redeem units. It can be a small amount, as is the case with Associate Investors Ltd., which charges a 1% redemption fee.

Redemption fees

Most funds can charge a redemption fee of up to 2% if an investor who purchased the fund on a no-load basis or at a commission rate of less than 2% redeems within a short time, say within to one year of purchase. In some cases management has the option of waiving this fee. This is often done as a good-will measure, depending on the circumstances.

Declining back-end loads

To compete with no-load funds, a number of management companies have introduced what are called declining back-end load funds or declining deferred-sales-charge funds. You don't pay a commission when you buy this type of fund. But you do pay a redemption fee if you redeem within a specific number of years. The redemption fee is highest in the first year you hold the fund and declines after that, eventually dropping to zero. The largest declining back-end load fund is Industrial Horizon Fund, which was launched during the 1987 RRSP season and which had $835 million in assets at the end of June 1988.

Table XIII on the next page shows its redemption charges:

These fees are not negotiable. Redemption fees charged on declining deferred-sales-charge funds vary widely. Maritime Life Growth Fund, for instance, charges 10% on first-year redemptions, declining to zero after the 10th year.

The salesperson is paid a commission by the fund at the time the sale is made. In Industrial Horizon's case, the commission is 4%. This type of fund is more popular with investment dealers than independent fund salespeople. Independents are reluctant to introduce their clients to a fund that doesn't charge a commission up front. As well, they are reluctant to limit their fee to 4%, particularly on smaller orders.

Industrial Horizon was introduced as an alternative to Industrial Growth Fund, one of the most popular and successful front-end load funds. In fact, Industrial Horizon was marketed as a clone of Industrial Growth without the front-end load. In addition to the sales fees there is a second important difference between the two funds that is overlooked by most investors and many salespeople. Industrial Growth's management expense ratio – total expenses of the fund as charged to the fund as a percentage of total assets – is less than 1.5%. Industrial Horizon's management expense ratio is 2.7%. The fund pays Mackenzie Financial Corp., the

Table XIII

**Industrial Horizon Fund
Redemption charges**

During the first year	4.5%
During the second year	4.0%
During the third year	3.5%
During the fourth year	3.0%
During the fifth year	2.5%
During the sixth year	2.0%
During the seventh year	1.5%
During the eighth year	1.0%
1.0% During the ninth year	0.5%
After that	nil

manager of the fund, a management fee of 2%. In addition the fund is responsible for all expenses relating to the management of the fund.

Mackenzie will pay 0.5% of total assets, or one-quarter of its management fee, to Industrial Horizon Partnership 1987, a company formed to distribute Industrial Horizon Fund to brokers and dealers. The bottom line is that the management fee of Industrial Horizon Fund includes a 0.5% ongoing sales fee. While it may not seem significant at first glance, it is when you consider the effect of compounding on an investment held for many years and its impact on the dollar amount you receive. In fact, long-term investors might be better off paying a load and getting the benefit of the lower management fee.

AGF Management Ltd. has several deferred-load funds, known as the Excel Group. Each fund holds shares in an AGF front-end load fund as its only investment. For example, Excel Canadian Equity Fund holds only shares of Canadian Security Growth Fund.

The Excel funds have a seven-year deferred load set at 4.2% the first year and declining by 0.6 percentage points each subsequent year, so that in the second year the load would be 3.6% and in the third year 3%.

The deferred load is charged against the initial investment, rather than the market value of the holding. This makes it a better deal than deferred-load funds that charge a commission against market value (assuming the unit value of the fund appreciates). The fund charges an annual distribution fee of 1% a year, so, in effect, the management fee on Excel funds is one percentage point higher than the management fee on AGF front-end load funds. After seven years, investors in Excel funds can switch to the corresponding AGF fund at no cost. The 1% distribution fee paid over seven years is equivalent to about a 6% front-end load, assuming a 15% average annual compound rate of return over seven years on a front-end load fund.

The Trimark Group and Dynamic Group have announced declining back-end load funds too.

Purchase and redemption fees

A few fund groups such as the Viking Group of Funds charge a commission both when you buy and when you sell. Viking Group of Funds has a 3.5% commission on purchases of up to $25,000 (which applies to the total cost of all Viking Fund purchases) and a redemption fee using the same scale. The total sales and redemption fee cannot exceed 9% of the amount invested.

Many fund groups apply a charge if you want to transfer your money to another fund within the group. Others allow transfers free of charge. While the fee can be as much as full commission rates, many groups charge a 2% fee for a transfer.

Management expense ratio

All fees, other than direct sales fees and specific fees such as RRSP trustee fees, are almost always reflected in the management expense ratio. This ratio, expressed as a percentage in prospectuses, includes the management fee and the expenses paid by the fund. Some funds pay all expenses out of the management fee. Others charge the expenses directly to the fund. However, the management expense ratio is all-inclusive and allows comparisons among funds.

Lately, however, there has been concern that the situation is changing and that some fees, such as management fees, will be charged directly to the client rather than to the fund. This would make it more difficult for investors to make valid comparisons. Management expense ratios vary widely. For some equity funds they are as low as 0.75%; others exceed 3%. Most range from 1.5% to 2%. Management expense ratios for income funds are marginally lower.

Trailer fees

The trend in the mutual fund industry is toward trailer fees. Trailer fees are paid by management on an ongoing basis to the selling broker to encourage ongoing service to the client and to discourage switching. Generally they are one-quarter of the management fee.

If you've purchased your mutual fund units from one dealer and later switch your account to another firm, your trailer will move to the new firm provided your account shows you are dealing with the second firm. That is why a fund salesperson may be insistent about having all your dealings under one roof.

If you have purchased funds and aren't happy with the advice you've been getting, find a salesperson you feel comfortable with. Even if you don't purchase additional funds, the salesperson may be happy to give you advice provided the funds in question pay a trailer and he or she becomes involved with your account.

Trailers are a point of contention in the industry. Some want them banned entirely as a hidden charge, while others argue they are a payment made by the fund company, not the client, to encourage ongoing service. Provincial securities commissions are likely to require the fund industry to provide more detailed disclosure about trailers and the rights, if any, investors have to direct them.

Additional fees

Depending on the funds you hold, you may face additional charges. For instance, MONY Equity Fund has an annual administration fee of up to $50 on holdings of less than $50,000. A few funds have nominal charges for pre-authorized purchases or cheques issued on redemption. Trustee fees for RRSPs are an additional charge for virtually all funds and are charged against your account or billed separately. The point is, fees vary widely, so you should know what they are before you commit to buy.

Load vs. no-load

Table XIV on page 89 compares the growth of an investment of $10,000 over 30 years in three funds which have different types of sales charges. The figures show what investors would receive if they redeemed at the beginning of the year.

We are assuming that each earns the same rate of return of 18% before sales charges and management fees.

The first fund is a front-end load fund with a management expense ratio of 1.75%, so its compound rate of return is 16.25%. We will assume the investor paid a 5% front-end load.

The second fund has a deferred declining sales charge of 4.5% in the first year decreasing by 0.5% each year to zero in the ninth year. This fund has a management expense ratio of 2.25%, so its compound rate of return is 15.75%.

The third fund is a no-load fund with a management expense ratio of 2%, so its compound rate of return is 16%.

The figures suggest that, all other things being equal, investors who expect to hold a fund for a long period and who are choosing between a

Table XIV

Comparing Fund Costs

Yr	Fund 1	Fund 2	Fund 3	Yr	Fund 1	Fund 2	Fund 3
1	$9,500	$9,550	$10,000	16	90,911	89,705	92,655
2	11,044	11,112	11,600	17	105,684	103,833	107,480
3	12,838	12,929	13,456	18	122,858	120,187	124,677
4	14,925	15,043	15,609	19	142,823	139,116	144,625
5	17,350	17,502	18,106	20	166,031	161,027	167,765
6	20,169	20,362	21,003	21	193,011	186,389	194,608
7	23,447	23,690	24,364	22	224,376	215,745	225,745
8	27,257	27,699	28,262	23	260,837	249,725	261,864
9	31,686	32,223	32,784	24	303,223	289,057	303,762
10	36,835	37,298	38,030	25	352,496	334,583	352,364
11	42,821	43,173	44,114	26	409,777	387,280	408,742
12	49,779	49,972	51,173	27	476,366	448,277	474,141
13	57,868	57,843	59,360	28	553,775	518,880	550,004
14	67,272	66,953	68,858	29	643,764	600,604	638,004
15	78,203	77,499	79,875	30	748,375	695,199	740,085

front-end load fund and a deferred declining-sales-charge fund with a higher management fee are better off paying the front-end load.

If the choice is between a front-end load fund and a no-load fund, the decision depends on the difference in management fees. For the short term, a no-load fund has the advantage, even if its management expense ratio is one-quarter point higher. But for the longer term, the difference is not significant.

Your best buy is a no-load fund with a low management fee. Very few funds meet this description. Two that do are MD Growth Investments Ltd. and CMA Investment Fund. However, they are available only to members of the Canadian Medical Association.

And many investors shouldn't shop on the basis of price alone. Rather, they should depend on professional advice to help them select funds.

CHAPTER ELEVEN

HOW TO PICK A FUND

INDIVIDUAL INVESTORS AND FUND ADVISORS SPEND HOURS AGONIZING over performance figures, attending information meetings and reading annual and quarterly reports and prospectuses searching for something that will help them pick one fund over another.

Unfortunately, there are no methods that will guarantee that any one fund will outperform another. The best you can do is choose funds whose investment policies are compatible with your own and which have performed well over time (or whose current managers have demonstrated acceptable performance).

Objectives

The first thing you have to do is determine what type of fund meets your objectives. For example, if you want long-term capital growth tied to the Canadian economy, look at Canadian equity funds. If you want stable growth based on income within your RRSP, look at bond funds, mortgage funds or both.

Examine past performance

Most funds are sold on the basis of past performance. But past performance is not a perfect indicator of future performance. It may be a fair indicator of how a specific manager performed under certain market conditions. But it is no guarantee of the future.

What a performance figure indicates is a fund's rate of return or average rate of return over a specific period of time. If you look at several ending dates you'll likely find different funds among the top performers. You should also realize that many funds have grown from a few million dollars to hundreds of millions. The management styles and stock market trading responsible for superior performance when a fund was small may not work as well in a larger fund.

Financial Times of Canada publishes a monthly survey of investment funds that includes six performance figures for each fund. Three are short-term returns covering the change in value of a fund, including dividends reinvested, for one-month, three-month and one-year periods. The other figures are average annual compound rates of return for three years, five years and 10 years. They show the average annual return of the fund each year, assuming all income is reinvested. Average annual compound rates of return are a more accurate method of measuring performance than simply taking the average annual performance of the fund.

Financial Times publishes two other products widely used by mutual fund professionals and to a lesser extent by individual investors. One is the Mutual Fund Sourcedisk and the other is the Mutual Fund Sourcebook.

The Mutual Fund Sourcedisk, which can be used on an IBM PC or compatible computer, is a computer disk updated monthly. It provides the performance information included in the Financial Times' monthly survey, plus additional historical performance information. It allows investors to rank funds globally or within fund types using a broad range of criteria.

The Mutual Fund Sourcebook includes performance information as well as details covering such matters as commission rates, trustee fees, addresses and managers.

Most people who work in the fund business emphasize the longer-term rates of return, reasoning that most investors buy funds as long-term investments. They feel that many investors are misled by short-term performance.

However, short-term performance is important, too, because it can act as an indicator of a change in a manager's investment strategy. For instance, if a top-performing fund started to lag behind its competition in a rising market, it might indicate that the manager is building cash in anticipation of a market correction. So if your fund started to fall behind other performers, you might want to investigate why. It might mean a change in investment strategy. Or it could signal something more serious, such as a change in fund manager.

It makes sense to look at long-, medium- and short-term performance if you're holding for long-term growth. If a fund has good long- and short-term performance but poor medium-term performance, don't reject it outright. Try to determine why performance fluctuated. It may be that the manager called the market wrong for a relatively short period but then corrected the error. Even though the error in strategy was corrected, it will be reflected in the performance figures for several years.

When judging the performance of specialty funds, particularly volatile ones such as golds and Japanese funds, short-term performance figures are probably more important than long-term figures. You are more likely to buy specialty funds for a relatively short-term hold. So you're more likely to base your decision on how such a fund has performed recently rather than over 10, five and possibly three years.

And if you're considering a relatively new fund, you only have short-term performance to examine. Just remember: There is little correlation between short-term and long-term performance. If you buy a fund on the basis of short-term performance, don't be surprised if its long-term performance fails to meet your expectations.

In fact, some investors buy funds that have good long-term performance but which have lagged the pack recently. Their view is that every dog has its day.

Besides performance you should also consider volatility, particularly when considering funds whose objective is growth or a combination of growth and income. The Financial Times' monthly survey of investment funds also ranks funds by volatility, or the stability of monthly rates of return. The survey uses two measures. One is a percentage figure; the second is a statistical measure called standard deviation. Standard deviation shows the relative volatility of monthly rates of return. The lower the figure, the less volatile the monthly rate of return. A money market fund would have a very low standard deviation; a gold fund would have a very high one.

The percentage figure ranks funds by volatility within fund groups. So, within Canadian growth and growth and income funds one would expect balanced funds to have a low percentage figure while gold funds and energy funds would have high percentage figures. Most funds fall in the middle range, between 15% and 85%. If you are trying to decide between two funds as long-term investments and they have similar performance histories, the fund with the lower volatility figure would be your choice.

On the other hand, if you're looking for a short-term trading position, you might want the fund that has shown the largest swings in performance as measured by the volatility rating.

Who is the manager?

You or your fund advisor also should look at who is managing the fund and consider his or her experience. This information is available from most fund management companies. Indeed, many fund salespeople place more emphasis on who the manager is than on the fund's recent performance record. After all, it doesn't make sense to buy a fund on the basis of its 10-year performance if the person who is responsible for that performance has left for another job. Similarly, it doesn't make sense to reject a fund with poor performance if a new manager with a superior track record is put in charge.

Besides looking at the manager, look at the management organization. Is there adequate back-up if the manager takes a vacation or quits? What type of analytical support is behind the manager? There is nothing wrong with investing in a fund whose manager has limited back-up. Just be prepared to be nimble if the manager leaves.

When should I switch?

No manager is infallible. From time to time a manager may make a bad decision that has an impact on performance. A manager may build cash prematurely in a rising market and consequently underperform the competition. Or he or she may not sell soon enough and tumble with the general market.

Don't make a decision to sell on the basis of short-term performance. You should, however, determine whether the manager has corrected any misjudgments and is back on track. It can be difficult knowing when it's an appropriate time to judge whether the manager has, in fact, made an error. Some managers habitually "sell too soon," only to outperform their competition in the subsequent market downturn. Three to five years is probably the minimum period over which to judge a fund manager.

What you can expect

Pick up the financial pages of any newspaper and you'll likely see ads for mutual funds. Generally, the results they display are impressive, showing 10-year average annual compound rates of return of 16%, 18%, even 22%. Some ads for newer funds emphasize short-term performance that may be significantly higher.

There are no guarantees that future results will be similar. However, on a historical basis, people who have invested for long-term growth using equity funds have done better than people who invested in guaranteed investments. Moreover, people who have invested in equity funds have outpaced inflation.

Over the 10 years ended June 30, 1987, the average annual compound rate of return for Canadian equity funds was 17.2%, while the average return for bond and mortgage funds was 11.1%. In comparison, an investment in Government of Canada treasury bills would have given an average return of 11%. Using the 10 years to June 30, 1988, which includes the October 1987 crash, the average return for Canadian equity funds was 14.5%, still substantially above a T-bill return of 11.1%.

No one knows what rates of return funds will achieve in the future. But given the structure of the economy, it seems safe to say that people who buy equities for the long term will continue to do better than people who take less risk and buy fixed-income investments.

Legal registration of funds

Open-end funds are either mutual fund corporations, mutual fund trusts, or insurance company variable life policies. Their common element is the underlying portfolio of securities or investments, which determines the share or unit value of the fund.

It doesn't really matter to most investors which of the three they own. But there are some subtle differences, particularly with insurance company variable life policies, that can have a bearing on making investment decisions.

For tax purposes, mutual fund trusts must "flow through" to investors all Canadian dividends, interest, capital gains and foreign income net of expenses. (The fund would generally charge expenses against foreign income and interest income to reduce the potential tax liability of unitholders.)

Mutual fund corporations also flow through Canadian dividends and capital gains. However, they are not allowed to flow through interest and foreign income. Rather, it is taxable in the fund's hands. But mutual fund corporations generally charge expenses against interest income and foreign income, effectively cutting their tax liability.

There are some circumstances in which a mutual fund corporation's income can become taxable in the fund's hands rather than flow through to shareholders. If 25% or more of the shares of a mutual fund corporation were held by one shareholder – an unlikely event – its income would be taxable. Similarly, if 25% or more of its income was interest income, it would be taxable in the corporation's hands. This can happen if a fund manager, anticipating a declining stock market, decides to hold a major portion of the portfolio in treasury bills and other short-term investments.

Having income taxed in the fund's hands is a disadvantage for RRSP holders, who would pay no tax if the income were flowed through. Even so, on a per-unit basis this is of little consequence, especially when weighed against the alternative of not preserving capital in a falling market.

Mutual fund corporations must hold annual meetings. There is no such requirement for trusts. This is not a significant difference in that both mutual fund corporations and trusts must issue detailed annual and semi-annual financial statements to investors. (Most of them issue quarterly reports as well.) Trusts generally don't issue certificates, although many will on request. This is of little importance to most people. In fact certificates can be a bother, particularly if you have distributions automatically reinvested to buy additional units in a fund. After a few years you could end up with a stack of certificates. Alternatively, you would be constantly having your certificates replaced to reflect your increased holdings.

In some circumstances having certificates can be helpful. For example, if you borrow money from a bank using your fund holdings as security, the bank may ask you to give it the certificate as security for the loan. However, the certificate isn't really necessary. You can assign the units as collateral so that the bank's name would appear on the fund's list of unitholders. Virtually all fund management companies have procedures covering this and can explain them to bank or trust company managers, if necessary.

All in all, it makes little difference whether you hold units in a mutual fund corporation or mutual fund trust. However, overtures have been made to Ottawa by the funds industry to allow mutual fund corporations to flow through dividends, interest and realized capital gains to shareholders in the same manner as mutual fund trusts.

Creditor-proof funds

Insurance company segregated funds are effectively insurance policies whose value varies with the underlying assets. On death or at maturity, the holder or his or her estate gets the greater of market value or 75% of the value of contributions. Moreover, as an insurance policy, the investment can be made creditor-proof under certain circumstances by designating a beneficiary within the immediate family. Also, these policies give holders the option of rolling into an annuity at guaranteed rates, although these rates are generally quite low.

For tax purposes, dividends, interest and capital gains received by insurance company segregated funds are flowed through to investors. But an important caveat for people who invest with borrowed money is that interest on money borrowed to buy a segregated fund may not be deductible from income for tax purposes.

All types of funds have similar mechanisms to protect investors. The securities are held by a custodian, generally a bank or trust company, and not by the fund management company. And the fund portfolio is the property of the investors. It is not part of the assets of the fund management company and cannot be used by the manager to support its business.

So if the fund management company goes bankrupt, the investors in the funds are protected.

Avoiding commissions

Should you buy a no-load fund and avoid commissions? The answer depends on your own personal situation. In some cases the answer is "absolutely." In other cases it's a definite "no." In many cases it's a "maybe." It all depends on your objectives, how much work you do on your own and whether you need professional advice.

Some no-load fund groups have employees who can provide advice. But the majority of funds specialists sell load funds and are paid commissions. If you decide to use a broker or fund specialist, make sure the person you pick has the expertise and can provide a level of service that justifies the commission you pay.

As far as performance is concerned, no-loads, as a group, are just as good as load funds. Both groups include funds that are excellent performers as well as funds that are poor performers. In fact, some investment managers manage both types of funds, but they are marketed through different fund-management distribution companies.

If you are a sophisticated, experienced investor who knows what you want, then by all means buy no-load funds and save yourself the commission. Even if you aren't an investment wizard but have a good idea about what suits your objectives – say you want a bond fund for your RRSP or a mortgage fund for income – then check out the no-loads offered by the banks and trust companies with which you deal.

The vast majority of no-loads are offered by banks and trust companies. However, a handful of investment counsellors such as Sceptre Investment Counsel Ltd. offer no-loads directly to the public. As well, several organizations such as the Canadian Medical Association and Ontario Teachers' Group offer families of funds to their members.

If you buy a fund from a bank or trust company the quality of advice you'll get, if any, depends on the expertise of the individual who comes to the counter. This can be a hit-or-miss situation. Some institutions are making efforts to train individuals at each branch about the mutual fund business.

For example, Central Trust Co. requires all its managers and term deposit officers to complete the Canadian Investment Funds Course. And the banking and trust industries are introducing training courses for employees who will deal with fund investors and potential investors. Currently however, and with few exceptions, financial institutions won't or can't give you the level of advice available from mutual fund specialists. In fact, some institutions forbid their employees from offering advice.

The onus is on you to determine whether the person advising you has the necessary training and experience. It is generally a good idea to ask for the manager. And don't be shy about inquiring whether he or she has taken the Canadian Investment Funds Course and has had other specialized training. Just remember that if you use no-load funds you've assumed the responsibility of monitoring performance and making changes to your fund portfolio when necessary. You've also assumed the task of making sure the portfolio of funds you've chosen meets your needs and objectives.

CHAPTER TWELVE

HOW TO PICK AN ADVISOR

THE MAJORITY OF FUND OWNERS IN CANADA BUY FUNDS THROUGH AN intermediary. It can be an investment dealer or stockbroker, a mutual fund specialist, a trust company employee, or an insurance agent selling insurance company segregated funds or mutual funds.

Some intermediaries will sell funds offered by several fund management companies; others will sell only a single group of funds. Firms that advertise themselves as independent dealers, such as Regal Capital Planners Ltd., offer funds from many of the major fund management companies. In contrast, sales representatives employed by the Investors Group will offer only the Investors funds. Similarly, many insurance agents will sell only the specific family of funds, that is affiliated with their insurance company. Stockbrokers will generally offer funds from the major fund management companies. In addition, some will offer funds affiliated with their firms. For instance, the betting in the investment industry is that brokerage houses owned by banks may soon be distributing bank-managed mutual funds along with other funds.

Should you use an advisor who offers a single family of funds or someone who offers many? All advisors will, or should, offer you the best they have. The question is whether a sales representative handling a single family of funds has the best. While many fund companies have top performers, none has a monopoly on top performance in all types of funds – RRSP equity, RRSP bonds, foreign equity, specialty funds and so on. An "independent" salesperson who handles many funds has access to a wider range than a "captive" representative who has only a single family to offer. Further, many of the top-performing funds are available only through independent salespeople. But as the ranking table indicates, some of the funds sold only through captive sales forces have done quite well, as have some of the no-load funds.

Much depends on the individual sales representative and whether he or she can tailor a fund portfolio to suit your needs. The key point is that if you are going to need advice and guidance, the sales person you choose must be an expert. A mutual fund specialist, whether employed by an investment dealer, independent fund-sales organization, insurance agency or part of a captive sales force should have a detailed understanding of how to use funds to meet clients' objectives. He or she should monitor fund performance closely and be in touch with fund management companies to be aware of any changes in strategy or investment personnel that may have an impact on client returns.

While there is a tendency among many fund salespeople not to second-guess portfolio managers, some salespeople demand detailed explanations about current investment policy. This helps them determine whether specific funds continue to meet the criteria on which they base their recommendations. Give the choice of a fund advisor a lot of thought. Making the wrong choice can be financially and emotionally expensive.

Licensing requirements

Sales of mutual funds are regulated by provincial securities commissions. Firms selling mutual funds must meet certain capital requirements and their officers and managers must demonstrate specific levels of expertise. Individuals selling mutual funds must also meet certain standards. To receive registration to sell mutual funds, individuals must complete an investment course. salespeople who are employed by investment dealers must have completed the Canadian Securities Course. This course covers the investment spectrum but includes a section on mutual funds. It also meets the requirement for licensing of people employed by mutual fund dealers. The Canadian Investment Funds Course is designed specifically for people seeking registration to sell mutual funds and as additional education for people who are registered to sell securities. During 1988 the banking and trust company associations decided to develop their own educational programs which would meet licensing requirements for their employees. Until recently bank and trust company employees marketing funds were considered exempt from registration. However the recent trend is to eliminate exemptions for sales of securities and require all people involved in selling securities to the public to meet minimum training levels.

The Canadian Investment Funds Course is sponsored by the education division of the Investment Funds Institute of Canada. IFIC, the umbrella organization of the fund industry, is recognized as such by provincial securities commissions. The educational standards of the industry are constantly being upgraded. However, the quality of people advising about funds varies widely, just as in any other profession. It's up to you to determine whether a specific fund salesperson meets your needs.

If you do most of your own work and know specifically which funds you want, just about any dealer can handle your order at a discounted commission. If all you want is execution of your purchase order and nothing else, expect to pay between one-third and one-half of the maximum commission, as stated in the fund prospectus, for the number of units you want.

If you want full service, including detailed advice and monitoring of your holdings, expect to pay higher commissions, up to but not necessarily the full rates. Full service should include an analysis of your investment objectives and needs, and recommendations of what funds meet these. Many sales representatives will confine their analysis to your investment needs; others will extend their analysis to include life insurance and other aspects of your finances such as tax returns, pension plans and your personal balance sheet.

You should determine in advance what type of ongoing service you can expect from a fund salesperson. Is his or her analysis of funds limited to reviewing rates of return? Or does the analysis include reviews of portfolio managers' investment strategies and comparisons with other funds? Many fund salespeople do this on their own, while others depend on specialists within their firms to do this work. But it is essential that your advisor have access to this type of information on a continuous basis in order to advise you whether conditions have changed. Your advisor should be able to give you detailed explanations behind all purchase recommendations, especially those that involve switching funds. He or she should also provide you with periodic statements of your holdings and their performance, generally monthly or quarterly, depending on how active you are in the market.

The use of personal computers has allowed many fund salespeople to develop their own report packages. These often include monthly statements showing how your funds have performed. Other reports include such items as projected returns using recent performance figures along with account histories and performance summaries of each fund held, plus a detailed portfolio summary and performance comparison of clients' holdings.

Not every investor wants detailed reports. What it really comes down to is making sure that you are comfortable with the salesperson you choose. Do his or her recommendations fit your investment objectives? Do they take into consideration your other investment holdings? Have the risks been explained in detail? Will your situation be monitored constantly and, if so, how? Will you get service even if you don't make any subsequent purchases? Does your advisor have substantial investment or business experience? Unfortunately, many fund salespeople may not fully appreciate the risks involved in the strategies they recommend.

Financial planning

Many people selling funds call themselves financial planners. However, financial planning is unregulated. Anyone can call himself or herself a financial planner, whether or not they know anything about the area and whether or not they produce a financial plan for their clients.

The fund industry is trying to set some standards. The Canadian Institute of Financial Planning, which is affiliated with IFIC, has developed a program of six correspondence courses covering areas relevant to financial planning. Successful completion of the course leads to the designation of chartered financial planner.

A voluntary association of personal financial planners, the Canadian Association of Financial Planners, has been formed as an industry group and has set some standards for membership. And provincial securities commissions have been considering having financial planners as a separate category of securities registration. Should the commissions proceed – and there is a wide range of opinion in the fund industry about whether they should – they will likely require that people who call themselves financial planners demonstrate their expertise either through completing specific courses or by demonstrating relevant experience.

CHAPTER THIRTEEN

INSIDE THE PROSPECTUS

WHILE VIRTUALLY EVERY FUND USES GLOSSY SALES MATERIAL TO promote itself, the offer to sell fund shares or units is made only through the fund's prospectus. This is a legal document that discloses all pertinent information about the fund.

When you first inquire about a fund you may be given the prospectus or, more likely, the condensed prospectus summary statement. No-load funds routinely send out prospectuses in response to requests for information. But many load funds do not because their salespeople prefer to stick with easier-to-understand brochures.

When you actually get down to buying a fund, the seller is required by law to provide a prospectus, the latest annual financial statements and subsequent quarterly statements, if any. Generally, these will be mailed to you with, or at the same time as, the slip confirming your purchase order.

Most people don't bother to read prospectuses and financial statements. And, frankly, the majority aren't worse off for it because they can get enough information from sales material or their sales person. Nevertheless, you might take the time to at least skim through the prospectus.

Each fund actually files two prospectuses, the second being a shorter form or summary statement of the first. It includes the main points of the full prospectus in plain language. Real estate funds are the exception. They file only the full prospectus.

The shorter version was introduced in response to requests from the fund industry. The view was that a condensed version would be more likely to be read and would save the funds a bundle on postal and printing costs.

You'll almost certainly receive the shorter version. If don't want to read it thoroughly, leaf through the first couple of pages of the section that summarizes the document.

There are a number of areas you can quickly look at. Make sure the fund's investment policies and objectives are compatible with yours. It's also important that you understand the fund's sales charges, if any, and whether they are negotiable.

And you should be aware of ongoing management fees. Every fund has management fees that, with the rare exception, are charged to the fund (and not to individual investors). Management fees cover the cost of portfolio management and other expenses of running a fund. As a percentage of fund assets they vary widely and can have a significant impact on the rate of return you receive.

Some funds absorb all expenses, such as legal and audit fees, as part of their management fees. Others charge certain expenses directly to the fund. If you want to directly compare expenses of different funds, check the management expense ratio. This takes into account all fees charged to the fund (excluding brokerage commissions) and allows for direct comparisons among funds.

The summary prospectus begins by telling you that it is only an outline of the information you should have before making a decision to buy and that additional information is available in the prospectus, which you can get by writing to the issuer.

The summary prospectus also explains your statutory rights. Generally speaking, you can back out of an agreement to buy mutual fund shares or units within two days after receipt of the simplified prospectus or within 48 hours after receiving the confirmation of the purchase of such securities. Very few people use this right of rescission. But if you read the prospectus and you find that, for example, the fund's investment objectives aren't compatible with yours, you have the right to withdraw from your agreement to purchase.

You have other rights too. Some provinces provide for cancelling the purchase and allow for damages if the prospectus includes misrepresentations. There are time limits, however, on exercising these rights.

The next item in a prospectus is the name and address of the fund and information about its incorporation. This is followed by a brief summary of the fund's investment policies.

The summary statement may include a section outlining risks. This isn't included in all short-form prospectuses. Rather, it is required only if a fund is speculative or has significant risk factors. The value of all funds, except money market funds, will fluctuate with changes in the value of their underlying securities. This is disclosed in all summary prospectuses. However, not every fund calls this a risk factor.

Following the summary statement is a description of the shares or units, which provides information on dividend rights, voting rights and the like.

Other important items include how the manager calculates the price at which sales are offered and redeemed, how the shares will be distributed, information on minimum purchases and sales charges, management fees, dividend records, the tax consequences of sales, rules governing dividends and redemptions, and the name and address of the auditor.

Some of this information may be found in the annual report, rather than the summary statement, because the rules about exactly where all this information must appear aren't rigid.

CHAPTER FOURTEEN

THE
LARGEST
FUNDS

TO MAKE THE TASK OF CHOOSING A FUND EASIER, WE HAVE INCLUDED A listing of the 100 largest funds offered in Canada. This is not to say you should restrict your search to these top 100 funds. But the list is representative of the more than 460 currently offered in Canada.

Before you begin comparing funds, go through the following steps every investor needs to take before deciding on a particular investment:

1. Get your financial house in order. Make sure your insurance needs are taken care of, your will is up to date, personal debts are paid off and your affairs are structured so you don't pay any more taxes than necessary. Eliminating personal debts is the best high-return, no-risk investment you can make. Also make sure you understand how different types of investment income are taxed so you can set up your mutual fund investment program in ways that will keep taxes to a minimum.

2. Next, list your specific investment objectives, such as saving for retirement, saving for your children's education or maximizing current income. With this in mind, choose the fund type or types that are most suitable for your goals. Remember, the shorter the saving time frame, the more conservative you should be. Conversely, if you can invest for the long-term, it's to your advantage to take some risk.

3. Then, decide on the strategies that can help you meet your objectives. These might include opening an RRSP to use tax-assisted dollars to save for retirement; beginning an accumulation or dollar-averaging plan; opening a withdrawal plan; or even borrowing money from the bank to invest. Of course, if you do borrow, don't overlook the risks should the market plummet. Also, consider the potential impact of tax reform on your expected returns.

4. At this point, decide whether to make all your own decisions about investment funds or whether you should seek an advisor. If you decide to use an advisor, make sure he or she is a specialist. Any broker or mutual fund salesperson can execute orders. Pick an experienced specialist who stays on top of developments in the fund industry and understands your objectives.

5. Finally, understand all the costs associated with your investment and the criteria used to choose a specific fund. Costs vary widely and can have a significant impact on rates of return. The time to investigate is before you buy, not after years of holding a fund. Two other things: make sure that a fund's objective is compatible with yours; and don't forget to compare a fund's performance with other funds that have similar objectives.

How the Top 100 works

The funds are listed alphabetically and ranked by assets. On August 31, 1988, these 100 funds controlled almost $27 billion in assets, representing about 82% of the total of the Canadian mutual fund industry.

Each listing includes much of the information you need to decide whether a fund meets your needs:

The name and address so you can contact the fund to obtain its prospectus and annual and latest quarterly reports.

The date the fund was established so you'll know how long it has been in operation.

The provinces in which the fund is available.

Whether the fund can be registered as an RRSP.

The maximum sales charge, if any.

The maximum redemption charge, if any.

The management expense ratio (the ratio of management and other administrative fees charges to the fund as a percentage of a fund's total assets, as reported in its latest annual report or prospectus.)

The total returns for each 12-month period ended August 31, 1988 going back as far as 14 years. These periods include some of the strongest markets as well as some weak ones. So you can determine, and compare, how funds have performed in bull and bear markets.

Rank	27	77
	AGF Preferred Income Fund	**AGF Japan Fund Limited**
	AGF Management Ltd.	AGF Management Ltd.
	31st Floor, T-D Tower	31st Floor, T-D Tower
	Toronto-Dominion Centre	Toronto Dominion Centre
	Toronto, Ont. M5K 1E9	Toronto, Ont. M5K 1E9
	(416) 367-1900	(416) 367-1900
		Toll-free: 1-800-387-1780
Type	Preferred Dividend Fund	International Equity Fund
Fund Established	April 10, 1984	Jan. 23, 1969
Where Sold	Everywhere in Canada	Everywhere in Canada
Sales Charge	9%	9%
Redemption Fee	None	None
Management Expense Ratio	0.77%	1.72%
RRSP Eligible	No	No
Net Assets ($ Millions)	264.7	95.3
Total Return(%)		
1988	3.6	4.6
1987	7.6	31.8
1986	10.2	92.9
1985		15.9
1984		22.6
1983		32.4
1982		-21.0
1981		57.0
1980		11.2
1979		3.4
1978		35.6
1977		25.3
1976		10.5
1975		30.1
1974		-20.3

Rank	60	41
	AGF Money Market Fund	**AGF Special Fund Limited**
	AGF Management Ltd.	AGF Management Ltd.
	31st Floor, T-D Tower	31st Floor, T-D Tower
	Toronto Dominion Centre	Toronto Dominion Centre
	Toronto, Ont. M5K 1E9	Toronto, Ont. M5K 1E9
	(416) 367-1900	(416) 367-1900
Type	Money Market Fund	U.S. Equity Fund
Fund Established	Dec. 1, 1975	Sept. 19, 1968
Where Sold	Everywhere in Canada	Everywhere in Canada
Sales Charge	9%	9%
Redemption Fee	None	None
Management Expense Ratio	0.59%	1.65%
RRSP Eligible	Yes	No
Net Assets ($ Millions)	101.7	181.9
Total Return(%)		
1988	8.4	-8.2
1987	7.8	10.5
1986	9.2	31.2
1985	10.8	23.4
1984	9.4	-10.9
1983	12.0	96.1
1982	18.2	-12.6
1981	14.7	50.6
1980	13.6	33.2
1979	9.7	30.7
1978	6.9	35.8
1977	8.4	19.4
1976		9.4
1975		40.4
1974		-17.4

26	84	72
AMD T-Bill Fund	**Altamira Canadian**	**American Growth Fund**
Suite 1600	**Balanced Fund**	**Limited**
121 King St. W.	Altamira Investment	AGF Management Ltd.
Toronto, Ont. M5H 3W6	Services Inc.	31st Floor, T-D Tower
	250 Bloor St. E., Suite 301	Toronto Dominion Centre
	Toronto, Ont, M4W 1E6	Toronto, Ont. M5K 1E9
	(416) 925-1623	(416) 367-1900

Money Market Fund	Balanced Fund	U.S. Equity Fund
Aug. 21, 1987	May, 1985	April 18, 1957
Everywhere in Canada	Everywhere in Canada.	Everywhere in Canada
1%	No-load	9%
None	None	None
Fiscal year not complete.	2%	1.58%
Yes	Yes	No
	83.9	105.4
	-14.3	-15.0
	12.5	8.4
	21.2	27.0
		33.3
		-6.0
		62.9
		-5.3
		43.2
		27.9
		17.6
		8.6
		3.4
		2.3
		16.6
		-20.4

Rank	70	93
	Bolton Tremblay Canada Cumulative 70 University Ave. Suite 1050, P.O. Box 11 Toronto, Ont. M5J 2M4	**Bolton Tremblay Income Fund** 70 University Ave. Suite 1050, P.O. Box 11 Toronto, Ont. M5J 2M4 (416) 595-5200
Type	Canadian Equity Fund	Preferred Dividend Fund
Fund Established	April 21, 1972	Sept. 7, 1976
Where Sold	Everywhere in Canada	Everywhere in Canada
Sales Charge	9%	5%
Redemption Fee	None	None
Management Expense Ratio	1.79%	1.06%
RRSP Eligible	Yes	Yes
Net Assets ($ Millions)	117.7	75.1
Total Return(%)		
1988	-7.7	3.1
1987	10.7	9.7
1986	19.4	7.7
1985	11.7	13.4
1984	-2.0	4.4
1983	80.0	30.2
1982	-32.4	14.3
1981	33.7	-0.4
1980	22.8	9.8
1979	28.4	7.3
1978	22.6	6.0
1977	19.7	
1976	26.7	
1975	8.9	
1974	-14.3	

18	62	6
Bolton Tremblay International Fund	**Bolton Tremblay Money Fund**	**CMA Investment Fund**
70 University Ave.	70 University Ave.	MD Management Limited
Suite 1050, P.O. Box 11	Suite 1050	1867 Alta Vista Drive
Toronto, Ont. M5J 2M4	P.O. Box 11	Ottawa, Ont. K1G 3Y6
(416) 595-5200	Toronto, Ont. M5J 2M4	(613) 731-4552
	(416) 595-5200	1-800-267-4022
International Equity Fund	Money Market Fund	Canadian Equity Fund
March 14, 1961	Nov. 12, 1981	March 1, 1966
Everywhere in Canada	Everywhere in Canada	Everywhere in Canada
9%	2%	No-load
None	None	None
1.77%	0.5%	1%
No	Yes	Yes
400.9	137.2	908.4
-15.2	8.7	6.1
19.5	8.2	20.5
41.1	9.4	20.5
25.4	11.0	33.9
1.1	9.1	2.3
67.6	11.7	62.0
-9.2		-12.1
45.5		12.1
12.9		17.8
17.2		30.3
12.5		10.4
8.0		-1.4
20.8		3.8
19.9		7.3
-10.7		-9.6

Rank	64	42
	CMA Short Term Deposit Fund MD Management Limited 1867 Alta Vista Dr. Ottawa, Ont. K1G 3Y6 (613) 731-4552 1-800-267-4022	**Canada Life Canadian Equity S-9** Canada Life Assurance Co. 330 University Ave. Toronto, Ont. M5G 1R8 (416) 597-1456
Type	Money Market Fund	Canadian Equity Fund
Fund Established	February, 1975	August, 1969
Where Sold	Everywhere in Canada.	Everywhere in Canada
Sales Charge	No-load	1%
Redemption Fee	None	2.5%
Management Expense Ratio	0.75%	2%
RRSP Eligible	Yes	Yes
Net Assets ($ Millions)	117.8	175.0
Total Return(%)		
1988	7.6	1.7
1987	7.1	14.0
1986	9.0	23.0
1985	10.5	31.0
1984	9.3	-1.0
1983	11.6	64.3
1982	17.5	-26.8
1981	13.3	19.4
1980	13.5	25.9
1979	10.1	36.2
1978	7.5	12.4
1977	9.3	3.8
1976	6.9	4.5
1975		
1974		

21	79	13
Canada Life Managed Fund S-35	**Canadian Investment Fund, Ltd.**	**Canadian Security Growth Fund Limited**
Canada Life Assurance Co.	630 Dorchester Blvd. W.	AGF Management Ltd.
330 University Ave.	Suite 2690	31st Floor, T-D Tower
Toronto, Ont. M5G 1R8	Montreal, Que. H3B 1X1	Toronto Dominion Centre
(416) 597-1456	(514) 866-5421	Toronto, Ont. M5K 1E9
	1-800-363-0260	(416) 367-1900
Balanced Fund	Canadian Equity Fund	Canadian Equity Fund
April 1, 1984	Nov. 16, 1932	June 12, 1963
Everywhere in Canada	Everywhere in Canada	Everywhere in Canada
1%	9%	9%
2.5%	None	None
2%	1.86%	1.68%
Yes	Yes	Yes
322.3	92.3	573.9
3.5	-7.8	-7.0
11.4	11.1	12.0
20.0	15.1	27.2
27.4	27.3	35.5
	-5.1	2.6
	66.4	80.4
	-22.7	-31.5
	14.7	31.8
	13.8	21.7
	30.7	40.9
	11.9	28.6
	3.4	8.6
	2.5	1.2
	7.6	5.6
	-7.4	-5.0

Rank	19	78
	Canadian Trusteed Income Fund	**Counsel Trust Real Estate Fund**
	AGF Management Ltd.	Counsel Trust Co.
	31st Floor, T-D Tower	36 Toronto St., Suite 300
	Toronto Dominion Centre	Toronto, Ont. M5C 2C5
	Toronto, Ont. M5K 1E9	(416) 365-3100
	(416) 367-1900	
Type	Bond Fund	Real Estate Fund
Fund Established	Aug. 15, 1962	July 10, 1981
Where Sold	Everywhere in Canada	B. C., Alberta, Sask., Ont., N.B. and N.S.
Sales Charge	9%	No Load
Redemption Fee	None	None
Management Expense Ratio	0.78%	0.68%
RRSP Eligible	Yes	Yes
Net Assets ($ Millions)	346.5	76.3
Total Return(%)		
1988	7.4	13.7
1987	5.8	14.6
1986	20.4	21.0
1985	31.4	
1984	3.5	
1983	31.2	
1982	18.4	
1981	-3.9	
1980	3.1	
1979	7.2	
1978	8.0	
1977	16.0	
1976	10.4	
1975	9.2	
1974	-4.9	

23	94	34
Cundill Value Fund Ltd.	**Dynamic American Fund**	**Dynamic Fund of**
1200 Sun Life Plaza	Dynamic Funds Mgmt. Ltd.	**Canada Ltd.**
1100 Melville St.	Dynamic Building	Dynamic Funds Mgmt. Ltd.
Vancouver, B.C. V6E 4A6	6 Adelaide St. E., 9th floor	6 Adelaide St. E., 9th Floor
(604) 685-4231	Toronto, Ont. M5C 1H6	Toronto, Ont. M5C 1H6
Toll-free: 1-800-663-0156	(416) 363-5621	(416) 363-5621
	Toll-free: 1-800-268-8186	Toll-free: 1-800-268-8186
Balanced Fund	U.S. Equity Fund	Canadian Equity Fund
Jan. 16, 1967	Aug. 31, 1979	1957
Everywhere in Canada	Everywhere in Canada	Everywhere in Canada
8.75%	9%	9%
None	None	None
1.96%	2%	2%
No	No	Yes
287.3	70.3	212.4
10.4	-8.1	-1.9
16.5	22.7	25.3
22.4	22.3	15.2
13.5	31.1	23.0
5.5	2.9	-6.5
66.7	58.5	65.2
0.0	-11.1	-31.1
40.0	39.7	23.7
6.6		26.8
43.2		45.2
42.1		31.7
19.5		11.8
18.0		8.9
-8.4		25.0
-17.9		1.4

Rank	80	71
	Dynamic Income Fund	**Dynamic Managed**
	Dynamic Funds Mgmt. Ltd.	**Portfolio Inc.**
	Dynamic Building	Dynamic Funds Mgmt. Ltd.
	6 Adelaide St. E., 9th Floor	6 Adelaide St. E., 9th Floor
	Toronto, Ont. M5C 1H6	Toronto, Ont. M5C 1H6
	(416) 363-5621	(416) 363-5621
	Toll-free: 1-800-268-8186	Toll-Free: 1-800-268-8186
Type	Bond Fund	Balanced Fund
Fund Established	Aug. 31, 1979	January 23, 1986
Where Sold	Everywhere in Canada	Everywhere in Canada
Sales Charge	5%	9%
Redemption Fee	None	None
Management Expense Ratio	1%	2%
RRSP Eligible	Yes	Yes
Net Assets ($ Millions)	85.6	101.0
Total Return(%)		
1988	6.6	-2.3
1987	8.2	30.0
1986	14.1	
1985	30.3	
1984	1.5	
1983	36.3	
1982	6.4	
1981	-2.0	
1980		
1979		
1978		
1977		
1976		
1975		
1974		

53	14	51
Empire Life Insurance Segregated Fund	**First Canadian Mortgage Fund**	**FuturLink Canadian Growth Fund**
The Empire Life Insurance Co. 243-259 King St. E. Kingston, Ont. K7L 3A8	55 Bloor St. W., 17th floor Toronto, Ont. M4W 3N5 (416) 927-6000	c/o 5415 Spring Garden Road Halifax, NS B3J 3J1 (902) 420-5936
Canadian Equity Fund	Mortgage Fund	Canadian Equity Fund
December, 1964	1974	Sept. 1, 1987
Not available in Nfld. and Nova Scotia.	Everywhere in Canada.	Everywhere in Canada
9%	No-load	No-load
None	None	None
1.2%	1%	2%
Yes	Yes	Yes
146.4	490.0	
3.5	9.2	
16.9	9.2	
23.5	11.5	
31.9	18.4	
-9.4	8.5	
85.9	21.4	
-26.0	18.3	
37.3	3.3	
22.6	8.7	
33.6	8.2	
25.9	9.1	
6.2	13.1	
7.9	8.6	
5.6		
-16.0		
7.4		

Rank	90	37
	General Trust Bond Fund	**Global Strategy Fund**
	General Trust Investment Funds	Worldwide Capital Management Ltd.
	1100 University St.	2 Bloor St. W., Suite 3400
	Montreal, Que. H3B 2G7	Toronto, Ont. M4W 1A1
	(514) 871-7530	(416) 927-0233
		1-800-587-1229
Type	Bond Fund	International Equity Fund
Fund Established	Nov. 18, 1966	August, 1985
Where Sold	Everywhere in Canada	Everywhere in Canada.
Sales Charge	No-load	9%
Redemption Fee	None	None
Management Expense Ratio	1.2%	2.14%
RRSP Eligible	Yes	No
Net Assets ($ Millions)	77.0	222.6
Total Return(%)		
1988	7.3	-17.3
1987	5.4	24.7
1986	17.8	
1985	32.9	
1984	1.6	
1983	31.9	
1982	14.3	
1981	-3.5	
1980	2.3	
1979	8.2	
1978	9.4	
1977	13.9	
1976	9.3	
1975	11.7	
1974	2.3	

97	55	17
Green Line Mortgage Fund	**Growth Equity Fund Ltd.**	**Industrial American Fund**
Toronto Dominion Sec. Inc.	AGF Management Ltd.	150 Bloor St. W., 4th Floor
T-D Tower, 9th Floor	31st Floor, T-D Tower	Toronto, Ont. M5S 3B5
Toronto Dominion Centre	Toronto Dominion Centre	(416) 922-5322
Toronto, Ont. M5K 1A2	Toronto, Ont. M5K 1E9	
(416) 982-6432	(416) 367-1900	
	Toll-free: 1-800-387-1780	

Mortgage Fund	Canadian Equity Fund	U.S. Equity Fund
Dec. 21, 1973	Oct. 22, 1964	July, 1975
Everywhere in Canada	Everywhere in Canada	Everywhere in Canada
No-load	9%	9%
None	None	None
1.15%	1.03%	1.81%
Yes	Yes	No
67.3	160.8	431.3
9.7	-17.0	-6.3
8.5	20.3	18.4
10.5	33.2	26.3
13.7	21.5	29.9
8.7	-7.6	-1.3
22.1	90.9	55.9
18.3	-49.8	-5.1
5.7	27.4	38.9
8.8	53.8	14.8
7.6	61.2	23.3
8.8	42.6	17.8
13.8	11.0	32.4
8.8	7.6	
	1.0	
	-20.5	

Rank	83	24
	Industrial Cash Management Fund 150 Bloor St. W., 4th Floor Toronto, Ont. M5S 3B5 (416) 922-5322	**Industrial Dividend Fund Limited** 150 Bloor St. W., 4th Floor Toronto, Ont. M5S 3B5 (416) 922-5322
Type	Money Market Fund	Canadian Equity Fund
Fund Established	July, 1984	March, 1950
Where Sold	Everywhere in Canada	Everywhere in Canada
Sales Charge	2%	9%
Redemption Fee	None	None
Management Expense Ratio	0.5%	1.99%
RRSP Eligible	Yes	Yes
Net Assets ($ Millions)	73.4	300.0
Total Return(%)		
1988	8.1	6.1
1987	7.8	27.4
1986	9.4	16.5
1985		33.2
1984		6.5
1983		69.7
1982		-21.4
1981		16.8
1980		-1.3
1979		40.8
1978		16.7
1977		19.5
1976		12.6
1975		
1974		

44	75	31
Industrial Equity Fund Limited	**Industrial Future Fund**	**Industrial Global Fund**
150 Bloor St. W., 4th Floor	150 Bloor St. W.	150 Bloor St. W., 4th Floor
Toronto, Ont. M5S 3B5	Suite 400	Toronto, Ont. M5S 3B5
(416) 922-5322	Toronto, Ont. M5S 2X9	(416) 922-5322
	(416) 922-5322	
Canadian Equity Fund	Canadian Equity Fund	International Equity Fund
January, 1969	Dec. 23, 1987	September, 1985
Everywhere in Canada	Everywhere in Canada	Everywhere in Canada
9%	5%	9%
None	None	None
2.00%	Fiscal year not complete	2%
Yes	Yes	No
180.8		239.5
-0.5		-1.4
31.4		32.1
18.1		
16.8		
0.3		
88.1		
-25.4		
10.5		
20.2		
27.1		
35.0		
20.0		
3.4		
9.7		
17.0		

Rank	1	7
	Industrial Growth Fund 150 Bloor St. W., 4th Floor Toronto, Ont. M5S 3B5 (416) 922-5322	**Industrial Horizon Fund** 150 Bloor St. W., 4th Floor Toronto, Ont. M5S 3B5 (416) 922-5322
Type	Canadian Equity Fund	Canadian Equity Fund
Fund Established	October, 1967	Jan. 28, 1987
Where Sold	Everywhere in Canada	Everywhere in Canada
Sales Charge	9%	No-load
Redemption Fee	None	None
Management Expense Ratio	1.47%	2.63%
RRSP Eligible	Yes	Yes
Net Assets ($ Millions)	1714.9	835.0
Total Return(%)		
1988	4.5	15.2
1987	27.7	
1986	16.4	
1985	27.1	
1984	2.8	
1983	77.7	
1982	-17.1	
1981	8.6	
1980	24.9	
1979	28.1	
1978	25.1	
1977	22.0	
1976	3.3	
1975	7.1	
1974	30.3	

40	**54**	**12**
Industrial Income Fund	**Industrial Pension Fund**	**Investors Bond Fund**
150 Bloor St. W., 4th Floor	150 Bloor St. W., 4th Floor	One Canada Centre
Toronto, Ont. M5S 3B5	Toronto, Ont. M5S 3B5	447 Portage Ave.
(416) 922-5322	(416) 922-5322	Winnipeg, Man. R3C 3B6
		(204) 943-0361
Balanced Fund	Canadian Equity Fund	Bond Fund
July, 1974	February, 1971	April, 1979
Everywhere in Canada	Everywhere in Canada	Everywhere in Canada
9%	9%	8.5%
None	None	None
1.25%	2%	1.37%
Yes	Yes	Yes
156.0	153.0	556.4
13.2	4.3	7.4
12.3	23.4	6.4
18.6	20.8	16.3
38.0	30.6	28.5
-0.5	0.6	0.0
39.0	84.0	28.3
5.9	-21.2	13.7
-7.0	11.6	-7.7
-5.0	-2.4	-1.1
7.3	37.4	
8.5	21.0	
15.6	22.6	
7.7	-6.8	
	2.7	
	40.0	

Rank	46	4
	Investors Canadian Equity Fund	**Investors Dividend Fund Ltd.**
	One Canada Centre	One Canada Centre
	447 Portage Ave.	447 Portage Ave.
	Winnipeg, Man. R3C 3B6	Winnipeg, Man. R3C 3B6
	(204) 943-0361	(204) 943-0361
Type	Canadian Equity Fund	Preferred Dividend Fund
Fund Established	September, 1983	November, 1961
Where Sold	Everywhere in Canada	Everywhere in Canada
Sales Charge	8.5%	8.5%
Redemption Fee	None	None
Management Expense Ratio	1.43%	1.28%
RRSP Eligible	Yes	No
Net Assets ($ Millions)	163.6	1000.0
Total Return(%)		
1988	-7.2	3.6
1987	10.1	9.9
1986	27.9	9.8
1985	25.5	24.2
1984		2.5
1983		55.3
1982		-14.9
1981		6.6
1980		4.5
1979		27.5
1978		8.6
1977		0.6
1976		5.5
1975		13.0
1974		-10.2

32	16	38
Investors Global Fund Ltd.	**Investors Growth Fund of Canada Ltd.**	**Investors International Mutual Fund Ltd.**
One Canada Centre	One Canada Centre	One Canada Centre
447 Portage Ave.	447 Portage Ave.	447 Portage Ave.
Winnipeg, Man. R3C 3B6	Winnipeg, Man. R3C 3B6	Winnipeg, Man. R3C 3B6
(204) 943-0361	(204) 943-0361	(204) 943-0361

International Equity Fund	Canadian Equity Fund	U.S. Equity Fund
October, 1986	Sept. 1, 1957	November, 1961
Everywhere in Canada	Everywhere in Canada	Everywhere in Canada
8.5%	8.5%	8.5%
None	None	None
1.42%	1.33%	1.35%
No	No	No
222.9	442.5	192.6
-14.9	-9.8	-14.4
	18.8	18.5
	25.5	25.3
	28.5	27.2
	-7.4	-12.2
	69.2	66.5
	-23.7	-14.8
	15.7	23.7
	28.5	25.2
	38.9	12.2
	5.2	11.6
	-1.1	4.7
	4.6	5.1
	14.2	21.8
	-10.9	-18.0

Rank	39	48
	Investors Japanese Growth Fund Ltd.	**Investors Money Market Fund**
	One Canada Centre	One Canada Centre
	447 Portage Ave.	447 Portage Ave.
	Winnipeg, Man. R3C 3G6	Winnipeg, Man. R3C 3B6
	(204) 943-0361	(204) 943-0361
Type	International Equity Fund	Money Market Fund
Fund Established	March 1971	May, 1985
Where Sold	Everywhere in Canada	Everywhere in Canada
Sales Charge	8.5%	No-load
Redemption Fee	None	None
Management Expense Ratio	1.33%	1.1%
RRSP Eligible	No	Yes
Net Assets ($ Millions)	178.1	142.8
Total Return(%)		
1988	4.5	8.3
1987	31.8	7.2
1986	87.9	8.9
1985	7.2	
1984	14.4	
1983	34.3	
1982	-15.7	
1981	66.0	
1980	1.1	
1979	-4.8	
1978	38.6	
1977	31.8	
1976	1.6	
1975	24.7	
1974	-21.9	

3	22	33
Investors Mortgage Fund	**Investors Mutual of Canada Ltd.**	**Investors Real Property Fund**
One Canada Centre	One Canada Centre	One Canada Centre
447 Portage Ave.	447 Portage Ave.	447 Portage Ave.
Winnipeg, Man. R3C 3B6	Winnipeg, Man. R3C 3B6	Winnipeg, Man. R3C 3B6
(204) 943-0361	(204) 943-0361	(204) 943-0361

Mortgage Fund	Balanced Fund	Real Estate Fund
August, 1973	October, 1948	November, 1983
Everywhere in Canada	Everywhere in Canada	Everywhere in Canada
8.5%	8.5%	8.5%
None	None	None
1.35%	1.3%	1.41%
Yes	No	Yes
1100.0	311.9	196.2
8.8	-1.9	8.2
8.4	18.4	10.0
11.4	12.7	10.0
18.5	21.6	9.8
7.0	-5.9	
23.8	68.6	
16.7	-19.7	
3.7	12.3	
7.6	21.7	
7.4	29.7	
9.6	7.4	
14.3	4.0	
8.0	8.5	
8.3	8.6	
	-9.1	

Rank	9	36
	Investors Retirement Mutual Fund One Canada Centre 447 Portage Ave. Winnipeg, Man. R3C 3B6 (204) 943-0361	**London Life Bond Fund** 255 Dufferin Ave. London, Ont. N6A 4K1 (519) 432-5281
Type	Canadian Equity Fund	Bond Fund
Fund Established	November, 1971	1961
Where Sold	Everywhere in Canada	Everywhere in Canada
Sales Charge	8.5%	5%
Redemption Fee	None	None
Management Expense Ratio	1.36%	0.98%
RRSP Eligible	Yes	Yes
Net Assets ($ Millions)	806.2	215.5

Total Return(%)		
1988	4.6	5.3
1987	20.4	4.2
1986	13.6	21.2
1985	26.7	41.3
1984	-3.9	2.0
1983	58.3	31.6
1982	-27.0	13.5
1981	15.8	-1.9
1980	27.9	3.8
1979	42.7	7.3
1978	8.2	7.6
1977	-1.4	14.8
1976	2.8	
1975	10.8	
1974	-7.0	

49	**86**	**66**
London Life Canadian Equity Fund 255 Dufferin Ave. London, Ont. N6A 4K1 (519) 432-5281	**London Life Mortgage Fund** 255 Dufferin Ave. London, Ont. N6A 4K1 (519) 432-5281	**Lotus Fund** M.K. Wong Management Ltd. 800-26 Wellington St. E. Toronto, Ont. M5E 1S2 (416) 361-3370
Canadian Equity Fund	Mortgage Fund	Balanced Fund
1961	1969	February, 1984
Everywhere in Canada	Everywhere in Canada	Everywhere in Canada
5%	5%	No-load
None	None	None
0.98%	1.34%	2%
Yes	Yes	Yes
153.7	78.1	122.1
-0.3	8.7	-6.1
21.0	9.3	10.4
19.0	13.7	19.6
28.7	22.9	25.7
-3.8	5.3	
65.3	41.9	
-21.3	15.5	
15.7	-10.0	
26.4	1.6	
44.0	5.3	
14.1	9.2	
-0.4	19.3	
4.3	6.0	
4.3	7.2	

Rank	10	73
	MD Growth Investments Limited MD Management Limited 1867 Alta Vista Drive Ottawa, Ont. K1G 3Y6 (613) 731-4552 1-800-267-4022	**MD Realty Fund** MD Management Limited 1867 Alta Vista Drive Ottawa, Ont. K1G 3Y6 (613) 731-4552 1-800-267-4022
Type	International Equity Fund	Real Estate Fund
Fund Established	July 18, 1969	June 30, 1983
Where Sold	Everywhere in Canada.	Everywhere in Canada.
Sales Charge	No-load	No-load
Redemption Fee	None	None
Management Expense Ratio	1%	1.9%
RRSP Eligible	No	Yes
Net Assets ($ Millions)	770.6	

Total Return(%)		
1988	-5.2	
1987	25.8	
1986	36.9	
1985	37.2	
1984	0.7	
1983	74.3	
1982	-16.9	
1981	42.9	
1980	16.2	
1979	33.6	
1978	34.8	
1977	44.5	
1976	17.4	
1975	29.2	
1974	-21.0	

65	87	45
MONY Canadian Growth Fund	**Mackenzie Equity Fund**	**Mackenzie Mortgage and Income Fund**
MONY Life Insurance Co. of Canada	150 Bloor St. W., 4th Floor	150 Bloor St. W., 4th Floor
797 Don Mills Rd., 15th Fl.	Toronto, Ont. M5S 3B5	Toronto, Ont. M5S 3B5
Don Mills, Ont. M3C 1V2	(416) 922-5322	(416) 922-5322
Canadian Equity Fund	Canadian Equity Fund	Bond/Mortgage Fund
July 5, 1974	May, 1973	December, 1974
Everywhere in Canada	Everywhere in Canada	Everywhere in Canada
No-load	9%	9%
4%	None	None
	2.00%	1.08%
Yes	Yes	Yes
123.8	76.8	156.2
-16.6	4.8	13.0
20.3	20.8	12.5
14.6	23.1	17.6
34.9	29.6	30.3
-5.6	3.0	4.3
85.3	67.9	27.6
-17.3	-26.8	14.2
17.5	25.7	0.9
26.2	25.1	8.0
33.8	44.6	8.0
13.6	14.5	8.0
0.9	-6.2	13.7
4.2	3.7	8.6
	13.4	

Rank	52	81
	Maritime Life Growth Fund The Maritime Life Assurance Co. 2701 Dutch Village Road Halifax, N.S. B3J 2X5 (902) 453-4300	**Montreal Trust RRSP/RRIF: Equity** 1 Place Ville-Marie P.O. Box 1900, Station B Montreal, Que. H3B 3L6 (514) 397-7326
Type	Canadian Equity Fund	Canadian Equity Fund
Fund Established	April, 1968	February, 1958
Where Sold	Everywhere in Canada	Everywhere in Canada
Sales Charge	No-load	No-load
Redemption Fee	10%	None
Management Expense Ratio	1.5%	1.78%
RRSP Eligible	Yes	Yes
Net Assets ($ Millions)	148.5	86.7
Total Return(%)		
1988	-11.1	-6.2
1987	15.2	21.0
1986	24.7	17.7
1985	34.8	25.0
1984	-2.8	-9.7
1983	73.2	69.3
1982	-30.9	-29.5
1981	15.1	17.2
1980	24.7	24.8
1979	40.1	40.5
1978	17.0	11.7
1977	5.4	2.0
1976	0.7	4.5
1975		8.5
1974		-9.1

88	**50**	**91**
Montreal Trust	**Mutual Diversifund 40**	**Mutual Diversifund 55**
RRSP/RRIF: Income	227 King St. S.	227 King St. S.
1 Place Ville Marie	Waterloo, Ont. N2J 4C5	Waterloo, Ont. N2J 4C5
P.O. Box 1900, Station B	(519) 888-2472	(519) 888-2472
Montreal, Que. H3B 3L6		
(514) 397-7326		

Bond Fund	Balanced Fund	Balanced Fund
February, 1958	Jan. 2, 1985	Jan. 2, 1985
Everywhere in Canada	Everywhere in Canada	Everywhere in Canada
No-load	6%	6%
None	None	None
1.36%	1.5%	1.5%
Yes	Yes	Yes
77.3	156.5	75.1
6.7	0.6	-1.0
8.2	6.8	7.7
17.9	19.7	20.9
23.1		
2.8		
43.6		
9.5		
-7.1		
3.2		
7.0		
6.3		
16.4		
9.2		
9.7		
-0.2		

Rank	98	69
	Mutual Equifund 227 King St. S. Waterloo, Ont. N2J 4C5 (519) 888-2472	**National Trust Equity Fund** National Trust 21 King St. E., 15th Floor Toronto, Ont. M5C 1B3 (416) 361-5553
Type	Canadian Equity Fund	Canadian Equity Fund
Fund Established	Jan. 2, 1985	Dec. 23, 1957
Where Sold	Everywhere in Canada	Everywhere in Canada.
Sales Charge	6%	No-load
Redemption Fee	None	None
Management Expense Ratio	1.5%	1%
RRSP Eligible	Yes	Yes
Net Assets ($ Millions)	70.2	115.5

Total Return(%)

1988	-6.2	-9.7
1987	7.9	14.6
1986	26.7	24.9
1985		31.0
1984		-5.9
1983		50.9
1982		-20.5
1981		19.9
1980		25.3
1979		40.7
1978		10.0
1977		-1.3
1976		-0.5
1975		7.6
1974		-12.9

95	92	29
Provident Stock Fund Ltd.	**Prudential Growth Fund Canada Ltd.**	**RoyFund Bond Fund**
One Canada Centre	200 Consilium Place	Suite 2990, South Tower
447 Portage Ave.	Scarborough, Ont.	Royal Bank Plaza, P.O.
Winnipeg, Man. R3C 3B6	M1H 3E6	Box 70
(204) 943-0361		Toronto, Ont. M5J 2J2
		(416) 865-0505
		Toll-free 1-800-387-1605
Specialty Equity Fund	Canadian Equity Fund	Bond Fund
December, 1967	July 29, 1970	1973
Everywhere in Canada	Everywhere in Canada	Everywhere in Canada
8.5%	8.5%	No-load
None	None	None
1.44%	0.98%	1.42%
No	Yes	Yes
70.2	73.9	236.6
-10.0	-15.6	7.8
16.6	27.9	6.8
21.3	23.7	15.7
17.7	27.9	23.9
-17.9	-5.8	1.0
89.6	74.7	23.4
-30.2	-35.5	8.6
25.2	14.8	0.9
35.2	24.3	13.3
37.6	44.5	6.5
9.1	13.1	8.0
-2.1	1.6	13.9
5.2	5.0	7.8
5.7	7.3	10.6
-9.8	-13.5	

Rank	8	67
	RoyFund Equity Ltd. Suite 2990, South Tower Royal Bank Plaza, P.O. Box 70 Toronto, Ont. M5J 2J2 (416) 865-0505 Toll-free: 1-800-387-1605	**RoyFund Money Market Fund** Suite 2900, South Tower Royal Bank Plaza, Box 70 Toronto, Ont. M5J 2J2 (416) 865-0505 Toll-free 1-800-387-1605
Type	Canadian Equity Fund	Money Market Fund
Fund Established	April, 1967	September, 1986
Where Sold	Everywhere in Canada	Everywhere in Canada
Sales Charge	No-load	No-load
Redemption Fee	None	None
Management Expense Ratio	1.88%	1.15%
RRSP Eligible	Yes	Yes
Net Assets ($ Millions)	860.1	107.3
Total Return(%)		
1988	-8.3	7.8
1987	12.1	
1986	34.9	
1985	35.2	
1984	-0.9	
1983	82.1	
1982	-40.7	
1981	24.4	
1980	37.6	
1979	48.1	
1978	15.5	
1977	1.7	
1976	4.1	
1975	9.3	
1974	-4.5	

61	100	25
Royal Trust Advantage Balanced Fund	**Royal Trust Advantage Income Fund**	**Royal Trust Bond Fund**
Royal Trust Co.	Royal Trust Co.	Royal Trust Co.
Suite 3900, Royal Trust Tower	Suite 3900, Royal Trust Tower	Suite 3900, Royal Trust Tower
Toronto-Dominion Centre	Toronto-Dominion Centre	Toronto-Dominion Centre
Toronto, Ont. M5W 1P9	Toronto, Ont. M5W 1P9	Toronto, Ont. M5W 1P9

Balanced Fund	Balanced Fund	Bond Fund
Dec. 11, 1986	Dec. 11, 1986	July 29, 1966
Everywhere in Canada	Everywhere in Canada	Everywhere in Canada
No-load	No-load	No-load
None	None	None
1.31%	1.29%	1.12%
Yes	Yes	Yes
132.6	66.2	287.9
0.2	3.1	7.3
		6.2
		16.5
		30.0
		1.3
		35.5
		11.7
		-2.1
		1.3
		7.3
		7.8
		15.9
		10.6
		11.1
		-2.9

Rank	20	28
	Royal Trust Canadian Money Market	**Royal Trust Canadian Stock Fund**
	Royal Trust Co.	Royal Trust Co.
	Suite 3900, Royal Trust Tower	Suite 3900, Royal Trust Tower
	Toronto-Dominion Centre	Toronto-Dominion Centre
	Toronto, Ont. M5W 1P9	Toronto, Ont. M5W 1P9
Type	Money Market Fund	Canadian Equity Fund
Fund Established	July 7, 1987	July 29, 1966
Where Sold	Everywhere in Canada	Everywhere in Canada
Sales Charge	No-load	No-load
Redemption Fee	None	None
Management Expense Ratio	Fiscal year not complete	1.48%
RRSP Eligible	Yes	Yes
Net Assets ($ Millions)		256.4
Total Return(%)		
1988		-5.7
1987		17.8
1986		11.3
1985		24.6
1984		-8.6
1983		79.0
1982		-34.1
1981		14.6
1980		28.8
1979		43.3
1978		11.0
1977		0.0
1976		3.8
1975		8.7
1974		-7.5

5	**76**	**89**
Royal Trust Mortgage Fund	**Sentinel Canada Equity Fund Limited**	**Sentinel Canada Money Market Fund**
Royal Trust Co.	Mackenzie Financial Corp.	Mackenzie Financial Corp.
Suite 3900, Royal Trust Tower	150 Bloor St. W., 4th Floor	150 Bloor St. W., 4th Floor
Toronto-Dominion Centre	Toronto, Ont. M5S 3B5	Toronto, Ont. M5S 3B5
Toronto, Ont. M5W 1P9	(416) 922-5322	(416) 922-5322
Mortgage Fund	Canadian Equity Fund	Money Market Fund
Oct. 1, 1968	May 7, 1986	Jan. 7, 1987
Everywhere in Canada	Everywhere in Canada	Everywhere in Canada
No-load	5%	No-load
None	None	None
1.36%	1.84%	0.67%
Yes	Yes	Yes
1016.8	100.3	90.0
9.2	-13.0	9.8
8.7	22.4	
11.3		
16.8		
8.6		
20.8		
18.7		
5.2		
7.9		
8.3		
9.3		
14.3		
9.6		
11.2		
5.4		

Rank	96	58
	Sentinel Global Fund Mackenzie Financial Corp. 150 Bloor St. W., 4th Floor Toronto, Ont. M5S 3B5 (416) 922-5322	**Sunset Fund** IBM Tower, Suite 2802 79 Wellington St. Toronto, Ont. M5K 1H1 (416) 862-2020 1-800-268-8690
Type	International Equity Fund	Balanced Fund
Fund Established	Sept. 4, 1986	June 25, 1985
Where Sold	Everywhere in Canada	Everywhere in Canada
Sales Charge	5%	9%
Redemption Fee	None	None
Management Expense Ratio	2.58%	2%
RRSP Eligible	No	Yes
Net Assets ($ Millions)	76.5	138.2
Total Return(%)		
1988	-21.3	1.7
1987		10.9
1986		
1985		
1984		
1983		
1982		
1981		
1980		
1979		
1978		
1977		
1976		
1975		
1974		

74	82	2
Sunset World Fund	**Templeton Canadian**	**Templeton Growth Fund**
IBM Tower, Suite 2802	**Fund**	**Ltd.**
79 Wellington St. W.	4 King St. W.	4 King St. W.
Toronto, Ont. M5K 1H1	P.O. Box 4070, Station A	P.O. Box 4070, Station A
(416) 862-2020	Toronto, Ont. M5W 1M3	Toronto, Ont. M5W 1M3
1-800-268-8690	(416) 364-4672	(416) 364-4672

International Equity Fund	Canadian Equity Fund	International Equity Fund
June 11, 1987	April 7, 1983	Sept. 1, 1954
Everywhere in Canada	Everywhere in Canada	Everywhere in Canada
9%	8.5%	8.5%
None	None	None
2.58%	2.01%	0.82%
No	Yes	No
	85.1	1279.1
	-11.4	-10.4
	19.0	19.3
	23.0	31.8
	20.9	28.1
	-10.1	6.7
		56.2
		-14.0
		28.3
		16.7
		24.2
		33.5
		43.3
		15.7
		22.3
		-12.3

Rank	15	11
	Trimark Canadian Fund	**Trimark Fund**
	One First Canadian Place	One First Canadian Place
	Suite 935, P.O. Box 189	Suite 935, P.O. Box 189
	Toronto, Ont. M5X 1A3	Toronto, Ont. M5X 1A3
Type	Canadian Equity Fund	International Equity Fund
Fund Established	July 10, 1981. First offered Sept. 1, 1981.	July 10, 1981. First offered Sept. 1, 1981.
Where Sold	Everywhere in Canada	Everywhere in Canada
Sales Charge	9%	9%
Redemption Fee	None	None
Management Expense Ratio	1.61%	1.59%
RRSP Eligible	Yes	No
Net Assets ($ Millions)	472.1	590.3
Total Return(%)		
1988	1.6	-0.5
1987	19.6	17.5
1986	18.1	31.2
1985	31.5	26.5
1984	-0.9	-1.6
1983	85.1	82.8
1982		
1981		
1980		
1979		
1978		
1977		
1976		
1975		
1974		

99	**30**	**47**
Trust Pret Revenu - H Fond	**United Accumulative Fund Ltd.**	**United Accumulative Retirement Fund**
850 Place d'Youville	200 King St. W.	200 King St. W.
Quebec City, Que.	Toronto, Ont. M5H 3W8	Toronto, Ont. M5H 3W8
G1R 3P6	(416) 598-7777	(416) 598-7777
(418) 692-1221		

Mortgage Fund	International Equity Fund	Canadian Equity Fund
Oct. 1, 1974	May 27, 1957	Nov. 30, 1971
Everywhere in Canada	Everywhere in Canada	Everywhere in Canada
No-load	9%	9%
None	None	None
1.24%	1.88%	1.88%
Yes	No	Yes
67.7	234.5	164.7
8.6	-14.9	-2.2
12.5	11.7	4.8
10.7	34.3	22.3
17.5	32.7	42.9
7.9	10.6	2.4
23.8	39.8	54.4
19.5	-17.9	-29.0
5.3	30.5	28.0
8.3	27.9	28.1
8.2	46.8	69.4
8.3	2.8	9.8
13.7	-2.4	-6.8
7.5	6.1	8.6
	6.8	3.1
	-17.2	-9.1

Rank	85	56
	United Venture Retirement Fund 200 King St. W. Toronto, Ont. M5H 3W8 (416) 598-7777	**Universal Savings Equity Fund Limited** 401 Bay St., Suite 1218 Toronto, Ont. M5H 2Y4 (416) 364-1145 1-800-268-9374
Type	Canadian Equity Fund	Canadian Equity Fund
Fund Established	Nov. 30, 1971	April, 1965
Where Sold	Everywhere in Canada	Everywhere in Canada
Sales Charge	9%	9%
Redemption Fee	None	None
Management Expense Ratio	1.93%	2%
RRSP Eligible	Yes	Yes
Net Assets ($ Millions)	82.3	136.6
Total Return(%)		
1988	-9.8	11.0
1987	13.7	17.1
1986	28.9	24.3
1985	31.9	31.1
1984	-4.5	1.3
1983	66.9	54.4
1982	-40.5	-13.4
1981	36.1	12.2
1980	43.7	17.4
1979	74.7	43.0
1978	16.6	27.5
1977	-4.8	3.7
1976	11.1	17.1
1975	13.1	6.9
1974	-19.1	-3.1

35	43	57
Viking Canadian Fund Ltd.	**Viking Commonwealth Fund Ltd.**	**Viking Dividend Fund Ltd.**
595 Bay St.	595 Bay St.	595 Bay St.
Toronto, Ont. M5G 2C6	Toronto, Ont. M5G 2C6	Toronto, Ont. M5G 2C6
(416) 343-5222	(416) 343-5222	(416) 343-5222

Canadian Equity Fund	Balanced Fund	Preferred Dividend Fund
September, 1971	April, 1932	June, 1978
Not for sale in Yukon, NWT and Nfld.	Not for sale in Yukon, NWT and Nfld.	Not for sale in Yukon, NWT and Nfld.
3.5%	3.5%	3.5%
None	None	None
1.673%	1.72%	1.13%
Yes	No	Yes
209.4	168.4	135.1
-2.6	-3.4	3.5
11.1	21.2	11.5
20.6	30.4	15.3
25.9	24.3	23.5
-2.4	0.7	6.2
66.8	55.0	55.4
-29.8	-7.7	-14.3
19.2	30.9	9.2
26.6	4.7	5.2
42.4	14.5	
11.0	11.8	
-0.4	20.7	
3.3	11.6	
7.7	9.7	
-9.9	-14.5	

Rank	63	68
	Viking Growth Fund Ltd. 595 Bay St. Toronto, Ont. M5G 2C6 (416) 343-5222	**Viking Income Fund** 595 Bay St. Toronto, Ont. M5G 2C6 (416) 343-5222

Type	International Equity Fund	Bond Fund
Fund Established	March, 1949	November, 1972
Where Sold	Not for sale in Yukon and NWT and Nfld.	Not for sale in Yukon, NWT and Nfld.
Sales Charge	3.5%	3.5%
Redemption Fee	None	None
Management Expense Ratio	1.73%	1.15%
RRSP Eligible	No	Yes
Net Assets ($ Millions)	126.6	113.0

Total Return(%)		
1988	-8.5	7.7
1987	15.2	7.3
1986	42.3	16.5
1985	27.6	30.9
1984	-2.6	0.5
1983	50.7	37.9
1982	-17.3	10.9
1981	32.2	-8.0
1980	10.0	-2.1
1979	19.8	5.5
1978	19.8	6.1
1977	23.9	14.9
1976	15.4	10.0
1975	20.6	10.6
1974	-19.0	

59

**Viking International
Fund Ltd.**
595 Bay St.
Toronto, Ont. M5G 2C6
(416) 343-5222

International Equity Fund

April, 1968

Not for sale in Yukon,
NWT and Nfld.

3.5%

None

1.71%

No

135.0

-5.2
10.4
32.4
21.1
6.0
54.2
-14.5
54.5
5.5
16.5
29.0
27.2
11.0
16.2
-25.2

CHAPTER FIFTEEN

THE BEST PERFORMERS

1 Year

1	First City Realfund*	**16.2**
2	Industrial Horizon Fund*	**15.2**
3	Counsel Trust Real Estate Fd*	**13.7**
4	Industrial Income Fund*	**13.2**
5	Rabin Budden Income Fund*	**13.1**
6	Mackenzie Mortgage & Income Fund*	**13.0**
7	Ethical Growth Fund*	**12.3**
8	Universal Svgs Income Fund*	**12.1**
9	Trust General Money Market*	**11.2**
10	Universal Svgs Equity Fund Ltd.*	**11.0**
11	Everest Bond Fund*	**10.8**
12	Cundill Value Fund Ltd.	**10.4**
13	Altamira Income Fund*	**10.4**
14	Imperial Realty Growth Fund*	**10.3**
15	Sentinel Cda Money Market Fd*	**9.8**
16	TD's Green Line Mtge Fund*	**9.7**
17	PH&N Bond Fund*	**9.5**
18	Talvest Money Fund*	**9.5**

* RRSP Eligible. One-year figures show percentage rate of return, including dividends and capital gains distributions, for year to August 31, 1988. Three-year, five-year and 10-year rates are average annual compound rates of return, including dividends and capital gains.

19	Canadian Protected Fund*	**9.4**
20	Elliott & Page Money Fund*	**9.4**
21	Prudential Income Fund Canada*	**9.3**
22	First Canadian Mortgage Fund*	**9.2**
23	Royal Trust Mortgage Fund*	**9.2**
24	Trans-Canada Shares Series B	**8.9**
25	Hallmark Bond Fund*	**8.9**
26	Montreal Trust Mortgage Fund*	**8.9**
27	Prudential Money Market Fund*	**8.8**
28	Confed Dolphin Mortgage Fund*	**8.8**
29	Investors Mortgage Fund*	**8.8**
30	Bolton Tremblay Money Fund*	**8.7**
31	London Life Mortgage Fund*	**8.7**
32	Guardian Short Term Money Fund*	**8.7**
33	Trimark Interest Fund*	**8.6**
34	Fiducie Pret Revenu Fonds H*	**8.6**
35	Sceptre Bond Fund*	**8.5**
36	Mtl Trust RRSP-Mortgage Sect*	**8.5**
37	Viking Money Market Fund*	**8.4**
38	AGF Money Market Fund*	**8.4**
39	AMD Money Market Fd*	**8.3**
40	AMD Fixed Income Fd*	**8.3**
41	St-Laurent Reer-Epargne-Plus*	**8.3**
42	Investors Money Market Fund*	**8.3**
43	CDA Money Market Fund*	**8.2**
44	Investors Real Property Fund*	**8.2**
45	CDA RSP Fixed Income Fund*	**8.2**
46	Industrial Cash Management Fd*	**8.1**
47	Ordre Ingenieurs Revenu Var*	**8.1**
48	Talvest Income Fund*	**8.1**
49	Allied Money Fund*	**8.1**
50	Dynamic Money Market Fund*	**8.1**

3 Year

1 AGF Japan Fund Ltd.	**38.6**
2 Universal Savings Pacific Fd	**37.6**
3 Investors Japanese Growth Fund	**37.3**
4 Royal Trust Japanese Fund	**36.6**
5 Trans-Canada Equity Fund*	**22.4**
6 Cambridge Growth Fund*	**20.9**
7 Natl Trust Global Fund I	**20.6**
8 Trans-Canada Shares Series B	**19.5**
9 MD Growth Investments Ltd.	**17.8**
10 Universal Svgs Equity Fund Ltd.*	**17.4**
11 Counsel Trust Real Estate Fd*	**16.4**
12 Trans-Canada Shares Series C*	**16.4**
13 Cundill Value Fund Ltd.	**16.4**
14 Industrial Dividend Fund Ltd.*	**16.3**
15 Mackenzie Equity Fund*	**15.9**
16 Industrial Pension Fund*	**15.8**
17 Industrial Growth Fund*	**15.8**
18 Industrial Equity Fund Ltd.*	**15.6**
19 CMA Investment Fund*	**15.5**
20 GoldenFund*	**15.5**
21 Imperial Realty Growth Fund*	**15.4**
22 Trimark Fund	**15.3**
23 Viking Commonwealth Fund	**15.1**
24 Cambridge Balanced Fund*	**15.1**
25 AGF HiTech Fund Ltd	**14.9**
26 Industrial Income Fund*	**14.7**
27 Bullock Amer Fund	**14.5**
28 Viking Growth Fund Ltd	**14.4**

* RRSP Eligible. One-year figures show percentage rate of return, including dividends and capital gains distributions, for year to August 31, 1988. Three-year, five-year and 10-year rates are average annual compound rates of return, including dividends and capital gains.

29	Mackenzie Mortgage & Income Fund*	**14.3**
30	Empire Life Segregated #1*	**14.3**
31	First City Realfund*	**14.1**
32	Dynamic Precious Metals Fund*	**14.0**
33	Guardian Global Equity Fd	**13.9**
34	NW Canadian Fund Ltd.*	**13.7**
35	CDA RSP Common Stock Fund*	**13.6**
36	PH&N Canadian Fund*	**13.5**
37	Talvest Growth Fund*	**13.0**
38	DK Enterprise Fund*	**12.8**
39	London Life Equity Fund*	**12.8**
40	Trimark Canadian Fund*	**12.8**
41	Investors Retirement Mutual*	**12.7**
42	Bolton Tremblay International	**12.6**
43	Cda Life Cdn&Intl Equity S-9*	**12.5**
44	Guardian Cdn Equity Fd*	**12.5**
45	Universal Savings American	**12.4**
46	PH&N Bond Fund*	**12.4**
47	Noram Convertible Securities	**12.4**
48	Dynamic Fund of Canada Ltd.*	**12.3**
49	Hallmark Canadian Fund*	**12.2**
50	Ont Teachers Grp Aggr Equity*	**12.2**

5 Year

1	AGF Japan Fund Ltd.	**30.4**
2	Universal Savings Pacific Fd	**26.6**
3	Investors Japanese Growth Fund	**26.0**
4	Trans-Canada Equity Fund*	**19.7**
5	Cambridge Growth Fund*	**18.3**
6	Natl Trust Global Fund I	**18.3**
7	Trans-Canada Shares Series B	**17.8**
8	MD Growth Investments Ltd.	**17.7**
9	Industrial Dividend Fund Ltd.*	**17.4**
10	Universal Svgs Equity Fund Ltd.*	**16.5**
11	Trans-Canada Shares Series C*	**16.5**
12	CMA Investment Fund*	**16.1**
13	Mackenzie Equity Fund*	**15.8**
14	Industrial Income Fund*	**15.7**
15	Industrial Pension Fund*	**15.3**
16	Mackenzie Mortgage & Income Fund*	**15.2**
17	Industrial Growth Fund*	**15.2**
18	CDA RSP Common Stock Fund*	**14.1**
19	Cambridge Balanced Fund*	**14.1**
20	Templeton Growth Fund	**14.0**
21	London Life Bond Fund*	**13.9**
22	Viking Commonwealth Fund	**13.8**
23	Trimark Fund	**13.8**
24	Cundill Value Fund Ltd.	**13.5**
25	United Accumulative Fund Ltd.	**13.4**
26	Trimark Canadian Fund*	**13.3**
27	Viking Growth Fund Ltd	**13.2**
28	Canadian Trusteed Income Fund*	**13.2**

* RRSP Eligible. One-year figures show percentage rate of return, including dividends and capital gains distributions, for year to August 31, 1988. Three-year, five-year and 10-year rates are average annual compound rates of return, including dividends and capital gains.

29	Dynamic American Fund	**13.2**
30	Universal Savings American	**13.2**
31	RoyFund Equity Ltd*	**13.2**
32	Cda Life Cdn&Intl Equity S-9*	**13.1**
33	Ont Teachers Grp Aggr Equity*	**13.1**
34	PH&N Bond Fund*	**13.0**
35	Canadian Security Growth Fund*	**13.0**
36	Associate Investors Ltd.*	**12.9**
37	United Accumulative Retirement*	**12.9**
38	Confed Dolphin Fund*	**12.8**
39	Talvest Bond Fund*	**12.8**
40	Guardian Balanced Fund*	**12.8**
41	Universal Svgs Income Fund*	**12.7**
42	Bolton Tremblay International	**12.6**
43	First City Realfund*	**12.6**
44	Industrial Equity Fund Ltd.*	**12.6**
45	MER Equity Fund*	**12.6**
46	Montreal Trust Intl Fund	**12.5**
47	Industrial American Fund	**12.5**
48	Trust General Bond Fund*	**12.5**
49	NW Canadian Fund Ltd.*	**12.4**
50	Talvest Growth Fund*	**12.3**

10 Year

1	MD Growth Investments Ltd.	**21.9**
2	AGF Japan Fund Ltd.	**21.7**
3	Cundill Value Fund Ltd.	**21.0**
4	AGF Special Fund Ltd.	**20.7**
5	Mackenzie Equity Fund*	**19.2**
6	Investors Japanese Growth Fund	**19.1**
7	United Venture Retirement Fund*	**18.9**
8	United Accumulative Retirement*	**18.8**
9	Empire Life Segregated #1*	**18.6**
10	Cdn Anaesthetists Mutual Accumul*	**18.6**
11	Universal Svgs Equity Fund Ltd.*	**18.4**
12	Bolton Tremblay International	**18.2**
13	Tradex Investment Fund Ltd.*	**18.1**
14	United Accumulative Fund Ltd.	**18.1**
15	Industrial American Fund	**18.0**
16	NW Canadian Fund Ltd.*	**18.0**
17	Industrial Growth Fund*	**17.9**
18	CMA Investment Fund*	**17.8**
19	Canadian Security Growth Fund*	**17.8**
20	Guardian Enterprise Fund*	**17.7**
21	RoyFund Equity Ltd*	**17.7**
22	London Life Equity Fund*	**17.2**
23	American Growth Fund Ltd.	**17.2**
24	Confed Dolphin Fund*	**17.1**
25	Ont Teachers Grp Aggr Equity*	**17.1**
26	Industrial Dividend Fund Ltd.*	**17.1**
27	Templeton Growth Fund	**17.0**
28	Jones Heward Fund Ltd.*	**17.0**

* RRSP Eligible. One-year figures show percentage rate of return, including dividends and capital gains distributions, for year to August 31, 1988. Three-year, five-year and 10-year rates are average annual compound rates of return, including dividends and capital gains.

29	PH&N U.S. Fund	**16.4**
30	Cda Life Cdn&Intl Equity S-9*	**16.4**
31	Growth Equity Fund Ltd.*	**16.3**
32	PH&N Canadian Fund*	**16.2**
33	CDA RSP Common Stock Fund*	**16.2**
34	Viking International Fund	**16.1**
35	MONY Canadian Growth Fund*	**16.1**
36	Industrial Pension Fund*	**16.0**
37	Ont Teachers Grp Diversified*	**16.0**
38	Montreal Trust Intl Fund	**15.9**
39	United Venture Fund Ltd.	**15.9**
40	Associate Investors Ltd.*	**15.7**
41	Guardian Global Equity Fd	**15.7**
42	Trans-Canada Equity Fund*	**15.7**
43	Viking Commonwealth Fund	**15.7**
44	Industrial Equity Fund Ltd.*	**15.7**
45	Cambridge Growth Fund*	**15.6**
46	Investors Growth Fund of Cda	**15.6**
47	Investors Retirement Mutual*	**15.6**
48	Dynamic Fund of Canada Ltd.*	**15.5**
49	Viking Growth Fund Ltd	**15.0**
50	National Trust Equity Fund*	**15.0**

CHAPTER SIXTEEN

DIRECTORY OF FUNDS

AGF Management Limited
31st Floor
T-D Bank Tower
Toronto, ON, M5K 1E9
(416) 367-1900

Money Market
AGF Special Fund
Japan
Option Equity
HiTech
Preferred Income
American Growth
Canadian Trusted Income
Corporate Investors Ltd.
Corporate Investors Stock
Canadian Gas & Energy
Canadian Security Growth
Growth Equity Fund Ltd.
Global Government Bond
Excel Canadian Equity
Excel American Equity
Excel Canadian Bond & MM

AIC Ltd.
101 Frederick St.
Suite 901
Kitchener, ON, N2H 6R2
(519) 578-6760

AIC Advantage

AMD Finsco Ltd.
145 King St. W.
3rd Floor
Toronto, ON, M5H 3T7
(416) 864-3886

AMD American Blue Chip Growth
AMD Canadian Blue Chip Growth
AMD Dividend
AMD Fixed Income
AMD Money Market
AMD U.S. Dollar Money Market
AMD T-Bill

Allied Capital Management Inc.
8 King St. E.
Suite 501
Toronto, ON, M5C 1B5
(416)869-7327

Allied Canadian
Allied Dividend
Allied Income
Allied International
Allied Money

Altamira Management Ltd.
20 Queen St. W., Suite 1606
Box 90,Cadillac Fairview Offic
Toronto, ON, M5H 3R3
(416) 971-9291

Altamira Income

**Bank of Montreal Investment
Management**
1 First Canadian Place
First Bank Tower
Toronto, ON, M5X 1A1
(416) 927-6606

First Cdn Mortgage

Bissett & Associates
750, Bow Valley Square Two
205-5th Ave. S.W.
Calgary, AB, T2P 2V7
(403) 266-4664

Bissett Canadian
Bissett Fiduciary

Bolton Tremblay Inc.
70 University Ave.
Suite 1050,
Toronto, ON, M5J 2M4
(416) 595-5200

International
Canada Cumulative
Planned Resources
Taurus
Preferred Income
Money

**Burns Fry Investment
Management**
P.O. Box 150, Suite 5000
One First Canadian Place
Toronto, ON, M5X 1H3
(416) 365-4000

Burns Fry
Burns Fry Canadian

CDSPI
2 Lansing Square
Suite 600
Willowdale, ON, M2J 4Z3
(416) 497-7117

Canada RSP Fixed Income
Canada RSP Common Stock
Canada Money Market
Canada RSP Balanced

CGF Fund Management
70 University Ave.
Suite 800
Toronto, ON, M5J 2M5
(416) 591-6000

CGF Venture
CGF Fund 4000
International Growth

CSA Management
Suite 2804, IBM Tower
T-D Centre, P.O. Box 68
Toronto, ON, M5K 1E7
(416)865-0326

Goldtrust
Goldfund

CT Investment Counsel Inc.
Suite 800
110 Yonge St.
Toronto, ON, M5C 1T4
(416) 869-9391

Everest Short-term Asset
Everest Bond
Everest Special Equity
Everest Balanced
Everest International

Calvin Bullock Ltd.
630 Dorchester Blvd.W.
Suite 2690
Montreal, PQ, H3B 1X1
(514) 866-5421

American
Income
Dividend
Canadian Investment
Growth

Canada Life
330 University Ave.
Toronto, ON, M5G 1R8
(416) 597-1456

Canadian Equity
U.S.& International Equity
Fixed Income
Money Market
Managed

Canada Trust
15th Floor
320 Bay St.
Toronto, ON, M5H 2P6
(416) 361-8180

Canada Trust Investment Equity
Canada Trust Investment Income
Canada Trust North American

Canadian Anaesthetists' Mutual Accum.
94 Cumberland St.
Suite 503
Toronto, ON, M5R 1A3
(416) 923-1449

Mutual Accumulating

Canadian General Life Insurance
P.O. Box 918
120 King St. W.
Hamilton, ON, L8N 3P6
(416)528-6766

Equity Fund A
Security Fund B
Money Market C

Capstone Consultants Limited
1 University Ave.
Suite 401
Toronto, ON, M5J 2P1
(416) 863-0687

Capstone Investment Trust
Capstone Intl. Investment
Capstone Cash Management

Central Capital Mgmt.
1 First Canadian Place
38th Floor
Toronto, ON, M5X 1G4
(416) 364-4400

Central Trust RRSP Equity
Central Trust RRSP Bond
Central Trust Mortgage
Central Select

Central Group of Funds
Box 7290
55 Broad Leaf Cresent
Ancaster, ON, L9G 3P2
(416) 648-2025

Univest Growth
Natural Resources Growth
All-Canadian Revenue Growth
All-Canadian Dividend

Chou Associates Management
70 Dragoon Crescent
Scarborough, Ontario, M1V 1N4
(416) 299-6749

Chou RRSP
Chou Associates

Co-Operative Trust Co. of Cda
333 - 3rd Ave. N.
Saskatoon, SK, S7K 2M2
(306) 244-1900

Co-operative Trust Growth
Co-operative Trust Income

Confederation Life Insurance
321 Bloor St. E.
7th Floor
Toronto, ON, M4W 1H1
(416) 323-8444

Confed Dolphin
Dolphin Mortgage

Counsel Trust Co.
36 Toronto St.
Suite 300
Toronto, ON, M5C 2C5
(416) 365-3100

Counsel Trust Real Estate

Dean Witter Reynolds
110 Yonge St.
Suite 1200
Toronto, ON, M5C 2S3
(416) 369-8919

Optimal Canadian

Dixon Krogseth Trust
Suite 2660
1066 West Hastings St.
Vancouver, BC, V6E 3X1
(604) 684-8541

DK Enterprise
DK American
Heritage

Dynamic Fund Management
6 Adelaide St. E.
9th Floor
Toronto, ON, M5C 1H6
(416) 363-5621

Dynamic American
Dynamic Fund of Canada
Dynamic Income
Dynamic Managed Portfolio
Dynamic Precious Metals
Dynamic Savings
Dynamic Dividend
Dynamic Global
Dynamic Global Bond

Eastland Realty Services
Suite 200
6112 Quinpool Road
Halifax, NS, B3L 1A3
(902) 429-0112

Canadian Property Inv. Trust

Elliott & Page
120 Adelaide St. W.
Suite 1120
Toronto, ON, M5H 1V1
(416) 365-8352

NAL-Investor Diversified
NAL-Investor Bond
NAL-Investor Blue Chip

Elliott & Page Ltd.
Suite 1120
120 Adelaide St. W.
Toronto, ON, M5H 1V1
(416) 365-8351

Elliott & Page Money

Empire Life Insurance Company
243-259 King St. E.
Kingston, ON, K7L 3A8
(613) 548-1881

Empire Life Ins. Segregated

First City Realfund
20 Adelaide St. E.
Suite 500
Toronto, ON, M5C 2T6
(416) 367-8484

First City Realfund

First City Trust
First City Building
777 Hornby St.
Vancouver, BC, V6Z 1S4
(604) 685-2489

First City Realfund
First City Growth
First City Income

First Grenadier Fund Management
224 Richmond St. W.
Toronto, ON, M5V 1V6
(416) 593-0144

Canadian Natural Resources

Futurefund Shares Inc.
P.O. Box 7290
55 Broad Leaf Cresent
Ancaster, ON, L9G 3N6
(416) 648-7363

Valuefund
Lifefund
Foodfund
Technofund
Goldenfund
Silverfund

G. T. Management Canada Ltd.
121 King St. W.
Suite 1750
Toronto, ON, M5H 3T9
(416) 363-9100

G.T. Global Choice

Greydanus, Boeckh & Assoc.
300 Dundas St.
London, ON, N6B 1T6
(519) 673-3020

Hallmark Bond
Hallmark Canadian

Guaranty Realty Investments
Box 95, Suite 933
595 Bay St., Tower C
Toronto, ON, M5G 2C2
(416) 975-4827

Guaranty Trust Property

Guardian Capital Group
Royal Bank Plaza, North Tower
19th Floor, P.O. Box 201
Toronto, ON, M5J 2J6
(416) 947-4087

Guardian Preferred Dividend
Guardian Enterprise
Guardian Growth
Guardian North American
Guardian Short Term Money
Guardian World Equity
Guardian Canadian

Guardian Timing Services
74 Victoria St.
Toronto, ON, M5C 2A5
(416) 863-1100

Canadian Protected
Salamander Trust
Protected Bond

Hodgson Robertson Laing Ltd.
Suite 1608
390 Bay St.
Toronto, ON, M5H 2Y2
(416) 368-1428

Waltaine Preferred Income
Waltaine
Waltaine Convertible Preferred

**Horgan Tattersall Investment
Counsel**
Suite 1904, P.O. Box 95
20 Queen St. W.
Toronto, ON, M5H 3R3
(416) 979-1818

Saxon World Growth
Saxon Stock
Saxon Small Capital
Saxon Balanced

Hume Fund Management
Suite 600
70 University Ave.
Toronto, ON, M5J 2M4
(416) 979-5640

Hume Growth & Income
Hume RRSP Growth & Income

I.A. Michael Investment Counsel
10 King St. E.
Suite 1010
Toronto, ON, M5C 1C3
(416) 365-9696

ABC Fully Managed

Imperial Advisors Ltd.
1600 Imperial Broadway Tower
363 Broadway
Winnipeg, MB, R3C 3N9
(204) 949-1220

Imperial Realty Growth
Imperial Mortgage & Income

Integra Capital Management
55 University Ave.
Suite 1100, P.O. Box 42
Toronto, ON, M5J 2H7
(416) 367-0404

Integra Balanced

Investors Syndicate Ltd.
1 Canada Centre
447 Portage Ave.
Winnipeg, MB, R3C 3B6
(204) 956-8536

Investors Growth Fund Cda
Investors International Mutual
Investors Japanese Growth
Investors Mutual Canada
Investors Retirement Mutual
Investors Dividend
Provident Stock
Investors Mortgage
Investors Money Market
Investors Bond
Investors Cdn Equity
Investors Real Property
Investors Global
Investors Summa

Jones Heward Investment Management
P.O. Box 200, 72nd Floor
1 First Canadian Place
Toronto, ON, M5X 1A6
(416) 365-4700

Jones Heward
Jones Heward American

Keltic Savings Corp.
1770 Market St.
Brunswick St. Level
Halifax, NS, B3J 3M3
(902) 429-9911

Keltic Investment Trust

Laurentian Financial
595 Bay St.
Toronto, ON, M5G 2C6
(416) 343-5222

Viking Commonwealth
Viking Dividend
Viking Growth
Viking Money Market
Viking International
Viking Income
Viking Canadian

Leon Frazer & Assoc.
8 King St. E.
Suite 2001
Toronto, ON, M5C 1B6
(416) 864-1120

Associate Investors Ltd.

London Life
255 Dufferin Ave.
Terminal 190
London, ON, N6A 4K1
(519) 432-5281

London Life Equity
London Life Bond
London Life Mortgage
London Life U.S. Equity
London Life Diversified

MD Management Limited
1867 Alta Vista Dr.
Ottawa, ON, K1G 3Y6
(613) 731-4552

CMA Investment
CMA Insured Annuity
CMA Short-term Deposit
MD Growth Investments
MD Realty

MD Management Ltd.
1867 Alta Vista Drive
Ottawa, ON, K1G 3Y6

MD Realty Fund

MK Wong Management Ltd.
1066 West Hastings St.
Suite 2520
Vancouver, BC, V6E 3X1
(604) 669-4555

MK Wong Lotus
MK Wong One Decision

MOF Management Ltd.
P.O. Box 10379, Pacific Centre
2020-609 Granville St.
Vancouver, BC, V7Y 1G6
(604) 688-8151

Multiple Opportunities

MONY Life Insurance
797 Don Mills Rd.
15th Floor
Don Mills, ON, M3C 1V2
(416) 429-2200

MONY Life Equity

MYW Financial Management
121 King St. W.
Suite 840, P.O. Box 114
Toronto, ON, M5H 3T9
(416) 360-5096

MYW Canadian Growth
MYW Canadian Balanced
MYW North American Growth
MYW Defensive Income

Mackenzie Financial Corp.
4th Floor
150 Bloor St. W.
Toronto, ON, M5S 2X9
(416) 922-5322

Industrial American
Industrial Dividend
Industrial Equity
Industrial Growth
Industrial Income
Industrial Pension
MacKenzie Equity
MacKenzie Mortgage & Income
Industrial Cash Management
Industrial Global
Industrial Horizon

MagnaTrends Asset Management
Box 449
2 First Canadian Place
Toronto, ON, M5X 1J7
(416) 860-0495

Century DJ

Mandate Mortgage Investment
1285 West Broadway
8th Floor
Vancouver, BC, V6H 3X8
(604) 731-2899

Mandate Mortgage Invest. Corp

Maritime Life Assurance Co.
P.O. Box 1030
2701 Dutch Village Road
Halifax, NS, B3J 2X5
(902) 453-4300

Maritime Life Growth
Maritime Life Balanced

Marlborough Group
Suite 200
250 Consumers Road
Willowdale, ON, M2J 4V6
(416) 494-3039

Marlborough

McLean Budden Ltd.
1155 University St.
Suite 1301
Montreal, PQ, H3B 1S2
(514) 866-8531

McLean Budden Balanced

Merritt Easton Rae Management
Suite 1703
1166 Alberni St.
Vancouver, BC, V6E 3Z3
(604) 688-9531

MER Equity
MER Growth
MER Money Market

Metropolitan Life
99 Bank St.
Ottawa, ON, K1P 5A3
(613) 560-7982

MVP Equity
MVP Bond
MVP Balanced

**Metropolitan Money
Management Ltd.**
10303 Jasper Ave.
Suite 2700
Edmonton, AB, T5J 3N6
(403) 421-2020

*Metropolitan Collective
Metropolitan Growth
Metropolitan Venture
Metrolopolitan Bond
Metropolitan Cdn. Mutual
Principal World
Principal Equity
Metropolitan Speculators*

Midland Doherty
121 King St. W.
15th Floor
Toronto, ON, M5H 3W6
(416) 369-7594

Resources of Canada

Montreal Trust
P.O. Box 1900, Station B
One Place Ville Marie
Montreal, PQ, H3B 3L6
(514) 397-7000

*RRSP: Equity Section
Investment Fund: Equity
Investment Fund: Dividend
Investment Fund: Income
Investment Fund: International
Investment Fund: Mortgage
RRSP: Mortgage Section
RRSP: Income Section
RRSP: Money Market*

Morgan Trust Co.
55 Yonge St.
7th Floor
Toronto, ON, M5E 1S4
(416) 366-8999

*Morgan Worldwide
Morgan Income
Morgan Growth
Morgan Dividend
Morgan Resource*

Mutual Diversico Ltd.
227 King St. S.
Waterloo, ON, N2J 4C5
(519) 888-3503

*Mutual Diversifund 25
Mutual Diversifund 40
Mutual Diversifund 55
Mutual Equifund
Mutual Money Market
Mutual Amerifund
Mutual Dividend*

NW Management
Suite 1200
595 Howe St.
Vancouver, BC, V6C 2T5
(604) 689-1211

*NW Equity
NW Canadian*

Natrusco Investment Funds
c/o National Trust
21 King St. E.
Toronto, ON, M5C 1B3
(416) 361-3841

National Trust Global Fund I

Noram Capital Management Inc.
Suite 1400
390 Bay St.
Toronto, ON, M5H 2Y2
(416) 364-2642

Noram Convertible Securities

North West Trust Co.
10205-101 Street
18th Floor, T-D Tower
Edmonton, AB, T5J 4G1
(403) 429-9300

North West Trust Equity

Northern Funds Management
120 Adelaide St. W.
Suite 2320
Toronto, On., M5H 1T1
(416) 367-3141

NFM U.S. Equity
NFM Canadian Equity
NFM Intl. Money Market & Inc.

Ontario Teacher's Group
60 Mobile Dr.
Toronto, ON, M4A 2P3
(416) 752-9410

Aggresive Equity Section
Balanced Section
Diversified Section
Fixed Value Section
Mortgage Section

Ordre Ingenieurs du Quebec
2020 University St.
14th Floor
Montreal, PQ, H3A 2A5
(514) 845-6141

Ferique Revenu Variable
Ferique Obligations
Ferique Actions
Ferique Equilibre

Pacific Management
2400 Park Place
666 Burrard St.
Vancouver, BC, V6C 3C7
(604) 661-5917

Pacific Growth
Pacific Retirement Balanced
Pacific U.S. Growth

Pagebrook Realty Fund
1004-1959 Upper Water St.
Halifax, NS, M5S 2B3
(416) 964-9619

Pagebrook Realty

Peter Cundill & Associates
1200 Sunlife Plaza
1100 Melville St.
Vancouver, BC, V6E 4A6
(604) 685-4231

Cundill Value
Cundill Security

Phillips, Hager, & North
Suite 1700
1055 W. Hastings St
Vancouver, BC, V6E 2H3
(604) 684-4361

PH&N RSP Equity
PH&N Bond
PH&N Dividend Income
Vintage
PH&N
PH&N Canadian

Prudential Fund Management
200 Consilium Place
Scarborough, ON, M1H 3E6
(416) 296-3040

Prudential Growth
Prudential Income
Prudential Money Market
Prudential Dividend

Putnam Management Co.
One Post Office Square
Boston, Mass., 02109
(617) 292-1103

Putnam Health Sciences Trust

Rabin, Budden Partners
390 Bay St.
Suite 1904
Toronto, ON, M5H 2Y2
(416) 865-1722

Rabin Budden Income
Rabin Budden Capital

RealCap Funds Management
Suite 604
2161 Yonge St.
Toronto, ON, M4S 3A6
(416) 486-7729

Realgrowth Cda Equity
Realgrowth Active Income
Realgrowth American Trend

Renaissance Assets Management
390 Bay St.
Suite 614
Toronto, ON, M5H 2Y2
(416) 367-8000

Renaissance Cda Bond & Bullion

Royal Trust
5th Floor, Royal Trust Tower
Toronto Dominion Centre
Toronto, ON, M5W 1P9
(416) 864-6574

Royal Trust American Stock
Royal Trust Bond
Royal Trust Canadian Stock
Royal Trust Energy
Royal Trust Mortgage
Royal Trust Preferred Share
Royal Trust Japanese Stock
Advantage Balanced
Advantage Income
Advantage Growth

Royfund Group
Suite 2990, South Tower
POB 70, Royal Bank Plaza
Toronto, ON, M5J 2J2
(416) 865-0505

Royfund Equity
Royfund Bond
Royfund Money Market

Sagit Management Ltd
Suite 900
789 West Pender St.
Vancouver, BC, V6C 1H2
(604) 685-3193

Cambridge Growth
Cambridge Resource
Trans-Canada Equity
Cambridge Balanced
Trans-Canada B
Trans-Canada C

Savings & Investment Trust
850 Place D'Youville
Quebec, PQ, G1P 3P6
(418) 692-1221

Fiducie Pret Revenue American
Fiducie Pret Revenue Canadien
Fiducie Pret Revenue Retraite
Fiducie Pret Revenue Fonds H

Sceptre Investment Counsel
26 Wellington St. E.
Suite 1200
Toronto, ON, M5E 1W4
(416) 367-9898

Sceptre Capital Protection
Sceptre Balanced
Sceptre Equity
Sceptre International

Scotia Securities Inc.
1 Richmond St. W.
Suite 200
Toronto, ON, M5H 3W4
(416) 866-4574

Scotia Stock & Bond
Scotia Income

Sea Management
Suite 1800
10130-103rd Street
Edmonton, Alta, T5J 3N9
(403) 428-6012

Principal Equity
Principal World

Sentinal Investment
Management Corp.
Sun Life Tower, Suite 1308
150 King St. W.
Toronto, ON, M5H 1J9
(416) 585-9111

Canadian Equity
Bond
Global
Money Market
American Equity

Sogefonds M.F.Q. Inc.
625 St. Amable St.
Quebec, Quebec, G1R 2G5
(418) 644-4225

Fonds M.F.Q. Actions
Fonds M.F.Q. Obligations
Fonds M.F.Q. Equilibre

Sovereign Life Ins.
606-4th St. S.W.
Calgary, Alta, T2P 1S9
(403) 292-1500

Sovereign Revenue Growth
Sovereign Capital Sec. Bond
Sovereign Save & Prosper Prop
Soveriegn Growth Equity

Spectrum Mutual Funds
150 King St. W.
Suite 907
Toronto, ON, M5H 1G9
(416) 979-6280

Spectrum Canadian Equity
Spectrum International Equity
Spectrum Dividend
Spectrum Cash Reserve
Spectrum Savings
Spectrum Diversified
Spectrum Interest

St. Lawrence Financial Corp.
425 Maisonneuve Blvd. W.
Suite 1740
Montreal, PQ, H3A 3G5
(514) 288-7545

Sections Actions
Section Diversifiee
Section Obligations
Section Epargne-plus

Sterling Trust
220 Bay St.
Toronto, ON, M5J 2K8
(416) 364-7495

Sterling Mortgage

T.A.L. Investment Counsel
1900 Place Du Canada
Montreal, PQ, H3B 2N2
(514) 875-7040

Timvest Growth
Timvest Diversified
Timvest American
Timvest Money
Timvest Bond
Timvest Income

Templeton Management Ltd.
4 King St. W.
P.O. Box 4070, Station A
Toronto, ON, M5W 1M3
(416) 364-4672

Templeton Growth
Templeton Canadian

The Citadel Assurance
1075 Bay St.
Toronto, ON, M5S 2W5
(416)928-8520

Citadel Premier Fund

Toronto-Dominion Bank
Investment Div.
Toronto-Dominion Centre
T-D Bank Tower, 9th Floor
Toronto, ON, M5K 1A2
(416) 982-8222

Green Line Mortgage
Green Line Cdn Index
Green Line U.S. Index

Tradex Investment Fund Ltd.
77 Metcalfe St.
Suite 309
Ottawa, ON, K1P 5L6
(613) 233-3394

Tradex Investment

**Trimark Investment
Management**
Box 189
1 First Canadian Place #935
Toronto, ON, M5X 1A3
(416) 362-7181

Trimark
Trimark Canadian
Trimark Income Growth
Trimark Interest

Trust General Du Canada
1100 University St.
11th Floor
Montreal, PQ, H3B 2G7
(514) 871-7530

Canadian Equity
Trust General Mortgage
Trust General Bond
U.S. Equity

Trust la Laurentienne du Canada
1981 McGill College Ave.
15th floor
Montreal, PQ, H3A 2Y2
(514) 284-7000

Placement-Actions
Placement-Obligations

20/20 Financial Inc.
IBM Tower, Suite 2802
79 Wellington St. W.
Toronto, ON, M5K 1J5
(416) 862-2020

Cdn Convertible Preferred
Cdn Convertible Debenture
Sunset
Sunset World

U.S.E. Funds Mgmt
Suite 1218
401 Bay St.
Toronto, ON, M5H 2Y4
(416) 364-1145

Universal Savings Equity
Universal Savings Income
Universal Savings Japan
Universal Savings American
Universal Savings Natural Res
Universal Savings Global

United Financial Management
Suite 1202
200 King St. W.
Toronto, ON, M5H 3W8
(416) 598-7777

United Accumulative Retirement
United Venture Retirement
United Mortgage
United Security
United Accumulative
United American
United Venture

Vancity Investment Services
515 West 10th Ave.
Vancouver, B.C., V5Z 4A8
(604) 877-7613

Ethical Growth

APPENDIX A

*A typical statement of investment
assets of a fund that invests in
a broad range of Canadian
common stocks*

**BOLTON
TREMBLAY
INTERNATIONAL
FUND**

Quarterly Report
March 31, 1988

Statement of Investment Portfolio
as at March 31, 1988 (unaudited)

COMMON SHARES AND CONVERTIBLE SECURITIES	Number of Shares/ Principal Amount	Market Value	% of Net Assets
Financial Services			
American Express Company	205,000	$ 6,105,869	1.4
The Asia Pacific Fund, Inc.	40,100	309,422	0.1
Banco Nazionale del Lavoro	240,000	3,319,494	0.7
Bayerische Hypotheken und Wechselbank — Warrants	17,000	1,365,094	0.3
Chemical New York Corporation	80,000	2,123,512	0.5
Deutsche Bank, A.G. — ADR	10,000	3,009,585	0.7
The France Fund, Inc.	150,000	1,550,966	0.3
Groupe Bruxelles Lambert S.A. — Warrants, expiring June 1, 1991	100,000	2,118,080	0.5
Lyonnaise des Eaux C.B. 6.65%	3,545,100	775,697	0.2
National Australia Bank Limited	1,624,504	7,581,216	1.7
New Tokyo Investment Trust plc	500,000	1,629,672	0.4
Nationale-Nederlanden N.V.	122,046	4,607,733	1.0
National Westminister Bank plc — Warrants, expiring July 26, 1990	2,000	2,432,266	0.5
Omnium Participations Financières et Industrielles Paribas	10,000	659,647	0.1
Salomon Inc.	120,000	3,222,306	0.7
Swiss Bank Corporation	12,000	3,591,205	0.8
Taisho Marine and Fire Insurance Co. Ltd. — ADR	40,000	4,676,665	1.1

COMMON SHARES AND CONVERTIBLE SECURITIES (cont'd.)	Number of Shares/ Principal Amount	Market Value	% of Net Assets
The Throgmorton Trust plc	400,000	3,817,383	0.9
The Traveler's Corporation	95,000	4,119,706	0.9
WorldWide Equities Limited, Class "A"	200,000	1,800,000	0.4
Communications			
Axel Springer Verlag AG	7,000	2,911,125	0.7
Cable & Wireless plc	300,000	2,100,000	0.5
Elsevier — NDU N.V.	160,000	5,313,719	1.2
McGraw Hill, Inc.	110,000	7,299,573	1.6
News International plc	450,000	2,700,070	0.6
Pearson plc	264,000	4,145,886	0.9
Wolters Kluwer	62,500	5,395,202	1.2
Consumer Products			
American Home Products Corporation	66,000	6,253,867	1.4
Borden, Inc.	135,000	8,646,059	1.9
Fuji Photo Film Co., Ltd. — ADR	140,000	11,386,099	2.6
McDonalds Corporation	82,100	4,409,189	1.0
Matsushita Electric Industrial — ADR	20,000	5,308,780	1.2
Minnesota Mining and Manufacturing Company	140,000	9,938,530	2.2
LVMH Moët-Hennessey Louis Vuitton	12,000	4,639,528	1.0
Nestle S.A. — Participation Certificate	4,500	5,451,975	1.2
PepsiCo Inc.	65,000	2,808,715	0.6
Reckitt & Colman Holdings plc	300,000	5,548,293	1.2
Sara Lee Corporation	184,500	9,168,294	2.1
Sanyo Shokai	315,000	4,177,164	0.9
Unilever NV — ADR	100,000	7,284,140	1.6
United Biscuits — Warrants, expiring June 25, 1991	1,500,000	2,125,981	0.5
Energy			
Royal Dutch Petroleum Co. — Warrants, expiring June 4, 1991	100,000	1,574,115	0.4
Health Care			
CIBA-Geigy — Participation Certificate	2,600	4,348,918	1.0
Everest & Jennings International, Class "A"	98,000	1,119,165	0.3
Johnson & Johnson	60,000	5,879,783	1.3
Industrial Products			
A. G. Bayer — ADR	30,000	5,891,635	1.3
Alcan Aluminium Limited	100,000	3,362,500	0.8

COMMON SHARES AND CONVERTIBLE SECURITIES (cont'd.)	Number of Shares/ Principal Amount	Market Value	% of Net Assets
Avery International Corporation	185,000	5,196,123	1.2
Boral Limited	800,000	2,893,903	0.7
Bowater Incorporated	124,000	5,071,120	1.1
Compagnie Générale d'Électricité	50,000	2,296,973	0.5
Digital Equipment Corporation	27,000	3,475,091	0.8
EG & G Inc.	130,000	5,918,364	1.3
General Electric Company	170,000	8,473,986	1.9
Hitachi Ltd. — ADR	55,000	7,715,479	1.7
International Business Machines Corporation	57,000	7,565,012	1.7
Koninklijke Nederlandse Papierfabrieken	50,000	4,547,032	1.0
LaFarge Coppee	15,206	3,626,256	0.8
Norsk Data — ADR	95,000	1,319,479	0.3
Papierwerke Waldhof Aschaff	28,000	4,069,439	0.9
The Plessey Company plc — ADR	65,000	2,327,221	0.5
Scott Paper Company	80,400	3,623,057	0.8
SKF, Class "B"	50,000	2,422,903	0.5
Stefanel Spa	40,000	244,105	0.1
Sundstrand Corporation	85,000	5,299,521	1.2
Vermont American Corporation, Class "A"	110,000	2,800,999	0.6
Merchandising			
ASDA/MFI Group, 4.75%, Convertible Debenture, due April 24, 2002	2,500,000*	6,489,490	1.5
Bik Bok Gruppen, Class "B"	350,000	843,047	0.2
Burton Group — Warrants, expiring February 27, 1991	500,000	499,396	0.1
Carrefour	4,700	2,138,382	0.5
Dairy Farm, 6.75%, Preferred	2,500,000	2,839,580	0.6
Federated Department Stores, Inc.	50,000	4,475,425	1.0
Ito Yokado — ADR	20,000	3,407,496	0.8
MacIntosh N.V.	87,150	2,297,162	0.5
Melville Corporation	95,000	7,608,994	1.7
Mutow	300,000	4,037,883	0.9
Shimachu Co. Ltd.	110,000	3,882,694	0.9
Storehouse plc	800,000	4,316,162	1.0
W.H. Smith & Son (Holdings) plc, Convertible Debenture, 7.125%, due March 13, 2002	2,500,000*	5,879,752	1.3
Takashimaya Co. Ltd.	56,000	1,069,559	0.3
The Limited Inc.	100,000	2,407,470	0.5
Industrial Services			
Adia S.A. — Participation Certificate	5,000	2,735,010	0.6
Brambles Industries Ltd.	473,966	3,943,968	0.9
British Airways plc — ADR	30,000	1,117,500	0.3
Browning Ferris Industries, Inc.	76,900	2,468,459	0.6

APPENDIX A

COMMON SHARES AND CONVERTIBLE SECURITIES (cont'd.)	Number of Shares/ Principal Amount	Market Value	% of Net Assets
GTI Holding N.V.	42,000	2,795,406	0.6
Ryder System, Inc.	108,778	3,911,410	0.9
TNT Limited	1,680,000	6,720,175	1.5
Yokohama Reito	300,000	4,512,710	1.0
Utilities			
China Light and Power Company Ltd. — ADR	1,560,000	4,641,602	1.1
Lyonnaise des Eaux	15,000	3,521,203	0.8
New York State Electric & Gas Corp.	160,000	4,271,716	1.0
Pacific Telesis Group	185,000	6,509,429	1.5
Rheinische Westfalische Elektricitatswerke — ADR	30,000	4,550,119	1.0
Veba	15,000	2,856,371	0.6
Management Companies			
ADT, Inc., 8.375%, Convertible Debenture, due January 3, 2001	$4,000,000 U.S.	5,531,008	1.3
BET plc	1,226,415	6,510,768	1.5
Hutchison Whampoa Ltd. — ADR	500,000	3,259,344	0.7
Jardine Strategic Holdings	1,224,000	1,636,576	0.4
Swire Pacific — ADR	840,000	4,563,082	1.0
SHORT-TERM NOTES — AT AMORTIZED COST		37,009,957	8.4
TOTAL INVESTMENT PORTFOLIO		$442,148,191	99.5
Other assets and liabilities, net		2,057,436	0.5
NET ASSETS		$444,205,627	100.0
NET ASSET VALUE PER UNIT, based on 65,879,680 units outstanding		$6.74	

*British Pounds Sterling

APPENDIX B

*A typical statement of investment
assets of a fund that invests in
Canadian bonds denominated in
foreign currencies as well as Canadian
dollar bonds*

DYNAMIC INCOME FUND
STATEMENT OF INVESTMENTS AND OTHER NET ASSETS
DECEMBER 31, 1987
(In thousands of dollars)

CANADA BONDS	Average Cost	Quoted Market Value	% of Net Assets
$3,000 Government of Canada 13.75% Aug. 01 89	$ 3,191	$ 3,161	3.8
3,350 Government of Canada 13.25% Feb. 01 90	3,580	3,551	4.3
2,000 Government of Canada 9.75% Oct. 01 97	1,890	1,962	2.4
6,650 Government of Canada 11.75% Oct. 01 08	7,495	7,282	8.9
6,550 Government of Canada 11.00% Jun. 01 09	6,791	6,828	8.3
	22,947	22,784	27.7

CORPORATE BONDS

	Average Cost	Quoted Market Value	% of Net Assets
4,400 Bank of Nova Scotia 16.125% Mar. 20 89 *	3,419	3,735	4.5
420 Bank of Nova Scotia 18.50% Sep. 15 89 *	334	366	0.4
2,185 Export Development Corporation 10.75% Feb. 01 90 **	3,278	2,968	3.6
4,140 Export Development Corporation, Eurobond 10.625% May 01 90 **	6,056	5,631	6.9
6,300 Export Development Corporation 13.125% Jun. 04 90	6,300	5,985	7.3
5,100 Federal Business Development Bank, Eurobond 18.25% Jul. 13 89 *	4,011	4,440	5.4
4,000 Federal Business Development Bank 13.125% Jun. 29 90	4,000	3,590	4.4
3,500 International Bank for Reconstruction and Development, 8.625% Oct. 15 16 **	4,405	4,038	4.9
900 Ivaco Inc., convertible 9.50% Apr. 15 10	767	873	1.1
1,500 Sceptre Resources Ltd., convertible 8.00% Sep. 30 02	1,500	1,189	1.4
1,950 Toronto Dominion Bank 16.125% Aug. 07 88 *	1,399	1,664	2.0
1,500 Toronto Dominion Bank, Eurobond 17.50% Oct. 27 89 *	1,278	1,293	1.6
2,700 Trimac Ltd., convertible Eurobond 7.25% Jun. 16 97	2,446	2,025	2.5
4,150 Trizec Corporation Ltd. 16.75% Sep. 12 88 *	2,985	3,541	4.3
	42,178	41,338	50.3

DYNAMIC INCOME FUND
STATEMENT OF INVESTMENTS AND OTHER NET ASSETS (Cont'd)
AT DECEMBER 31, 1987
(In thousands of dollars)

	Average Cost	Quoted Market Value	% of Net Assets
PROVINCIAL GUARANTEED BONDS			
$6,450 Province of Alberta,			
Eurobond 7.375% Dec. 09 91 **	$ 8,352	$ 7,924	9.7
4,350 Province of Ontario 9.375% Nov. 30 08 **	5,423	5,422	6.6
	13,775	13,346	16.3
OTHER			
300 Sceptre Resources Ltd., Deposit Receipts	1,500	1,035	1.3
	80,400	78,503	95.6
SHORT TERM NOTES	1,199	1,199	1.5
AVERAGE COST AND QUOTED MARKET VALUE OF INVESTMENTS	81,599	79,702	97.1
OTHER ASSETS NET OF LIABILITIES		2,370	2.9
NET ASSETS AT MARKET VALUE		82,072	100.0

* A qualified Canadian investment payable with respect to both principal and interest in New Zealand dollars.
** A qualified Canadian investment payable with respect to both principal and interest in U.S. dollars.

APPENDIX C

How an investment would have grown if $100 a month was invested in a typical equity fund that invested in the Canadian market during the 10 years ending June 30, 1988

Month	Return	Cumulative Contribution	Value of Plan
1978-06		$100	$95
07	7.3%	$200	$197
08	7.0%	$300	$306
09	2.5%	$400	$408
10	-4.4%	$500	$486
11	2.0%	$600	$590
12	5.3%	$700	$716
1979-01	3.5%	$800	$836
02	1.4%	$900	$943
03	4.6%	$1,000	$1,081
04	1.6%	$1,100	$1,194
05	2.7%	$1,200	$1,321
06	4.9%	$1,300	$1,481
07	-2.2%	$1,400	$1,543
08	8.5%	$1,500	$1,769
09	2.4%	$1,600	$1,906
10	-7.9%	$1,700	$1,850
11	6.0%	$1,800	$2,056
12	2.7%	$1,900	$2,207
1980-01	8.8%	$2,000	$2,497
02	4.0%	$2,100	$2,690
03	-10.5%	$2,200	$2,503
04	4.0%	$2,300	$2,698
05	5.7%	$2,400	$2,948
06	4.6%	$2,500	$3,179

Month	Return	Cumulative Contribution	Value of Plan
07	6.7%	$2,600	$3,488
08	4.0%	$2,700	$3,723
09	0.2%	$2,800	$3,825
10	1.6%	$2,900	$3,980
11	5.4%	$3,000	$4,290
12	0.3%	$3,100	$4,397
1981-01	-0.9%	$3,200	$4,454
02	0.5%	$3,300	$4,572
03	6.9%	$3,400	$4,982
04	-1.5%	$3,500	$5,002
05	-0.2%	$3,600	$5,088
06	-1.0%	$3,700	$5,130
07	-3.1%	$3,800	$5,066
08	-3.6%	$3,900	$4,980
09	-9.2%	$4,000	$4,619
10	-1.5%	$4,100	$4,647
11	5.6%	$4,200	$5,000
12	0.8%	$4,300	$5,137
1982-01	-6.8%	$4,400	$4,884
02	-3.3%	$4,500	$4,818
03	-3.0%	$4,600	$4,769
04	-2.7%	$4,700	$4,733
05	-2.1%	$4,800	$4,728
06	-7.0%	$4,900	$4,492
07	3.5%	$5,000	$4,743
08	10.3%	$5,100	$5,325
09	0.3%	$5,200	$5,434
10	9.2%	$5,300	$6,030
11	2.6%	$5,400	$6,283
12	6.7%	$5,500	$6,799
1983-01	5.9%	$5,600	$7,294
02	3.4%	$5,700	$7,637
03	2.5%	$5,800	$7,921
04	6.0%	$5,900	$8,489
05	2.0%	$6,000	$8,757
06	-0.5%	$6,100	$8,809

Month	Return	Cumulative Contribution	Value of Plan
07	1.9%	$6,200	$9,076
08	0.3%	$6,300	$9,198
09	1.0%	$6,400	$9,381
10	-3.7%	$6,500	$9,133
11	5.2%	$6,600	$9,703
12	0.4%	$6,700	$9,835
1984-01	-1.2%	$6,800	$9,813
02	-2.9%	$6,900	$9,624
03	-0.9%	$7,000	$9,636
04	-2.8%	$7,100	$9,465
05	-3.2%	$7,200	$9,255
06	-0.6%	$7,300	$9,295
07	-4.8%	$7,400	$8,941
08	9.0%	$7,500	$9,842
09	1.3%	$7,600	$10,064
10	-2.0%	$7,700	$9,954
11	0.3%	$7,800	$10,074
12	2.3%	$7,900	$10,397
1985-01	7.9%	$8,000	$11,316
02	-0.7%	$8,100	$11,329
03	-0.7%	$8,200	$11,342
04	2.5%	$8,300	$11,720
05	6.1%	$8,400	$12,527
06	0.7%	$8,500	$12,714
07	0.9%	$8,600	$12,929
08	1.5%	$8,700	$13,217
09	-4.7%	$8,800	$12,687
10	1.9%	$8,900	$13,028
11	6.9%	$9,000	$14,021
12	3.4%	$9,100	$14,593
1986-01	0.6%	$9,200	$14,772
02	-0.7%	$9,300	$14,762
03	6.1%	$9,400	$15,762
04	-0.6%	$9,500	$15,762
05	0.8%	$9,600	$15,988
06	-1.3%	$9,700	$15,868

Month	Return	Cumulative Contribution	Value of Plan
07	-3.2%	$9,800	$15,457
08	4.5%	$9,900	$16,255
09	-0.2%	$10,000	$16,313
10	1.1%	$10,100	$16,580
11	1.5%	$10,200	$16,921
12	-1.2%	$10,300	$16,818
1987-01	7.0%	$10,400	$18,092
02	3.4%	$10,500	$18,801
03	6.8%	$10,600	$20,171
04	0.6%	$10,700	$20,390
05	1.0%	$10,800	$20,679
06	2.0%	$10,900	$21,191
07	4.9%	$11,000	$22,334
08	-0.3%	$11,100	$22,373
09	-2.1%	$11,200	$22,003
10	-15.4%	$11,300	$18,716
11	-0.4%	$11,400	$18,740
12	3.7%	$11,500	$19,535
1988-01	-1.3%	$11,600	$19,369
02	3.4%	$11,700	$20,120
03	3.6%	$11,800	$20,941
04	1.0%	$11,900	$21,251
05	-1.6%	$12,000	$21,014
06	4.1%		$21,978

A withdrawal plan where $100,000
was invested in an equity fund that
invested in the Canadian market
and $1,000 a month was withdrawn
during the 10 years ending June30, 1988

Month	Return	Cumulative Contribution	Value of Plan
1978-06		$97,000	
07	7.3%	$103,117	$1,000
08	7.0%	$109,368	$2,000
09	2.5%	$111,062	$3,000
10	-4.4%	$105,216	$4,000
11	2.0%	$106,273	$5,000
12	5.3%	$110,903	$6,000
1979-01	3.5%	$113,804	$7,000
02	1.4%	$114,419	$8,000
03	4.6%	$118,629	$9,000
04	1.6%	$119,554	$10,000
05	2.7%	$121,769	$11,000
06	4.9%	$126,748	$12,000
07	-2.2%	$122,979	$13,000
08	8.5%	$132,375	$14,000
09	2.4%	$134,489	$15,000
10	-7.9%	$122,862	$16,000
11	6.0%	$129,241	$17,000
12	2.7%	$131,760	$18,000
1980-01	8.8%	$142,369	$19,000
02	4.0%	$147,011	$20,000
03	-10.5%	$130,568	$21,000
04	4.0%	$134,811	$22,000
05	5.7%	$141,518	$23,000
06	4.6%	$147,077	$24,000

Month	Return	Cumulative Contribution	Value of Plan
07	6.7%	$155,948	$25,000
08	4.0%	$161,225	$26,000
09	0.2%	$160,517	$27,000
10	1.6%	$162,036	$28,000
11	5.4%	$169,797	$29,000
12	0.3%	$169,276	$30,000
1981-01	-0.9%	$166,814	$31,000
02	0.5%	$166,678	$32,000
03	6.9%	$177,170	$33,000
04	-1.5%	$173,500	$34,000
05	-0.2%	$172,181	$35,000
06	-1.0%	$169,387	$36,000
07	-3.1%	$163,139	$37,000
08	-3.6%	$156,298	$38,000
09	-9.2%	$140,995	$39,000
10	-1.5%	$137,936	$40,000
11	5.6%	$144,600	$41,000
12	0.8%	$144,817	$42,000
1982-01	-6.8%	$134,003	$43,000
02	-3.3%	$128,590	$44,000
03	-3.0%	$123,745	$45,000
04	-2.7%	$119,355	$46,000
05	-2.1%	$115,833	$47,000
06	-7.0%	$106,708	$48,000
07	3.5%	$109,423	$49,000
08	10.3%	$119,672	$50,000
09	0.3%	$118,977	$51,000
10	9.2%	$128,939	$52,000
11	2.6%	$131,332	$53,000
12	6.7%	$139,127	$54,000
1983-01	5.9%	$146,305	$55,000
02	3.4%	$150,280	$56,000
03	2.5%	$153,012	$57,000
04	6.0%	$161,130	$58,000
05	2.0%	$163,417	$59,000
06	-0.5%	$161,625	$60,000

Month	Return	Cumulative Contribution	Value of Plan
07	1.9%	$163,773	$61,000
08	0.3%	$163,262	$62,000
09	1.0%	$163,816	$63,000
10	-3.7%	$156,828	$64,000
11	5.2%	$163,986	$65,000
12	0.4%	$163,625	$66,000
1984-01	-1.2%	$160,677	$67,000
02	-2.9%	$155,026	$68,000
03	-0.9%	$152,678	$69,000
04	-2.8%	$147,469	$70,000
05	-3.2%	$141,718	$71,000
06	-0.6%	$139,868	$72,000
07	-4.8%	$132,123	$73,000
08	9.0%	$143,025	$74,000
09	1.3%	$143,871	$75,000
10	-2.0%	$139,937	$76,000
11	0.3%	$139,301	$77,000
12	2.3%	$141,447	$78,000
1985-01	7.9%	$151,653	$79,000
02	-0.7%	$149,558	$80,000
03	-0.7%	$147,470	$81,000
04	2.5%	$150,161	$82,000
05	6.1%	$158,284	$83,000
06	0.7%	$158,439	$84,000
07	0.9%	$158,940	$85,000
08	1.5%	$160,310	$86,000
09	-4.7%	$151,722	$87,000
10	1.9%	$153,668	$88,000
11	6.9%	$163,257	$89,000
12	3.4%	$167,814	$90,000
1986-01	0.6%	$167,783	$91,000
02	-0.7%	$165,589	$92,000
03	6.1%	$174,741	$93,000
04	-0.6%	$172,692	$94,000
05	0.8%	$173,126	$95,000
06	-1.3%	$169,793	$96,000

Month	Return	Cumulative Contribution	Value of Plan
07	-3.2%	$163,382	$97,000
08	4.5%	$169,809	$98,000
09	-0.2%	$168,427	$99,000
10	1.1%	$169,198	$100,000
11	1.5%	$170,714	$101,000
12	-1.2%	$167,713	$102,000
1987-01	7.0%	$178,467	$103,000
02	3.4%	$183,524	$104,000
03	6.8%	$194,973	$105,000
04	0.6%	$195,172	$106,000
05	1.0%	$196,027	$107,000
06	2.0%	$198,981	$108,000
07	4.9%	$207,819	$109,000
08	-0.3%	$206,297	$110,000
09	-2.1%	$201,010	$111,000
10	-15.4%	$169,115	$112,000
11	-0.4%	$167,472	$113,000
12	3.7%	$172,732	$114,000
1988-01	-1.3%	$169,421	$115,000
02	3.4%	$174,164	$116,000
03	3.6%	$179,446	$117,000
04	1.0%	$180,291	$118,000
05	-1.6%	$176,467	$119,000
06	4.1%	$182,768	$120,000

APPENDIX E

Survey of Annual Rates of Return
of Canadian Mutual Funds
through June 30, 1988

Fund	1988	1987	1986	1985	1984	1983	1982	1981	1980	1979
EQUITY FUNDS – RRSP-ELIGIBLE										
AIC Advantage Fund	-9.2	16.7	–	–	–	–	–	–	–	–
AMD Cdn Blue Chip Growth Fd	-9.4	13.3	–	--	–	–	–	–	–	–
All-Canadian Compound Fund	-9.3	15.3	16.8	18.3	3.8	26.9	4.8	39.1	8.3	19.5
All-Canadian Dividend Fund	-9.3	15.3	16.7	17.6	3.0	24.5	4.8	39.4	8.5	19.7
Allied Canadian Fund	-28.6	23.9	–	–	–	–	–	–	–	–
Associate Investors Ltd.	-0.3	14.9	15.0	33.7	4.2	74.6	-30.6	21.6	15.4	38.3
Bolton Tremblay Cda Cum Fund	-7.7	10.7	19.4	11.7	-2.0	80.0	-32.4	33.7	22.8	28.4
Bullock Growth Fund	-6.0	4.4	34.0	5.6	-14.2	75.3	-46.1	36.6	38.1	35.5
CDA RSP Balanced Fund	0.5	13.0	19.2	24.5	0.4	49.9	-22.7	8.7	-1.5	–
CDA RSP Common Stock Fund	-4.9	22.4	25.7	31.4	0.6	65.4	-21.5	12.8	14.5	38.1
CGF Fund 4000	-13.4	13.0	28.0	22.5	-1.4	35.9	-7.8	24.1	11.5	12.5
CGF Venture Fund	-20.2	15.2	-20.3	4.5	-2.5	28.5	-12.2	-2.6	14.3	28.4
CMA Investment Fund	6.1	20.5	20.5	33.9	2.3	62.0	-12.1	12.1	17.8	30.3
Caisse de Sec du Spectacle	-0.4	7.9	19.4	26.3	-4.1	43.9	1.3	11.4	–	–
Cambridge Balanced Fund	6.9	10.3	29.4	26.7	0.1	26.5	8.3	6.3	4.7	12.9
Cambridge Growth Fund	-0.4	26.3	40.7	31.5	-0.3	47.9	-16.9	27.2	-1.4	19.6
Cambridge Resource Fund	-7.7	27.5	17.9	10.6	-0.3	48.6	-13.4	0.2	11.2	23.1
Canadian Gas & Energy Fund Ltd	-15.5	69.4	-15.4	-3.5	-11.3	70.9	-52.4	10.2	56.8	69.3
Canadian Investment Fund Ltd.	-7.8	11.1	15.1	27.3	-5.1	66.4	-22.7	14.7	13.8	30.7
Canadian Natural Resource Fd	-14.3	–	–	–	–	–	–	–	–	–
Canadian Protected Fund	9.4	5.2	22.3	–	–	–	–	–	–	–
Canadian Security Growth Fund	-7.0	12.0	27.2	35.5	2.6	80.4	-31.5	31.8	21.7	40.9
Capital Growth Fund Ltd.	-13.5	18.6	10.0	26.2	-8.9	61.3	-11.5	20.4	25.6	40.7
Capstone Investment Trust	-10.6	10.1	24.6	26.9	-3.8	36.4	1.1	–	–	–
Cda Life Bal Eqty Income E-2	0.3	14.3	26.9	33.9	-0.6	65.7	-25.7	19.0	26.8	36.5
Cda Life Cdn&Intl Equity S-9	1.7	14.0	23.0	31.0	-1.0	64.3	-26.8	19.4	25.9	36.2
Cda Life Managed Fund S-35	3.5	11.4	20.0	27.4	–	–	–	–	–	–
Cdn Anaesthetists Mutual Accum	-3.7	20.4	21.7	27.2	-2.6	59.5	-25.3	30.4	30.8	54.4
Cdn Convertible Preferred Fd	1.2	14.3	–	–	–	–	–	–	–	–
Cdn Gen Life Ins Equity Fd A	-9.7	14.3	26.3	38.5	-1.8	58.3	-23.1	24.0	27.7	38.1
Chou RRSP Fund	7.1	–	–	–	–	–	–	–	–	–
Confed Dolphin Fund	-3.4	16.3	24.9	33.9	-2.6	74.6	-31.4	12.3	30.1	51.9
Corporate Investors Ltd.	-3.0	22.3	2.4	27.7	3.3	63.0	-21.9	17.6	8.5	24.3
Corporate Investors Stock Fund	-31.4	13.9	43.0	26.4	-1.5	81.2	-45.5	30.8	38.1	51.8
Counsel Trust Real Estate Fd	13.7	14.6	21.0	–	–	–	–	–	–	–

Fund	1988	1987	1986	1985	1984	1983	1982	1981	1980	1979
Crown Life Commitment Fund	-4.7	–	–	–	–	–	–	–	–	–
Crown Life Pensions Balanced	2.9	11.0	–	–	–	–	–	–	–	–
Crown Life Pensions Equity	-3.6	18.2	26.9	36.0	-12.1	53.6	-28.1	12.3	13.3	39.7
Cundill Security Fund	2.1	22.6	10.3	24.2	3.4	57.1	-24.5	16.8	–	–
DK All Seasons Fund	-16.9	-12.8	50.7	-0.3	-13.5	42.5	-35.7	31.5	23.6	57.7
DK Enterprise Fund	-10.8	19.8	34.4	4.8	-18.4	68.7	-36.9	15.4	40.1	75.2
Dynamic Fund of Canada Ltd.	-1.9	25.3	15.2	23.0	-6.5	65.2	-31.1	23.7	26.8	45.2
Dynamic Managed Portfolio	-2.3	30.0	–	–	–	–	–	–	–	–
Dynamic Precious Metals Fund	-7.2	73.2	-7.9	1.1	–	–	–	–	–	–
Empire Life Segregated #1	3.5	16.9	23.5	31.9	-9.4	85.9	-26.0	37.3	22.6	33.6
Ethical Growth Fund	12.3	9.1	–	–	–	–	–	–	–	–
Everest Special Equity Fund	-19.5	–	–	–	–	–	–	–	–	–
F.M.O.Q. Fonds de Placement	-0.8	23.3	12.7	21.4	–	–	–	–	–	–
F.M.O.Q. Omnibus	2.9	17.5	15.6	25.1	0.7	42.4	4.6	5.9	–	–
Ficadre Actions	-13.4	19.4	31.0	–	–	–	–	–	–	–
Ficadre Equilibre	-3.7	14.7	14.9	–	–	–	–	–	–	–
Fiducie Pret Revenu Retraite	-1.4	11.1	16.0	17.2	3.6	44.5	-7.9	-1.5	10.8	24.9
Fiducie Pret Revenue Canadien	-14.8	17.8	11.1	12.2	-3.8	78.4	-35.6	8.8	15.5	34.7
First City Growth Fund	-9.2	–	–	–	–	–	–	–	–	–
First City Realfund	16.2	11.4	14.6	13.2	7.8	–	–	–	–	–
Fonds Desjardins Actions	-11.0	8.7	16.2	24.9	-10.4	76.2	-29.0	20.9	20.6	39.6
Fonds Desjardins Equilibre	-0.6	–	–	–	–	–	–	–	–	–
FoodFund	-9.4	5.6	36.6	–	–	–	–	–	–	–
Global Strategy Corp	-17.2	24.9	–	–	–	–	–	–	–	–
GoldenFund	-14.1	55.2	15.5	–	–	–	–	–	–	–
Green Line Cdn Index Fund	-6.2	23.3	–	–	–	–	–	–	–	–
Growth Equity Fund Ltd.	-17.0	20.3	33.2	21.5	-7.6	90.9	-49.8	27.4	53.8	61.2
Guardian Balanced Fund	5.9	14.7	11.5	29.8	3.8	50.3	-5.6	3.8	10.4	19.9
Guardian Cdn Equity Fd	-7.6	14.5	34.5	23.6	-7.7	59.7	-24.4	18.4	29.6	30.1
Guardian Enterprise Fund	-1.9	8.9	24.4	24.4	0.2	86.9	-24.6	23.0	36.4	30.6
Hallmark Canadian Fund	-4.2	12.7	30.9	–	–	–	–	–	–	–
Hume RRSP Growth&Income Fund	-14.3	12.5	21.2	–	–	–	–	–	–	–
Imperial Realty Growth Fund	10.3	24.9	11.5	7.0	–	–	–	–	–	–
Industrial Dividend Fund Ltd.	6.1	27.4	16.5	33.2	6.5	69.7	-21.4	16.8	-1.3	40.8
Industrial Equity Fund Ltd.	-0.5	31.4	18.1	16.8	0.3	88.1	-25.4	10.5	20.2	27.1
Industrial Growth Fund	4.5	27.7	16.4	27.1	2.8	77.7	-17.1	8.6	24.9	28.1
Industrial Horizon Fund	15.2	–	–	–	–	–	–	–	–	–
Industrial Pension Fund	4.3	23.4	20.8	30.6	0.6	84.0	-21.2	11.6	-2.4	37.4
Investors Cdn Equity Fund	-7.2	10.1	27.9	25.5	–	–	–	–	–	–
Investors Gr Tr Pooled Equity	-3.0	15.7	15.4	27.0	-4.8	64.9	-27.0	16.4	26.7	43.8
Investors Real Property Fund	8.2	10.0	10.0	9.8	–	–	–	–	–	–
Investors Retirement Mutual	4.6	20.4	13.6	26.7	-3.9	58.3	-27.0	15.8	27.9	42.7
Investors Summa Fund Ltd	-3.1	–	–	–	–	–	–	–	–	–
Jones Heward Fund Ltd.	-3.9	11.8	29.4	31.6	-5.7	73.8	-34.7	31.4	26.4	47.4
Keltic Investment Trust	-10.1	12.0	29.4	9.6	-10.9	78.9	-39.4	-39.8	67.1	–
LifeFund	-17.3	10.1	26.6	–	–	–	–	–	–	–
London Life Equity Fund	-0.3	21.0	19.0	28.7	-3.8	65.3	-21.3	15.7	26.4	44.0
Lotus Fund	-6.1	10.4	19.6	25.7	–	–	–	–	–	–
MER Equity Fund	-6.0	15.4	23.2	25.6	7.7	–	–	–	–	–

Fund	1988	1987	1986	1985	1984	1983	1982	1981	1980	1979
MER Heartland Equity Fund	-7.1	–	–	–	–	–	–	–	–	–
MONY Balanced Fund	-0.9	–	–	–	–	–	–	–	–	–
MONY Canadian Growth Fund	-16.6	20.3	14.6	34.9	-5.6	85.3	-17.3	17.5	26.2	33.8
Mackenzie Equity Fund	4.8	20.8	23.1	29.6	3.0	67.9	-26.8	25.7	25.1	44.6
Maritime Life Balanced Fund	1.9	–	–	–	–	–	–	–	–	–
Maritime Life Growth Fund	-11.1	15.2	24.7	34.8	-2.8	73.2	-30.9	15.1	24.7	40.1
Marlborough Fund	-16.0	13.7	23.0	25.5	-10.4	74.0	-32.3	17.2	20.5	48.5
Metropolitan Cdn Mutual Fd	-13.6	10.5	26.4	–	–	–	–	–	–	–
Metropolitan Growth Fund	-17.1	7.0	24.7	18.9	-4.1	54.7	-31.6	20.8	16.5	43.5
Metropolitan Var-Balanced Fd	-4.1	–	–	–	–	–	–	–	–	–
Metropolitan Variable-Equity	-11.8	–	–	–	–	–	–	–	–	–
Montreal Trust Equity Fund	-3.9	22.3	14.6	24.5	-9.6	66.1	-30.2	17.1	25.4	42.3
Morgan Growth Fund	-6.8	-4.7	41.8	24.5	–	–	–	–	–	–
Morgan Resource Fund	7.0	48.8	–	–	–	–	–	–	–	–
Mtl Trust RRSP-Equity Sectn	-6.2	21.0	17.7	25.0	-9.7	69.3	-29.5	17.2	24.8	40.5
Multiple Opportunities Fund	-27.2	93.5	–	–	–	–	–	–	–	–
Mutual Diversifund 25	3.0	6.4	15.9	–	–	–	–	–	–	–
Mutual Diversifund 40	0.6	6.8	19.7	–	–	–	–	–	–	–
Mutual Diversifund 55	-1.0	7.7	20.9	–	–	–	–	–	–	–
Mutual Equifund	-6.2	7.9	26.7	–	–	–	–	–	–	–
NW Canadian Fund Ltd.	-8.0	18.4	35.0	32.0	-7.4	83.8	-29.4	27.3	25.4	40.5
National Trust Cdn Common Shar	-3.5	18.6	25.0	25.9	-3.4	47.4	-20.3	19.3	24.5	41.4
National Trust Equity Fund	-9.7	14.6	24.9	31.0	-5.9	50.9	-20.5	19.9	25.3	40.7
Natl Trust Feb Pro Fund	0.9	13.3	18.9	7.5	–	–	–	–	–	–
Natl Trust Jan Pro Fund	4.6	8.8	17.7	8.0	–	–	–	–	–	–
Natural Resources Growth Fund	-12.4	50.3	-8.1	0.1	-11.1	41.6	-10.1	19.4	17.7	26.0
One Decision Fund	-4.6	10.3	–	–	–	–	–	–	–	–
Ont Teachers Grp Aggr Equity	-4.5	18.4	24.8	38.4	-5.4	75.3	-28.9	22.2	27.2	35.6
Ont Teachers Grp Balanced	1.8	13.3	–	–	–	–	–	–	–	–
Ont Teachers Grp Diversified	-4.7	17.3	21.3	34.7	-4.8	68.2	-26.6	18.6	26.9	35.8
Ordre Ingenieurs Actions	-2.8	23.7	17.0	30.8	-7.6	85.3	-37.6	24.1	23.9	27.2
Ordre Ingenieurs Equilibre	2.8	17.2	16.1	25.8	-0.5	51.6	-14.9	–	–	–
PH&N Canadian Fund	-2.9	16.1	29.7	28.1	-5.5	88.7	-40.9	36.5	25.4	33.0
PH&N Pooled Pension Trust	-4.7	18.7	23.8	28.6	-3.5	85.8	-34.6	19.7	24.3	27.9
PH&N RRSP Fund	-6.3	16.5	29.0	29.3	-7.2	95.3	-38.9	22.2	22.7	26.2
Pacific Growth Fund	-10.8	8.2	19.9	16.0	-13.7	67.8	-28.1	19.4	21.0	33.4
Pacific Retirement Bal Fund	-3.0	2.0	16.3	21.8	-8.9	50.7	-8.2	8.4	12.8	–
Planned Resources Fund Ltd.	-14.0	25.0	5.9	4.0	-3.9	73.3	-33.8	25.0	36.2	62.6
Prudential Growth Fund Canada	-15.6	27.9	23.7	27.9	-5.8	74.7	-35.5	14.8	24.3	44.5
Rabin Budden Capital Fund	-14.7	12.5	–	–	–	–	–	–	–	–
Rabin Budden Income Fund	13.1	12.6	–	–	–	–	–	–	–	–
Renaissance Cda Bond&Bullion	-6.9	2.6	4.8	–	–	–	–	–	–	–
RoyFund Equity Ltd	-8.3	12.1	34.9	35.2	-0.9	82.1	-40.7	24.4	37.6	48.1
Royal Trust Adv Balanced Fd	0.3	–	–	–	–	–	–	–	–	–
Royal Trust Cdn Stock Fund	-5.7	17.8	11.3	24.6	-8.6	79.0	-34.1	14.6	28.8	43.3
Royal Trust Energy Fund	-11.4	66.6	-23.7	0.1	-10.3	39.2	-41.8	–	–	–
Saxon Balanced Fund	-13.1	4.5	–	–	–	–	–	–	–	–
Saxon Small Cap	-9.1	11.8	–	–	–	–	–	–	–	–
Saxon Stock Fund	-12.9	5.5	–	–	–	–	–	–	–	–
Sceptre Balanced Fund	3.4	13.4	–	–	–	–	–	–	–	–

Fund	1988	1987	1986	1985	1984	1983	1982	1981	1980	1979
Sceptre Equity fund	4.4	–	–	–	–	–	–	–	–	–
Scotia Stock And Bond Fund	4.8	–	–	–	–	–	–	–	–	–
Sentinel Cda Equity Fund	-13.0	22.4	–	–	–	–	–	–	–	–
SilverFund	-23.7	53.2	-16.3	–	–	–	–	–	–	–
Spectrum Canadian Equity Fd	-3.3	–	–	–	–	–	–	–	–	–
Spectrum Diversified Fund	1.6	–	–	–	–	–	–	–	–	–
St-Laurent Reer-Actions	-13.6	16.4	–	–	–	–	–	–	–	–
St-Laurent Reer-Diversifiee	5.0	8.1	–	–	–	–	–	–	–	–
Sunset Fund	1.7	10.9	–	–	–	–	–	–	–	–
Talvest Diversified Fund	4.6	18.3	–	–	–	–	–	–	–	–
Talvest Growth Fund	-1.8	27.2	15.4	27.5	-2.8	52.8	-29.8	40.6	5.7	37.3
TechnoFund	-19.8	-5.3	8.1	–	–	–	–	–	–	–
Templeton Canadian Fund	-11.4	19.0	23.0	20.9	-10.1	–	–	–	–	–
Tradex Investment Fund Ltd.	-3.2	20.1	21.1	26.1	0.4	62.4	-26.2	27.6	24.7	55.1
Trans-Canada Equity Fund	-1.0	26.1	47.0	34.2	-0.3	54.0	-25.5	15.6	8.2	22.0
Trans-Canada Shares Series C	3.5	16.9	30.3	32.4	2.7	27.7	-3.8	17.8	5.3	14.1
Trimark Canadian Fund	1.6	19.6	18.1	31.5	-0.9	85.1	–	–	–	–
Trust General Balanced Fund	-0.2	–	–	–	–	–	–	–	–	–
Trust General Canadian Equity	-8.2	14.8	19.7	26.1	-4.9	63.5	-36.2	17.6	23.7	48.0
Trust La Laurentienne Action	-6.0	13.4	–	–	–	–	–	–	–	–
United Accumulative Retirement	-2.2	4.8	22.3	42.9	2.4	54.4	-29.0	28.0	28.1	69.4
United Venture Retirement Fund	-9.8	13.7	28.9	31.9	-4.5	66.9	-40.5	36.1	43.7	74.7
Universal Svgs Equity Fund Ltd	11.0	17.1	24.3	31.1	1.3	54.4	-13.4	12.2	17.4	43.0
Universal Svgs Natural Resourc	-4.1	51.2	-11.7	4.3	-3.6	81.6	-39.2	2.1	53.2	30.2
Univest Growth Fund	-7.9	10.2	22.1	20.7	-5.3	35.6	-12.2	35.9	8.4	14.7
ValueFund	-12.7	6.9	19.4	–	–	–	–	–	–	–
Viking Canadian Fund Ltd	-2.6	11.1	20.6	25.9	-2.4	66.8	-29.8	19.2	26.6	42.4
Vintage Fund	-10.2	25.1	–	–	–	–	–	–	–	–
Waltaine Balanced Fund	1.0	13.3	16.0	21.9	1.5	37.1	1.6	7.7	25.2	28.3
HIGHEST IN GROUP	16.2	93.5	50.7	42.9	7.8	95.3	8.3	40.6	67.1	21.5
LOWEST IN GROUP	-31.4	-12.8	-23.7	-3.5	-18.4	24.5	-52.4	-39.8	-2.4	12.5
AVERAGE OF GROUP	-4.8	17.9	19.8	23.6	-3.4	63.3	-24.5	18.8	22.8	38.0

EQUITY FUNDS – NOT RRSP-ELIGIBLE

Fund	1988	1987	1986	1985	1984	1983	1982	1981	1980	1979
AGF HiTech Fund Ltd	-12.5	18.7	46.2	-0.1	–	–	–	–	–	–
AGF Japan Fund Ltd.	4.6	31.8	92.9	15.9	22.6	32.4	-21.0	57.0	11.2	3.4
AGF Option Equity Fund	-11.2	6.0	12.0	25.5	-1.3	29.8	3.0	19.8	–	–
AGF Special Fund Ltd.	-8.2	10.5	31.2	23.4	-10.9	96.1	-12.6	50.6	33.2	30.7
AMD Amer Blue Chip Growth Fd	-16.0	12.6	–	–	–	–	–	–	–	–
Allied International Fund	-27.7	47.0	–	–	–	–	–	–	–	–
American Growth Fund Ltd.	-15.0	8.4	27.0	33.3	-6.0	62.9	-5.3	43.2	27.9	17.6
Bolton Tremblay International	-15.2	19.5	41.1	25.4	1.1	67.6	-9.2	45.5	12.9	17.2
Bullock Amer Fund	-20.7	21.2	56.0	16.8	-16.2	62.6	-16.0	46.4	17.9	-0.9
CGF Int'l Growth Fund	-12.9	13.7	37.2	14.4	3.4	30.3	1.5	45.5	-3.0	14.4
Cda Life U.S.&Intl Eqty S-34	-7.4	13.3	31.7	27.8	–	–	–	–	–	–
Century DJ Mutual Fund	-25.6	14.3	–	–	–	–	–	–	–	–
Chou Associates Fund	-5.2	–	–	–	–	–	–	–	–	–

Fund	1988	1987	1986	1985	1984	1983	1982	1981	1980	1979
Crown Life Pen Foreign Equity	-6.0	19.2	26.7	31.1	-5.9	30.9	4.8	–	–	–
Cundill Value Fund Ltd.	10.4	16.5	22.4	13.5	5.5	66.7	0.0	40.0	6.6	43.2
DK American Fund	-23.4	9.2	29.4	34.1	-25.8	45.2	-21.6	29.9	30.9	25.2
Dynamic American Fund	-8.1	22.7	22.3	31.1	2.9	58.5	-11.1	39.7	–	–
Dynamic Global Fund	-13.9	–	–	–	–	–	–	–	–	–
Fiducie Pret Revenu American	-22.3	15.0	35.4	24.3	-3.5	37.0	-7.5	21.7	8.6	12.0
Global Strategy Fund	-17.3	24.7	–	–	–	–	–	–	–	–
Green Line U.S. Fund	-7.8	–	–	–	–	–	–	–	–	–
Guardian American Eqty Fd	-13.1	12.8	14.5	10.5	-12.7	41.1	-7.4	28.0	38.9	24.8
Guardian Global Equity Fd	-13.9	13.3	51.3	20.2	-7.6	39.1	-20.0	52.7	32.3	16.6
Guardian North American Fund	-24.0	3.1	24.7	13.1	-12.3	45.1	-1.6	29.0	34.6	25.9
Hume Growth & Income Fund	-23.7	3.2	45.3	–	–	–	–	–	–	–
Industrial American Fund	-6.3	18.4	26.3	29.9	-1.3	55.9	-5.1	38.9	14.8	23.3
Industrial Global Fund	-1.4	32.1	–	–	–	–	–	–	–	–
Investors Global Fund Ltd	-14.9	–	–	–	–	–	–	–	–	–
Investors Growth Fund of Cda	-9.8	18.8	25.5	28.5	-7.4	69.2	-23.7	15.7	28.5	38.9
Investors International Mutual	-14.4	18.5	25.3	27.2	-12.2	66.5	-14.8	23.7	25.2	12.2
Investors Japanese Growth Fund	4.5	31.8	87.9	7.2	14.4	34.3	-15.7	66.0	1.1	-4.8
Investors Mutual of Canada Ltd	-1.9	18.4	12.7	21.6	-5.9	68.6	-19.7	12.3	21.7	29.7
Jones Heward American Fund	-17.5	14.6	39.0	20.2	2.2	–	–	–	–	–
MD Growth Investments Ltd.	-5.2	25.8	36.9	37.2	0.7	74.3	-16.9	42.9	16.2	33.6
MD Perpetual Growth Fd II	-20.9	–	–	–	–	–	–	–	–	–
MD Perpetual Growth Fund	3.8	–	–	–	–	–	–	–	–	–
MER Growth Fund	-15.9	1.9	19.5	16.9	7.5	–	–	–	–	–
MER Heartland Growth Fund	-14.7	–	–	–	–	–	–	–	–	–
MONY Global Fund	-18.5	–	–	–	–	–	–	–	–	–
Metropolitan Collective Mut	-27.7	6.1	28.9	14.9	-1.0	60.0	-5.4	30.9	23.4	21.7
Metropolitan Speculators	-20.6	29.1	–	–	–	–	–	–	–	–
Metropolitan Venture Fund	-21.6	17.8	35.1	11.9	-12.0	45.7	-5.7	38.6	15.1	14.7
Montreal Trust Intl Fund	-15.5	18.7	37.8	36.2	-4.1	42.5	-1.8	23.3	13.5	23.8
Morgan Worldwide Fund	-20.2	13.1	29.9	11.2	–	–	–	–	–	–
Mutual Amerifund	-3.6	9.3	–	–	–	–	–	–	–	–
NW Equity Fund Ltd.	-15.1	6.3	26.1	26.6	-7.4	55.0	-5.5	29.1	15.4	17.4
National Trust Pooled Non-Cdn	-14.5	5.5	51.2	30.0	-16.3	45.8	5.4	27.8	6.5	10.0
Natl Trust Global Fund P	-17.7	26.5	68.6	19.5	10.4	–	–	–	–	–
Natrusco Common Share Fund	-12.5	17.0	21.3	18.1	-3.6	71.1	-29.1	19.8	14.1	40.2
Noram Convertible Securities	3.9	30.5	4.7	–	–	–	–	–	–	–
PH&N U.S. FUND	-10.6	8.1	28.8	32.4	-15.8	86.2	-4.2	38.8	14.8	16.3
PH&N U.S. Pooled Pension Fund	-8.8	8.7	28.7	33.4	-8.4	82.0	-3.6	–	–	–
Pacific U.S. Growth Fund	-15.3	11.0	18.2	12.4	-20.4	24.2	-15.4	22.2	21.4	14.3
Provident Stock Fund Ltd.	-10.0	16.6	21.3	17.7	-17.9	89.6	-30.2	25.2	35.2	37.6
Royal Trust A Fund	-15.6	16.8	31.8	21.9	-11.9	45.4	-5.6	22.9	11.1	15.5
Royal Trust Adv Growth Fund	-4.4	–	–	–	–	–	–	–	–	–
Royal Trust J Fund	-4.7	42.4	87.7	–	–	–	–	–	–	–
Salamander Trust	-4.9	-6.5	30.2	18.5	–	–	–	–	–	–

Fund	1988	1987	1986	1985	1984	1983	1982	1981	1980	1979
Saxon World Growth	-10.8	31.6	–	–	–	–	–	–	–	–
Sceptre International Fund	-4.6	–	–	–	–	–	–	–	–	–
Sentinel Global Fund	-21.3	–	–	–	–	–	–	–	–	–
Spectrum Intl Equity Fund	-17.7	–	–	–	–	–	–	–	–	–
Talvest American Fund	-15.7	17.8	–	–	–	–	–	–	–	–
Taurus Fund Ltd.	-22.7	1.1	23.8	11.9	-4.3	58.2	-9.9	57.9	25.4	20.7
Templeton Growth Fund	-10.4	19.3	31.8	28.1	6.7	56.2	-14.0	28.3	16.7	24.2
Trans-Canada Shares Series B	8.9	19.8	30.9	28.1	3.6	36.2	-12.0	12.4	4.4	20.5
Trimark Fund	-0.5	17.5	31.2	26.5	-1.6	82.8	–	–	–	–
Trust General U.S. Equity	-20.9	18.3	39.9	29.6	-14.1	–	–	–	–	–
United Accumulative Fund Ltd.	-14.9	11.7	34.3	32.7	10.6	39.8	-17.9	30.5	27.9	46.8
United American Fund Ltd.	-17.3	6.3	32.3	29.2	9.3	38.7	-10.0	36.2	11.1	19.9
United Venture Fund Ltd.	-18.5	4.3	27.4	30.3	-3.1	55.5	-31.5	38.8	40.5	53.9
Universal Savings American	-5.8	18.9	26.8	27.6	2.5	37.4	4.2	61.5	-3.5	–
Universal Savings Global Fd	-11.4	19.0	–	–	–	–	–	–	–	–
Universal Savings Pacific Fd	-8.0	34.8	110.0	13.2	10.1	23.4	–	–	–	–
Viking Commonwealth Fund	-3.4	21.2	30.4	24.3	0.7	55.0	-7.7	30.9	4.7	14.5
Viking Growth Fund Ltd	-8.5	15.2	42.3	27.6	-2.6	50.7	-17.3	32.2	10.0	19.8
Viking International Fund	-5.2	10.4	32.4	21.1	6.0	54.2	-14.5	54.5	5.5	16.5
HIGHEST IN GROUP	10.4	47.0	110.0	37.2	22.6	96.1	5.4	66.0	40.5	53.9
LOWEST IN GROUP	-27.7	-6.5	4.7	-0.1	-25.8	23.4	-31.5	12.3	-3.5	-4.8
AVERAGE OF GROUP	-12.2	16.5	35.8	22.7	-3.3	53.1	-10.6	35.0	17.3	21.8

BOND AND MORTGAGE FUNDS

Fund	1988	1987	1986	1985	1984	1983	1982	1981	1980	1979
AGF Global Government Bd Fd	1.6	–	–	–	–	–	–	–	–	–
AMD Fixed Income Fd	8.3	4.7	14.7	–	–	–	–	–	–	–
All-Canadian Revenue Grwth Fnd	6.6	9.0	6.1	20.0	5.5	22.5	11.3	8.2	8.4	14.9
Allied Income Fund	5.9	16.1	–	–	–	–	–	–	–	–
Altamira Income Fund	10.4	7.5	11.8	21.8	3.2	26.8	13.8	3.9	11.4	9.2
Bullock Bond Fund	6.1	4.0	9.2	11.0	9.3	10.7	6.8	-2.5	11.8	–
CDA RSP Fixed Income Fund	8.2	8.1	14.0	21.2	4.8	32.2	15.3	-0.7	5.7	7.3
Canadian Trusteed Income Fund	7.4	5.8	20.4	31.4	3.5	31.2	18.4	-3.9	3.1	7.2
Cda Life Fixed Income S-19	6.9	6.4	14.8	24.7	2.5	37.0	12.8	-4.6	2.4	6.7
Cdn Convertible Debenture Fd	1.3	12.0	–	–	–	–	–	–	–	–
Cdn Gen Life Ins Security B	3.4	2.9	15.9	31.8	1.6	40.7	-4.9	7.7	12.4	16.6
Confed Dolphin Mortgage Fund	8.8	8.4	10.4	17.1	8.8	25.4	15.4	4.4	9.9	8.5
Crown Life Pensions Bond Fund	9.3	3.9	15.7	20.1	-6.0	33.6	7.5	-5.9	1.6	6.9
Crown Life Pensions Mortgage	8.6	8.6	13.2	21.7	7.8	38.4	15.8	-6.9	3.7	4.6
Dynamic Income Fund	6.6	8.2	14.1	30.3	1.5	36.3	6.4	-2.0	–	–
Everest Bond Fund	10.8	–	–	–	–	–	–	–	–	–
Fd Des Prof Du Que-Bonds	5.9	8.7	15.9	21.5	5.4	29.7	14.8	1.3	11.8	7.3
Ficadre Obligations	7.9	8.1	10.2	–	–	–	–	–	–	–
Fiducie Pret Revenu Fonds H	8.5	12.5	10.7	17.5	7.9	23.8	19.4	5.3	8.3	8.2
First Canadian Mortgage Fund	9.2	9.2	11.5	18.4	8.5	21.4	18.3	3.3	8.7	8.2
First City Income Fund	6.5	–	–	–	–	–	–	–	–	–
Fonds Desjardins Hypotheques	9.5	8.8	11.2	18.9	5.8	25.1	17.3	3.6	7.6	8.1

Fund	1988	1987	1986	1985	1984	1983	1982	1981	1980	1979
Fonds Desjardins Obligations	7.1	5.4	15.9	29.8	-3.2	37.6	13.7	-14.1	0.5	5.7
Guardian Strategic Income	5.1	–	–	–	–	–	–	–	–	–
Hallmark Bond Fund	8.9	7.0	16.1	–	–	–	–	–	–	–
Industrial Income Fund	13.2	12.3	18.6	38.0	-0.5	39.0	5.9	-7.0	-5.0	7.3
Investors Bond Fund	7.4	6.4	16.3	28.5	0.0	28.3	13.7	-7.7	-1.1	–
Investors Gr Tr Fixed Income	9.5	9.3	12.4	20.4	7.1	27.4	15.1	0.7	5.4	7.7
Investors Group Trust Bond	9.4	8.3	17.4	29.5	0.6	30.8	14.4	-5.8	-1.5	–
Investors Mortgage Fund	8.8	8.4	11.4	18.5	7.0	23.8	16.7	3.7	7.6	7.4
London Life Bond Fund	5.3	4.2	21.2	41.3	2.0	31.6	13.5	-1.9	3.8	7.3
London Life Mortgage Fund	8.7	9.3	13.7	22.9	5.3	41.9	15.5	-10.0	1.6	5.3
MER Heartland Bond Fund	9.0	–	–	–	–	–	–	–	–	–
MONY Bond Fund	4.9	–	–	–	–	–	–	–	–	–
Mackenzie Mortgage & Income Fu	13.0	12.5	17.6	30.3	4.3	27.6	14.2	0.9	8.0	8.0
Metropolitan Bond Fund	-3.2	7.9	13.3	27.1	-4.8	31.4	2.3	-3.1	0.0	–
Metropolitan Variable-Bond	2.1	–	–	–	–	–	–	–	–	–
Montreal Trust Income Fund	6.6	7.7	19.5	25.1	-0.8	35.0	11.4	-7.1	2.7	6.7
Montreal Trust Mortgage Fund	8.9	8.2	10.7	16.6	7.7	20.2	17.5	5.2	8.3	6.9
Morgan Income Fund	7.1	6.5	16.5	20.6	–	–	–	–	–	–
Mtl Trust RRSP-Income Sectn	6.7	8.2	17.9	23.1	2.8	43.6	9.5	-7.1	3.2	7.0
Mtl Trust RRSP-Mortgage Sect	8.5	8.2	10.5	16.4	7.6	19.9	17.0	5.2	8.1	6.8
National Trust Income Fund	7.8	7.3	16.3	30.0	-2.3	43.0	9.6	-7.7	2.6	7.1
National Trust Pooled Bond &Pr	8.3	5.7	17.0	26.3	1.4	33.5	13.4	-3.2	5.7	7.5
National Trust Pooled Mortgage	11.3	10.0	12.2	15.3	10.9	21.9	18.9	5.2	8.7	8.3
Ordre Ingenieurs Obligations	6.3	8.4	15.3	26.2	1.8	45.7	13.9	-13.0	-0.6	8.0
PH&N Bond Fund	9.5	9.4	18.6	34.0	-3.2	44.8	9.0	-8.9	0.3	8.4
Protected Bond Fund	7.2	3.1	–	–	–	–	–	–	–	–
Prudential Income Fund Canada	9.3	7.3	13.3	22.6	4.9	32.1	11.7	-0.9	3.0	6.9
RoyFund Bond Fund	7.8	6.8	15.7	23.9	1.0	23.4	8.6	0.9	13.3	6.5
Royal Trust Adv Income Fd	3.1	–	–	–	–	–	–	–	–	–
Royal Trust Bond Fund	7.3	6.2	16.5	30.0	1.3	35.5	11.7	-2.1	1.3	7.3
Royal Trust Mortgage Fund	9.1	8.7	11.3	16.8	8.6	20.8	18.7	5.2	7.9	8.3
Sceptre Bond Fund	8.5	7.4	–	–	–	–	–	–	–	–
Scotia Income Fund	6.9	–	–	–	–	–	–	–	–	–
Sentinel Cda Bond Fund	6.5	8.0	–	–	–	–	–	–	–	–
Spectrum Interest Fund	6.0	–	–	–	–	–	–	–	–	–
St-Laurent Reer-Obligations	7.9	7.4	–	–	–	–	–	–	–	–
TD's Green Line Mtge Fund	9.7	8.5	10.5	13.7	8.7	22.1	18.3	5.7	8.8	7.6
Talvest Bond Fund	7.9	9.3	16.0	30.2	2.5	40.7	12.3	-0.2	5.2	8.9
Talvest Income Fund	8.1	8.6	10.3	19.1	5.8	22.3	16.6	7.1	9.4	7.9
Trst Laurentienne Obligation	6.4	9.5	–	–	–	–	–	–	–	–
Trust General Bond Fund	7.3	5.4	17.8	32.9	1.6	31.9	14.3	-3.5	2.3	8.2
Trust General Mortgage Fund	7.9	9.1	12.7	21.7	7.7	23.9	17.1	1.0	4.7	8.5
United Mortgage	7.9	7.6	8.9	15.0	9.2	14.8	17.6	6.6	11.3	8.7
United Security Fund	5.2	8.1	15.0	27.0	-0.1	21.9	11.4	0.9	2.8	6.4
Universal Svgs Income Fund	12.1	7.0	15.7	36.4	-3.7	50.8	7.9	-11.7	-1.6	5.7
Viking Income Fund	7.7	7.3	16.5	30.9	0.5	37.9	10.9	-8.0	-2.1	5.5
Waltaine Income Fund	2.8	8.3	–	–	–	–	–	–	–	–
HIGHEST IN GROUP	13.2	16.1	21.2	41.3	10.9	50.8	19.4	8.2	13.3	16.6
LOWEST IN GROUP	-3.2	2.9	6.1	11.0	-6.0	10.7	-4.9	-14.1	-5.0	4.6
AVERAGE OF GROUP	7.4	7.9	14.3	24.3	3.4	30.6	13.0	-1.4	5.0	7.7

Fund	1988	1987	1986	1985	1984	1983	1982	1981	1980	1979
PREFERRED DIVIDEND FUNDS										
AGF Preferred Income Fund	3.6	7.6	10.2	–	–	–	–	–	–	–
AMD Dividend Fund	1.5	6.2	8.6	–	–	–	–	–	–	–
Allied Dividend Fund	0.5	5.5	–	–	–	–	–	–	–	–
Bolton Tremblay Income Fund	3.1	9.7	7.7	13.4	4.4	30.2	14.3	-0.4	9.8	7.3
Bullock Dividend Fund	0.0	6.2	10.7	–	–	–	–	–	–	–
Dynamic Dividend Fund	5.9	11.1	–	–	–	–	–	–	–	–
Guardian Pfd Dividend Fund	3.9	8.7	–	–	–	–	–	–	–	–
Investors Dividend Fund	3.6	9.9	9.8	24.2	2.5	55.3	-14.9	6.6	4.5	27.5
Montreal Trust Dividend Fund	-4.7	–	–	–	–	–	–	–	–	–
Morgan Dividend Fund	-3.9	12.0	–	–	–	–	–	–	–	–
Mutual Dividend Fund	3.7	8.6	–	–	–	–	–	–	–	–
PH&N Dividend Income Fund	2.0	18.8	10.2	20.3	0.8	56.7	-11.1	9.5	6.5	19.7
Prudential Dividend Fund	6.4	–	–	–	–	–	–	–	–	–
Royal Trust Preferred Fund	0.7	7.2	–	–	–	–	–	–	–	–
Spectrum Dividend Fund	3.4	–	–	–	–	–	–	–	–	–
Viking Dividend Fund Ltd	3.5	11.5	15.3	23.5	6.2	55.4	-14.3	9.2	5.2	–
Waltaine Conv Preferred Fund	-5.0	13.6	–	–	–	–	–	–	–	–
HIGHEST IN GROUP	6.4	18.8	15.3	24.2	6.2	56.7	14.3	9.5	9.8	27.5
LOWEST IN GROUP	-5.0	5.5	7.7	13.4	0.8	30.2	-14.9	-0.4	4.5	7.3
AVERAGE OF GROUP	1.7	9.8	10.4	20.4	3.5	49.4	-6.5	6.2	6.5	18.2
MONEY MARKET FUNDS										
AGF Money Market Fund	8.4	7.8	9.2	10.8	9.4	12.0	18.2	14.7	13.6	9.7
AMD Money Market Fd	8.3	7.9	9.6	–	–	–	–	–	–	–
AMD US Dollar Money Mkt(US$)	6.2	–	–	–	–	–	–	–	–	–
Allied Money Fund	8.1	7.9	–	–	–	–	–	–	–	–
Bolton Tremblay Money Fund	8.7	8.2	9.4	11.0	9.1	11.6	–	–	–	–
CDA Money Market Fund	8.2	7.5	9.6	11.0	9.5	11.5	16.1	14.1	11.6	8.2
CMA Short-Term Deposit Fund	7.6	7.1	9.0	10.5	9.3	11.6	17.5	13.3	13.5	10.1
Cda Life Money Market S-29	7.3	6.0	7.7	10.0	9.3	12.4	17.2	14.7	12.3	9.1
Cdn Gen Life Ins Money Mkt C	7.2	–	–	–	–	–	–	–	–	–
Crown Life Pen Short Term	9.3	7.4	10.0	10.8	9.0	11.3	17.1	–	–	–
Dynamic Money Market Fund	8.0	7.2	8.9	10.3	–	–	–	–	–	–
Elliott & Page Money Fund	9.4	9.1	10.6	–	–	–	–	–	–	–
Everest Short Term Asset Fd	7.8	–	–	–	–	–	–	–	–	–
Ficadre Monetaire	7.0	7.5	8.9	–	–	–	–	–	–	–
Guardian Short Term Money Fund	8.7	7.7	9.3	10.7	9.3	11.4	17.7	13.9	9.6	9.8
Industrial Cash Management Fd	8.1	7.8	9.5	–	–	–	–	–	–	–
Investors Money Market Fund	8.3	7.2	8.9	–	–	–	–	–	–	–
MER Money Market Fund	4.0	6.7	9.0	10.6	7.8	–	–	–	–	–
MONY T-Bill Fund	6.9	–	–	–	–	–	–	–	–	–
Mutual Money Market Fund	7.7	6.2	8.6	–	–	–	–	–	–	–
Ordre Ingenieurs Revenu Var	8.1	8.4	9.3	11.6	9.3	14.3	17.0	13.2	11.2	9.2
PH&N Money Market Fund	8.3	–	–	–	–	–	–	–	–	–
Prudential Money Market Fund	8.8	–	–	–	–	–	–	–	–	–
RoyFund Money Market Fd	7.8	–	–	–	–	–	–	–	–	–
Sentinel Cda Money Market Fd	9.7	–	–	–	–	–	–	–	–	–
Spectrum Cash Reserve Fund	8.0	–	–	–	–	–	–	–	–	–

Fund	1988	1987	1986	1985	1984	1983	1982	1981	1979	1978
St-Laurent Reer-Epargne-Plus	8.3	9.0	–	–	–	–	–	–	–	–
Talvest Money Fund	9.5	4.9	–	–	–	–	–	–	–	–
Trimark Interest Fund	8.6	–	–	–	–	–	–	–	–	–
HIGHEST IN GROUP	11.2	9.1	10.6	11.6	9.5	14.3	18.2	14.7	13.6	10.1
LOWEST IN GROUP	4.0	4.9	7.7	10.0	7.8	11.3	16.1	13.2	9.6	8.2
AVERAGE OF GROUP	8.1	7.5	9.3	10.7	9.1	12.0	17.3	14.0	12.0	9.4
MARKET INDICES										
91 Day Canada T Bill	8.7	8.0	9.3	10.7	10.0	10.7	16.5	14.8	12.9	10.2
Consumer Price Index	4.1	4.6	4.1	4.0	4.8	5.4	11.8	12.3	9.4	9.3
MYW Weighted 50 Mid-Term Index	8.6	7.7	17.2	34.0	-1.1	41.8	10.5	-6.1	–	–
Standard & Poor's 500 Index	-15.3	20.6	38.2	34.9	2.2	53.3	-5.0	26.0	15.4	18.4
TSE Total Return Index	-5.2	24.6	17.4	26.6	-6.1	86.6	-39.1	18.8	32.6	49.9

Survey of Performance
of Canadian Mutual Funds
through June 30, 1988

This survey shows the per cent change in investment over three months, six months, and one year and the average annual compound rate of return over three years, five years and ten years. The column labeled "%" shows the percentile ranking by volatility within the grouping. For example, a percentile ranking of 5 for the fund means that 95% of the funds in the group are more volatile while 4% are less volatile. The column labeled "St.D" shows the standard deviation. This measure indicates the amount by which a fund's rate of return is likely to diverge from its average monthly rate of return. A fund with a standard deviation of 6 is twice as volatile as a fund with a standard deviation of 3.

Fund	3 mo.	6 mo.	1 yr.	3 yr.	5 yr.	10 yr.	%	St.D.
EQUITY FUNDS – RRSP ELIGIBLE								
AGF Excel Cdn Equity Fund	5.2	3.3	–	–	–	–	N/A	–
AIC Advantage Fund	6.8	1.5	-9.2	–	–	–	N/A	–
AMD Cdn Blue Chip Growth Fd	5.8	2.1	-9.4	–	–	–	N/A	–
All-Canadian Compound Fund	1.3	2.4	-9.3	6.9	8.4	13.6	28	3.77
All-Canadian Dividend Fund	1.3	2.3	-9.3	6.8	8.1	13.3	27	3.77
Allied Canadian Fund	4.8	-2.9	-28.6	–	–	–	N/A	–
Associate Investors Ltd.	4.7	4.9	-0.3	9.6	12.9	15.7	26	3.53
Bolton Tremblay Cda Cum Fund	7.0	4.3	-7.7	6.9	6.0	13.1	46	4.26
Bolton Tremblay Cdn Balanced	3.6	2.6	–	–	–	–	N/A	–
Bolton Tremblay Discovery	2.3	0.8	–	–	–	–	N/A	–
Bullock Growth Fund	7.3	3.3	-6.0	9.6	3.6	11.2	86	5.20
CDA RSP Balanced Fund	4.0	2.5	0.5	10.6	11.1	–	6	2.07
CDA RSP Common Stock Fund	8.6	4.5	-4.9	13.6	14.1	16.2	55	4.48
CGF Fund 4000	4.0	0.9	-13.4	7.8	8.6	11.4	79	4.92
CGF Venture Fund	4.7	2.0	-20.2	-9.8	-5.7	1.9	99	6.97
CMA Investment Fund	6.1	6.1	6.1	15.5	16.1	17.8	26	3.53
Caisse de Sec du Spectacle	2.5	1.8	-0.4	8.7	9.2	–	14	2.57
Cambridge Balanced Fund	1.1	1.4	6.9	15.1	14.1	12.8	5	2.03
Cambridge Growth Fund	4.8	4.1	-0.4	20.9	18.3	15.6	32	3.92
Cambridge Resource Fund	5.4	8.5	-7.7	11.5	8.9	10.4	96	6.30
Canadian Gas & Energy Fund Ltd	2.4	0.8	-15.5	6.6	0.8	9.5	97	6.45
Canadian Investment Fund Ltd.	5.7	3.0	-7.8	5.7	7.3	12.1	57	4.53
Canadian Natural Resource Fd	1.6	0.0	-14.3	–	–	–	N/A	–
Canadian Protected Fund	0.5	1.3	9.4	12.1	–	–	2	1.59
Canadian Security Growth Fund	5.1	3.5	-7.0	9.8	13.0	17.8	38	4.10
Capital Growth Fund Ltd.	5.9	4.2	-13.5	4.1	5.4	14.7	67	4.73
Capstone Investment Trust	5.5	1.2	-10.6	7.0	8.4	–	77	4.85
Cda Life Bal Eqty Income E-2	8.0	6.0	0.3	13.3	14.1	17.3	73	4.81
Cda Life Cdn & Intl Equity S-9	8.6	5.8	1.7	12.5	13.1	16.4	51	4.40

Fund	3 mo.	6 mo.	1 yr.	3 yr.	5 yr.	10 yr.	%	St.D.
Cda Life Managed Fund S-35	4.8	3.5	3.5	11.4	–	–	15	2.73
Cdn Anaesthetists Mutual Accum	8.1	4.5	-3.7	12.2	11.8	18.6	36	4.02
Cdn Convertible Preferred Fd	3.4	2.7	1.2	–	–	–	N/A	–
Cdn Gen Life Ins Equity Fd A	3.0	0.7	-9.7	9.2	12.1	16.8	56	4.51
Chou RRSP Fund	3.1	2.9	7.1	–	–	–	N/A	–
Confed Dolphin Fund	6.0	4.9	-3.4	11.9	12.8	17.1	33	3.97
Corporate Investors Ltd.	4.7	2.9	-3.0	6.7	9.9	12.4	23	3.19
Corporate Investors Stock Fund	3.2	-1.3	-31.4	3.8	6.8	14.2	84	5.15
Counsel Trust Real Estate Fd	0.5	1.8	13.7	16.4	–	–	1	1.52
Crown Life Commitment Fund	5.3	1.7	-4.7	–	–	–	N/A	–
Crown Life Pensions Balanced	2.8	2.1	2.9	–	–	–	N/A	–
Crown Life Pensions Equity	5.5	2.6	-3.6	13.1	11.6	13.0	52	4.44
Cundill Security Fund	3.8	3.9	2.1	11.3	12.1	–	20	3.13
DK All Seasons Fund	3.8	2.2	-16.9	3.0	-1.2	8.3	94	6.15
DK Enterprise Fund	0.4	-4.1	-10.8	12.8	4.2	14.0	91	5.71
Dynamic Fund of Canada Ltd.	4.1	3.6	-1.9	12.3	10.2	15.5	29	3.80
Dynamic Managed Portfolio	1.7	1.9	-2.3	–	–	–	N/A	–
Dynamic Precious Metals Fund	-0.8	0.8	-7.2	14.0	–	–	97	6.37
Empire Life Segregated #1	9.3	7.8	3.5	14.3	12.3	18.6	59	4.55
Ethical Growth Fund	7.9	3.9	12.3	–	–	–	N/A	–
Everest Balanced Fund	4.4	8.3	–	–	–	–	N/A	–
Everest Special Equity Fund	3.2	0.1	-19.5	–	–	–	N/A	–
F.M.O.Q. Fonds de Placement	5.1	4.2	-0.8	11.3	–	–	24	3.38
F.M.O.Q. Omnibus	4.1	3.7	2.9	11.8	12.0	–	9	2.24
Fd Des Prof Du Que-Balanced	1.2	1.6	–	–	–	–	N/A	–
Ficadre Actions	6.5	2.1	-13.4	10.6	–	–	80	4.94
Ficadre Equilibre	5.1	3.0	-3.7	8.2	–	–	16	2.81
Fidelity Cap Balanced Fund	5.2	5.9	–	–	–	–	N/A	–
Fidelity Cap Conservation Fd	5.8	6.5	–	–	–	–	N/A	–
Fidelity Cap. Builder Fund	6.5	6.5	–	–	–	–	N/A	–
Fiducie Pret Revenu Retraite	2.1	1.6	-1.4	8.3	9.1	10.8	8	2.15
Fiducie Pret Revenue Canadien	4.9	1.4	-14.8	3.7	3.8	8.9	68	4.74
First City Growth Fund	5.6	1.3	-9.2	–	–	–	N/A	–
First City Realfund	0.9	6.5	16.2	14.1	12.6	–	3	1.64
Fonds Desjardins Actions	5.7	3.7	-11.0	4.0	4.7	12.3	58	4.53
Fonds Desjardins Equilibre	2.4	2.1	-0.6	–	–	–	N/A	–
FoodFund	0.8	1.5	-9.4	9.3	–	–	25	3.42
Global Strategy Corp	-4.0	-3.5	-17.2	–	–	–	N/A	–
Global Strategy RRSP	2.8	2.6	–	–	–	–	N/A	–
Global Strategy RRSP Access	2.3	2.1	–	–	–	–	N/A	–
GoldenFund	-3.1	-3.0	-14.1	15.5	–	–	92	5.89
Green Line Cdn Index Fund	6.3	4.5	-6.2	–	–	–	N/A	–
Growth Equity Fund Ltd.	4.8	8.9	-17.0	10.0	8.3	16.3	89	5.51
Guardian Balanced Fund	4.9	3.5	5.9	10.6	12.8	13.5	7	2.13
Guardian Cdn Equity Fd	7.8	3.9	-7.6	12.5	10.2	14.6	83	5.11
Guardian Enterprise Fund	6.3	1.8	-1.9	10.0	10.6	17.7	79	4.92
Hallmark Canadian Fund	1.4	1.5	-4.2	12.2	–	–	22	3.19
Hume Canadian Equity Fund	8.0	6.8	–	–	–	–	N/A	–
Hume RRSP Growth&Income Fund	4.5	2.3	-14.3	5.3	–	–	75	4.83
Imperial Realty Growth Fund	1.4	1.4	10.3	15.4	–	–	4	1.89

Fund	3 mo.	6 mo.	1 yr.	3 yr.	5 yr.	10 yr.	%	St.D.
Industrial Dividend Fund Ltd.	8.5	9.3	6.1	16.3	17.4	17.1	65	4.69
Industrial Equity Fund Ltd.	5.8	4.4	-0.5	15.6	12.6	15.7	47	4.31
Industrial Future Fund	4.0	4.4	–	–	–	–	N/A	–
Industrial Growth Fund	6.2	6.8	4.5	15.8	15.2	17.9	35	4.01
Industrial Horizon Fund	5.4	6.0	15.2	–	–	–	N/A	–
Industrial Pension Fund	8.3	9.1	4.3	15.8	15.3	16.0	71	4.79
Integra Balanced Fund	3.0	3.3	–	–	–	–	N/A	–
Investors Cdn Equity Fund	6.6	6.8	-7.2	9.3	–	–	76	4.83
Investors Gr Tr Pooled Equity	6.2	5.0	-3.0	9.0	9.4	14.9	37	4.02
Investors Retirement Mutual	7.6	7.7	4.6	12.7	11.7	15.6	39	4.11
Investors Summa Fund Ltd	5.1	4.5	-3.1	–	–	–	N/A	–
Jones Heward Fund Ltd.	8.9	5.2	-3.9	11.6	11.5	17.0	85	5.20
Keltic Investment Trust	5.4	0.0	-10.1	9.2	4.9	–	54	4.45
LifeFund	0.0	-0.7	-17.3	4.8	–	–	31	3.86
London Life Diversified fund	4.7	3.6	–	–	–	–	N/A	–
London Life Equity Fund	9.6	6.3	-0.3	12.8	12.2	17.2	68	4.73
Lotus Fund	3.8	2.7	-6.1	7.4	–	–	21	3.14
MER Equity Fund	6.4	5.3	-6.0	10.1	12.6	–	48	4.31
MER Heartland Equity Fund	6.0	4.9	-7.1	–	–	–	N/A	–
MONY Balanced Fund	2.4	2.6	-0.9	–	–	–	N/A	–
MONY Canadian Growth Fund	4.0	3.0	-16.6	4.8	7.9	16.1	43	4.19
Mackenzie Equity Fund	8.0	8.3	4.8	15.9	15.8	19.2	60	4.59
Maritime Life Balanced Fund	4.4	2.9	1.9	–	–	–	N/A	–
Maritime Life Growth Fund	6.9	1.8	-11.1	8.5	10.8	14.9	64	4.63
Marlborough Fund	8.3	2.9	-16.0	5.5	5.7	12.6	88	5.50
Metropolitan Cdn Mutual Fd	6.0	5.1	-13.6	6.5	–	–	72	4.80
Metropolitan Growth Fund	3.3	1.6	-17.1	3.4	4.8	10.4	49	4.31
Metropolitan Var-Balanced Fd	2.1	0.3	-4.1	–	–	–	N/A	–
Metropolitan Variable-Equity	7.2	2.8	-11.8	–	–	–	N/A	–
Montreal Trust Equity Fund	7.0	4.2	-3.9	10.4	8.7	13.9	66	4.71
Morgan Growth Fund	7.4	0.0	-6.8	8.0	–	–	63	4.63
Morgan Resource Fund	7.7	4.9	7.0	–	–	–	N/A	–
Mtl Trust RRSP-Equity Sectn	6.1	1.2	-6.2	10.2	8.6	14.0	82	5.10
Multiple Opportunities Fund	-2.3	-6.0	-27.2	–	–	–	N/A	–
Mutual Canadian Index Fund	5.9	5.0	–	–	–	–	N/A	–
Mutual Diversifund 25	2.2	2.2	3.0	8.3	–	–	3	1.87
Mutual Diversifund 40	3.5	3.2	0.6	8.8	–	–	12	2.52
Mutual Diversifund 55	4.4	3.8	-1.0	8.9	–	–	18	2.97
Mutual Equifund	6.6	5.5	-6.2	8.6	–	–	78	4.88
NFM Canadian Equity Fund	7.6	-2.6	–	–	–	–	N/A	–
NW Canadian Fund Ltd.	6.3	4.9	-8.0	13.7	12.4	18.0	69	4.76
National Trust Cdn Common Shar	6.5	4.1	-3.5	12.7	11.7	15.7	70	4.77
National Trust Equity Fund	6.3	3.9	-9.7	8.9	9.8	15.0	85	5.19
Natl Trust Feb Pro Fund	4.3	3.0	0.9	10.8	–	–	13	2.55
Natl Trust Jan Pro Fund	5.2	1.5	4.6	10.2	–	–	15	2.72
Natural Resources Growth Fund	-0.4	0.2	-12.4	6.6	1.5	9.3	93	5.93
One Decision Fund	4.2	3.0	-4.6	–	–	–	N/A	–
Ont Teachers Grp Aggr Equity	4.8	4.3	-4.5	12.2	13.1	17.1	50	4.38

Fund	3 mo.	6 mo.	1 yr.	3 yr.	5 yr.	10 yr.	%	St.D.
Ont Teachers Grp Balanced	2.5	2.6	1.8	–	–	–	N/A	–
Ont Teachers Grp Diversified	4.2	4.0	-4.7	10.7	11.7	16.0	44	4.25
Ordre Ingenieurs Actions	7.5	4.4	-2.8	12.1	11.2	14.4	62	4.63
Ordre Ingenieurs Equilibre	4.0	3.6	2.8	11.8	11.9	–	10	2.34
PH&N Canadian Fund	6.2	4.7	-2.9	13.5	12.1	16.2	62	4.62
PH&N Pooled Pension Trust	6.5	3.7	-4.7	11.9	11.7	14.9	61	4.59
PH&N RRSP Fund	6.8	4.7	-6.3	12.1	11.1	14.3	74	4.81
Pacific Growth Fund	6.0	4.6	-10.8	5.0	3.0	10.4	90	5.60
Pacific Retirement Bal Fund	5.2	4.2	-3.0	4.8	5.0	–	19	3.05
Planned Resources Fund Ltd.	7.0	4.6	-14.0	4.4	2.6	13.7	95	6.29
Prudential Diversif Invstmt	2.8	2.1	–	–	–	–	N/A	–
Prudential Growth Fund Canada	4.1	1.2	-15.6	10.1	10.0	14.1	87	5.46
Prudential Nat Res Fd Of Cda	10.1	11.7	–	–	–	–	N/A	–
Prudential Precious Metals	-0.8	-0.7	–	–	–	–	N/A	–
Rabin Budden Capital Fund	5.1	4.0	-14.7	–	–	–	N/A	–
Rabin Budden Income Fund	2.4	6.9	13.1	–	–	–	N/A	–
Renaissance Cda Bond&Bullion	-6.9	-6.8	-6.9	–	–	11	2.40	
RoyFund Balanced Fund	3.2	3.6	–	–	–	–	N/A	–
RoyFund Equity Ltd	5.2	2.3	-8.3	11.5	13.2	17.7	44	4.22
Royal Trust Adv Balanced Fd	3.2	2.5	0.3	–	–	–	N/A	–
Royal Trust Energy Fund	2.8	-0.3	-11.4	4.0	0.2	–	98	6.92
Saxon Balanced Fund	3.4	4.0	-13.1	–	–	–	N/A	–
Saxon Small Cap	2.2	2.8	-9.1	–	–	–	N/A	–
Saxon Stock Fund	3.3	3.3	-12.9	–	–	–	N/A	–
Sceptre Balanced Fund	4.3	2.7	3.4	–	–	–	N/A	–
Sceptre Equity fund	9.5	5.9	4.4	–	–	–	N/A	–
Scotia Stock And Bond Fund	1.8	2.2	4.8	–	–	–	N/A	–
Sentinel Cda Equity Fund	5.2	4.0	-13.0	–	–	–	N/A	–
SilverFund	-1.6	-3.7	-23.7	-0.7	–	–	100	9.01
Spectrum Canadian Equity Fd	3.7	2.5	-3.3	–	–	–	N/A	–
Spectrum Diversified Fund	2.4	2.0	1.6	–	–	–	N/A	–
St-Laurent Reer-Actions	6.0	2.1	-13.6	–	–	–	N/A	–
St-Laurent Reer-Diversifiee	2.1	1.5	5.0	–	–	–	N/A	–
Sunset Fund	3.6	3.6	1.7	–	–	–	N/A	–
Talvest Diversified Fund	5.5	4.2	4.6	–	–	–	N/A	–
Talvest Growth Fund	7.4	5.6	-1.8	13.0	12.3	14.6	41	4.13
TechnoFund	0.3	0.5	-19.8	-6.4	–	–	81	4.98
Templeton Canadian Fund	4.0	1.8	-11.4	9.1	7.1	–	53	4.44
Tradex Investment Fund Ltd.	7.9	4.6	-3.2	12.1	12.3	18.1	40	4.12
Trans-Canada Equity Fund	2.9	1.6	-1.0	22.4	19.7	15.7	32	3.91
Trans-Canada Shares Series C	1.7	1.3	3.5	16.4	16.5	14.1	17	2.90
Trimark Canadian Fund	5.2	6.1	1.6	12.8	13.3	–	50	4.35
Trimark Income Growth Fund	3.5	2.9	–	–	–	–	N/A	–
Trust General Balanced Fund	3.0	1.3	-0.2	–	–	–	N/A	–
Trust General Canadian Equity	8.3	2.7	-8.2	8.0	8.6	13.0	56	4.51
Trust La Laurentienne Action	5.8	3.9	-6.0	–	–	–	N/A	–
United Accumulative Retirement	3.3	3.1	-2.2	7.8	12.9	18.8	21	3.18
United Venture Retirement Fund	3.6	4.3	-9.8	9.7	10.7	18.9	38	4.07
Universal Svgs Equity Fund Ltd	8.3	8.4	11.0	17.4	16.5	18.4	45	4.25
Universal Svgs Natural Resourc	2.1	1.0	-4.1	8.6	5.2	11.2	91	5.66

Fund	3 mo.	6 mo.	1 yr.	3 yr.	5 yr.	10 yr.	%	St.D.
Univest Growth Fund	0.7	0.2	-7.9	7.4	7.2	11.0	30	3.81
ValueFund	2.1	1.9	-12.7	3.7	–	–	42	4.13
Viking Canadian Fund Ltd	5.7	5.1	-2.6	9.3	9.9	15.0	34	3.99
Vintage Fund	6.1	3.9	-10.2	–	–	–	N/A	–
Waltaine Balanced Fund	2.3	2.4	1.0	9.9	10.4	14.8	9	2.25
HIGHEST IN GROUP	10.1	11.7	16.2	22.4	19.7	19.2		
LOWEST IN GROUP	-6.9	-6.8	-31.4	-9.8	-5.7	1.9		
AVERAGE OF GROUP	4.4	3.1	-4.8	9.8	9.9	14.5		

EQUITY FUNDS – NOT RRSP-ELIGIBLE

Fund	3 mo.	6 mo.	1 yr.	3 yr.	5 yr.	10 yr.	%	St.D.
AGF Excel Amern Equity Fund	3.2	2.7	–	–	–	–	N/A	–
AGF HiTech Fund Ltd	-0.7	-2.8	-12.5	14.9	–	–	67	5.24
AGF Japan Fund Ltd.	-6.9	-8.8	4.6	38.6	30.4	21.7	89	5.79
AGF Option Equity Fund	-0.1	1.7	-11.2	1.8	5.5	–	7	3.38
AGF Special Fund Ltd.	5.4	4.9	-8.2	10.0	7.9	20.7	45	4.97
AMD Amer Blue Chip Growth Fd	2.9	5.1	-16.0	–	–	–	N/A	–
Allied International Fund	3.8	5.6	-27.7	–	–	–	N/A	–
American Growth Fund Ltd.	3.3	2.8	-15.0	5.4	8.0	17.2	51	5.09
Bolton Tremblay International	-0.1	0.6	-15.2	12.6	12.6	18.2	16	4.26
Bullock Amer Fund	4.4	2.6	-20.7	14.5	8.0	13.1	100	6.89
CGF Int'l Growth Fund	2.6	-0.5	-12.9	10.7	9.9	13.1	31	4.65
Cda Life U.S.&Intl Eqty S-34	3.9	2.3	-7.4	11.4	–	–	27	4.56
Century DJ Mutual Fund	2.8	-1.6	-25.6	–	–	–	N/A	–
Chou Associates Fund	4.1	2.5	-5.2	–	–	–	N/A	–
Crown Life Pen Foreign Equity	2.2	3.6	-6.0	12.4	11.9	–	35	4.71
Cundill Value Fund Ltd.	4.3	5.5	10.4	16.4	13.5	21.0	4	2.88
DK American Fund	1.5	-0.7	-23.4	2.7	1.5	10.1	93	5.86
Dynamic American Fund	1.9	2.4	-8.1	11.3	13.2	–	25	4.54
Dynamic Global Fund	-2.9	-2.4	-13.9	–	–	–	N/A	–
Everest International Fund	-3.1	1.0	–	–	–	–	N/A	–
Fidelity Intl Portfolio Fund	-1.7	-2.0	–	–	–	–	N/A	–
Fiducie Pret Revenu American	3.7	4.3	-22.3	6.6	7.7	10.5	69	5.28
Fonds Desjardins International	0.1	0.7	-17.0	9.2	7.7	11.2	53	5.09
G.T. Global Choice Fund	-1.9	-0.9	–	–	–	–	N/A	–
Global Strategy Americas	2.7	1.3	-18.0	–	–	–	N/A	–
Global Strategy Europe	-3.6	-4.9	-25.7	–	–	–	N/A	–
Global Strategy Far East	-5.7	-4.9	-8.8	–	–	–	N/A	–
Global Strategy Fund	-1.7	-3.0	-17.3	–	–	–	N/A	–
Green Line U.S. Fund	4.1	6.0	-7.8	–	–	–	N/A	–
Guardian American Eqty Fd	5.1	5.4	-13.1	3.9	1.6	12.1	44	4.96
Guardian Global Equity Fd	-4.0	-1.0	-13.9	13.9	10.4	15.7	29	4.59
Guardian North American Fund	4.3	6.2	-24.0	-0.8	-0.6	11.7	85	5.67
Guardian Pacific Rim Corp	-4.0	-2.6	–	–	–	–	N/A	–
Hume Growth & Income Fund	4.4	4.6	-23.7	4.6	–	–	96	6.14
Industrial American Fund	5.1	6.6	-6.3	11.9	12.5	18.0	49	5.07
Industrial Global Fund	1.6	0.9	-1.4	–	–	–	N/A	–
Investors Global Fund Ltd	-1.6	-1.3	-14.9	–	–	–	N/A	–
Investors Growth Fund of Cda	6.1	5.8	-9.8	10.4	9.8	15.6	33	4.67
Investors International Mutual	1.7	1.8	-14.4	8.3	7.3	13.3	75	5.51
Investors Japanese Growth Fund	-8.0	-9.6	4.5	37.3	26.0	19.1	78	5.62

Fund	3 mo.	6 mo.	1 yr.	3 yr.	5 yr.	10 yr.	%	St.D.
Investors Mutual of Canada Ltd	5.3	5.4	-1.9	9.4	8.4	13.7	11	3.75
Jones Heward American Fund	4.3	1.9	-17.5	9.5	10.1	–	76	5.57
London Life U.S. Equity Fund	5.1	3.7	–	–	–	–	N/A	–
MD Growth Investments Ltd.	2.8	5.1	-5.2	17.8	17.7	21.9	56	5.11
MD Perpetual Growth Fd II	0.4	-6.8	-20.9	–	–	–	N/A	–
MD Perpetual Growth Fund	0.4	0.6	3.8	–	–	–	N/A	–
MER Growth Fund	7.2	5.4	-15.9	0.8	5.2	–	62	5.14
MER Heartland Growth Fund	8.5	8.0	-14.7	–	–	–	N/A	–
Metropolitan Collective Mut	3.2	2.9	-27.7	-0.4	2.4	12.8	64	5.15
Metropolitan Speculators	1.5	-2.0	-20.6	–	–	–	N/A	–
Metropolitan Venture Fund	3.9	2.9	-21.6	7.7	4.2	11.9	71	5.36
Montreal Trust Intl Fund	4.5	4.7	-15.5	11.4	12.5	15.9	42	4.96
Morgan Worldwide Fund	2.4	0.6	-20.2	5.4	–	–	20	4.40
Mutual Amerifund	3.4	6.9	-3.6	–	–	–	N/A	–
NFM U.S. Equity Fund	5.0	10.1	–	–	–	–	N/A	–
NW Equity Fund Ltd.	9.2	7.0	-15.1	4.4	5.9	13.1	82	5.63
National Trust Pooled Non-Cdn	2.4	1.6	-14.5	10.9	8.2	13.1	80	5.63
Natl Trust Global Fund P	-2.7	-2.4	-17.7	20.6	18.3	–	36	4.85
Natrusco Common Share Fund	4.6	3.8	-12.5	7.5	7.2	12.6	47	5.07
Noram Convertible Securities	-0.2	0.6	3.9	12.4	–	–	0	2.16
PH&N U.S. FUND	5.8	6.4	-10.6	7.5	6.7	16.4	95	5.92
PH&N U.S. Pooled Pension Fund	5.9	6.8	-8.8	8.4	9.3	–	91	5.80
Pacific U.S. Growth Fund	2.8	4.3	-15.3	3.6	-0.1	5.9	87	5.69
Provident Stock Fund Ltd.	5.2	4.4	-10.0	8.4	4.3	14.3	55	5.10
Royal Trust A Fund	3.3	2.8	-15.6	9.1	6.9	11.7	40	4.94
Royal Trust Adv Growth Fund	3.4	2.5	-4.4	–	–	–	N/A	–
Royal Trust Global Invest	-4.0	-1.8	–	–	–	–	N/A	–
Royal Trust J Fund	-9.9	-12.1	-4.7	36.6	–	–	84	5.67
Salamander Trust	-1.9	-1.4	-4.9	5.0	–	–	5	2.93
Saxon World Growth	0.1	0.9	-10.8	–	–	–	N/A	–
Sceptre International Fund	5.2	7.7	-4.6	–	–	–	N/A	–
Sentinel Amer Fund	4.6	6.1	–	–	–	–	N/A	–
Sentinel Global Fund	-1.9	-3.6	-21.3	–	–	–	N/A	–
Spectrum Intl Equity Fund	-0.9	-2.8	-17.7	–	–	–	N/A	–
St-Laurent Placmt-Actions	10.3	5.3	–	–	–	–	N/A	–
Sunset World Fund	1.2	1.0	–	–	–	–	N/A	–
Talvest American Fund	5.6	5.1	-15.7	–	–	–	N/A	–
Taurus Fund Ltd.	5.2	3.8	-22.7	-1.1	0.7	13.4	73	5.37
Templeton Growth Fund	1.0	3.7	-10.4	12.1	14.0	17.0	15	4.25
Trans-Canada Shares Series B	2.5	2.3	8.9	19.5	17.8	14.4	2	2.72
Trimark Fund	4.8	9.6	-0.5	15.3	13.8	–	65	5.24
Trust General U.S. Equity	5.3	2.9	-20.9	9.4	7.8	–	60	5.13
United Accumulative Fund Ltd.	1.1	1.8	-14.9	8.5	13.4	18.1	13	4.25
United American Fund Ltd.	4.1	2.8	-17.3	5.2	10.4	14.0	22	4.40
United Venture Fund Ltd.	4.4	6.9	-18.5	2.7	6.5	15.9	38	4.90
Universal Savings American	3.3	5.3	-5.8	12.4	13.2	–	58	5.11
Universal Savings Global Fd	-1.4	-0.8	-11.4	–	–	–	N/A	–
Universal Savings Pacific Fd	-4.3	-3.7	-8.0	37.6	26.6	–	98	6.32
Universal Sector Canadian Fd	8.0	8.0	–	–	–	–	N/A	–

Fund	3 mo.	6 mo.	1 yr.	3 yr.	5 yr.	10 yr.	%	St.D.
Universal Sector Global Fund	-1.4	-1.0	–	–	–	–	N/A	–
Universal Sector Pacific Fd	-4.2	-3.7	–	–	–	–	N/A	–
Universal Sector Resource Sh	2.0	0.7	–	–	–	–	N/A	–
Universal Sectors Amer Fund	3.1	5.2	–	–	–	–	N/A	–
Viking Commonwealth Fund	2.8	2.8	-3.4	15.1	13.8	15.7	9	3.45
Viking Growth Fund Ltd	4.8	4.5	-8.5	14.4	13.2	15.0	18	4.35
Viking International Fund	3.5	3.4	-5.2	11.5	12.2	16.1	24	4.47
HIGHEST IN GROUP	10.3	10.1	10.4	38.6	30.4	21.9		
LOWEST IN GROUP	-9.9	-12.1	-27.7	-1.1	-0.6	5.9		
AVERAGE OF GROUP	1.9	1.9	-12.2	11.2	10.1	14.9		

BOND AND MORTGAGE FUNDS

Fund	3 mo.	6 mo.	1 yr.	3 yr.	5 yr.	10 yr.	%	St.D.
AGF Excel Cdn Bond Fund	1.4	1.8	–	–	–	–	N/A	–
AGF Global Government Bd Fd	-6.3	-8.2	1.6	–	–	–	N/A	–
AMD Fixed Income Fd	1.6	1.6	8.3	9.2	–	–	74	1.98
All-Canadian Revenue Grwth Fnd	0.9	1.5	6.6	7.2	9.3	11.1	24	1.13
Allied Income Fund	0.0	-4.6	5.9	–	–	–	N/A	–
Altamira Income Fund	1.4	1.9	10.4	9.9	10.8	11.8	40	1.32
Bolton Tremblay Bond & Mtg	1.8	2.9	–	–	–	–	N/A	–
Bullock Bond Fund	0.8	0.5	6.1	6.4	7.9	–	64	1.90
CDA RSP Fixed Income Fund	1.5	1.5	8.2	10.1	11.1	11.3	46	1.54
Canadian Trusteed Income Fund	1.5	1.8	7.4	11.0	13.2	11.9	98	2.51
Cda Life Fixed Income S-19	1.4	1.4	6.9	9.3	10.8	10.4	54	1.71
Cdn Convertible Debenture Fd	2.7	3.4	1.3	–	–	–	N/A	–
Cdn Gen Life Ins Security B	1.2	1.8	3.4	7.2	10.6	12.1	56	1.72
Confed Dolphin Mortgage Fund	-0.2	0.7	8.8	9.2	10.7	11.6	10	0.73
Crown Life Pensions Bond Fund	2.8	3.3	9.3	9.5	8.2	8.1	70	1.97
Crown Life Pensions Mortgage	0.6	0.8	8.6	10.1	11.9	11.0	26	1.16
Dynamic Income Fund	1.7	2.4	6.6	9.6	11.7	–	44	1.51
Everest Bond Fund	0.7	1.4	10.8	–	–	–	N/A	–
Fd Des Prof Du Que-Bonds	0.9	1.1	5.9	10.1	11.3	11.9	42	1.37
Ficadre Obligations	1.1	1.9	7.9	8.7	–	–	28	1.20
Fiducie Pret Revenu Fonds H	1.2	0.7	8.5	10.6	11.4	12.1	34	1.26
First Canadian Mortgage Fund	0.1	1.2	9.2	10.0	11.3	11.5	16	0.79
First City Income Fund	2.6	2.3	6.5	–	–	–	N/A	–
Fonds Desjardins Hypotheques	0.3	1.2	9.5	9.8	10.8	11.4	12	0.74
Guardian Strategic Income	-1.0	-0.4	5.1	–	–	–	N/A	–
Hallmark Bond Fund	1.2	1.9	8.9	10.6	–	–	72	1.97
Hume Canadian Bond Fund	1.1	2.1	–	–	–	–	N/A	–
Industrial Income Fund	3.0	3.2	13.2	14.7	15.7	11.2	68	1.92
Investors Bond Fund	1.5	1.8	7.4	10.0	11.3	–	82	2.12
Investors Gr Tr Fixed Income	0.6	1.7	9.5	10.4	11.7	11.3	18	0.81
Investors Group Trust Bond	1.7	2.1	9.4	11.6	12.6	–	80	2.11
Investors Mortgage Fund	0.4	1.5	8.8	9.5	10.7	11.2	14	0.77
London Life Bond Fund	2.3	2.0	5.3	10.0	13.9	12.1	100	3.09
London Life Mortgage Fund	0.1	1.9	8.7	10.5	11.8	10.7	36	1.30
MER Heartland Bond Fund	1.3	1.8	9.0	–	–	–	N/A	–
MONY Bond Fund	2.6	2.4	4.9	–	–	–	N/A	–

Fund	3 mo.	6 mo.	1 yr.	3 yr.	5 yr.	10 yr.	%	St.D.
Mackenzie Mortgage & Income Fu	3.4	3.9	13.0	14.3	15.2	13.3	58	1.76
Metropolitan Bond Fund	0.7	1.7	-3.2	5.8	7.5	–	88	2.18
Metropolitan Variable-Bond	-2.7	-2.6	2.1	–	–	–	N/A	–
Montreal Trust Income Fund	0.4	0.7	6.6	11.1	11.2	10.1	66	1.90
Montreal Trust Mortgage Fund	0.3	1.4	8.9	9.3	10.4	10.9	6	0.62
Morgan Income Fund	1.1	1.5	7.1	10.0	–	–	32	1.25
Mtl Trust RRSP-Income Sectn	0.9	0.7	6.7	10.8	11.5	10.8	52	1.70
Mtl Trust RRSP-Mortgage Sectn	0.3	1.3	8.5	9.1	10.2	10.7	4	0.59
National Trust Income Fund	1.3	1.8	7.8	10.4	11.3	10.5	78	2.09
National Trust Pooled Bond & Pr	1.4	2.1	8.3	10.2	11.4	11.1	62	1.89
National Trust Pooled Mortgage	1.2	2.3	11.3	11.1	11.9	12.2	2	0.57
Ordre Ingenieurs Obligations	1.2	1.5	6.3	9.9	11.3	10.2	60	1.80
PH&N Bond Fund	1.4	2.2	9.5	12.4	13.0	11.2	90	2.20
Protected Bond Fund	1.3	2.1	7.2	–	–	–	N/A	–
Prudential Income Fund Canada	1.4	2.1	9.3	9.9	11.3	10.7	30	1.21
RoyFund Bond Fund	1.1	1.8	7.8	10.0	10.8	10.5	50	1.65
Royal Trust Adv Income Fd	2.2	2.1	3.1	–	–	–	N/A	–
Royal Trust Bond Fund	1.4	1.7	7.3	9.9	11.8	10.9	84	2.15
Royal Trust Mortgage Fund	0.0	1.1	9.1	9.7	10.9	11.4	8	0.73
Sceptre Bond Fund	0.9	1.0	8.5	–	–	–	N/A	–
Scotia Income Fund	1.5	1.4	6.9	–	–	–	N/A	–
Sentinel Cda Bond Fund	0.5	0.9	6.5	–	–	–	N/A	–
Spectrum Interest Fund	1.0	1.5	6.0	–	–	–	N/A	–
St-Laurent Placmt-Obligatns	1.2	1.6	–	–	–	–	N/A	–
St-Laurent Reer-Obligations	1.4	1.2	7.9	–	–	–	N/A	–
Talvest Income Fund	1.0	2.1	8.1	9.0	10.3	11.4	22	0.91
Trst Laurentienne Obligation	2.3	1.5	6.4	–	–	–	N/A	–
Trust General Bond Fund	1.5	1.5	7.3	10.0	12.5	11.2	92	2.30
Trust General Mortgage Fund	-0.1	1.3	7.9	9.9	11.7	11.2	20	0.88
United Mortgage	0.5	1.9	7.9	8.1	9.7	10.7	0	0.48
United Security Fund	0.8	1.8	5.2	9.4	10.7	9.5	48	1.58
Universal Svgs Income Fund	1.7	1.9	12.1	11.5	12.7	10.5	96	2.42
Viking Income Fund	1.2	1.7	7.7	10.4	12.1	9.9	76	2.08
Waltaine Income Fund	1.2	2.1	2.8	–	–	–	N/A	–
HIGHEST IN GROUP	3.4	3.9	13.2	14.7	15.7	13.3		
LOWEST IN GROUP	-6.3	-8.2	-3.2	5.8	7.5	8.1		
AVERAGE OF GROUP	1.0	1.4	7.4	10.0	11.3	11.1		

PREFERRED DIVIDEND FUNDS

Fund	3 mo.	6 mo.	1 yr.	3 yr.	5 yr.	10 yr.	%	St.D.
AGF Preferred Income Fund	0.5	1.7	3.6	7.1	–	–	N/A	1.15
AMD Dividend Fund	0.9	0.8	1.5	5.4	–	–	N/A	1.26
Allied Dividend Fund	1.0	1.1	0.5	–	–	–	N/A	–
Bolton Tremblay Income Fund	2.1	2.7	3.1	6.8	7.6	9.7	N/A	1.48
Bullock Dividend Fund	2.8	1.9	0.0	5.6	–	–	N/A	2.20

Fund	3 mo.	6 mo.	1 yr.	3 yr.	5 yr.	10 yr.	%	St.D.
Dynamic Dividend Fund	2.3	3.3	5.9	–	–	–	N/A	–
Guardian Pfd Dividend Fund	0.1	1.0	3.9	–	–	–	N/A	–
Investors Dividend Fund	3.3	3.9	3.6	7.7	9.7	11.6	N/A	2.03
Montreal Trust Dividend Fund	2.8	2.0	-4.7	–	–	–	N/A	–
Morgan Dividend Fund	2.9	2.7	-3.9	–	–	–	N/A	–
Mutual Dividend Fund	0.4	1.3	3.7	–	–	–	N/A	–
PH&N Dividend Income Fund	6.0	2.3	2.0	10.1	10.1	12.1	N/A	2.99
Prudential Dividend Fund	2.0	3.3	6.4	–	–	–	N/A	–
Royal Trust Preferred Fund	2.1	0.7	0.7	–	–	–	N/A	–
Spectrum Dividend Fund	2.5	2.7	3.4	–	–	–	N/A	–
Viking Dividend Fund Ltd	3.3	3.6	3.5	10.0	11.8	–	N/A	2.16
Waltaine Conv Preferred Fund	3.5	2.6	-5.0	–	–	–	N/A	–
HIGHEST IN GROUP	6.0	3.9	6.4	10.1	11.8	12.1		
LOWEST IN GROUP	0.1	0.7	-5.0	5.4	7.6	9.7		
AVERAGE OF GROUP	2.3	2.2	1.7	7.5	9.8	11.1		

MONEY MARKET FUNDS

Fund	3 mo.	6 mo.	1 yr.	3 yr.	5 yr.	10 yr.	%	St.D.
AGF Excel Money Market Fund	0.6	1.7	–	–	–	–	N/A	–
AGF Money Market Fund	0.7	2.0	8.4	8.5	9.1	11.3	N/A	0.09
AMD Canadian T-Bill Fund	0.7	2.1	–	–	–	–	N/A	–
AMD Money Market Fd	0.7	2.0	8.3	8.6	–	–	N/A	0.08
AMD US Dollar Money Mkt(US$)	0.5	1.5	6.2	–	–	–	N/A	–
Allied Money Fund	0.7	2.1	8.1	–	–	–	N/A	–
Bolton Tremblay Money Fund	0.7	2.1	8.7	8.8	9.3	–	N/A	0.09
CDA Money Market Fund	0.7	1.9	8.2	8.4	9.2	10.7	N/A	0.18
CMA Short-Term Deposit Fund	0.8	1.6	7.6	7.9	8.7	10.9	N/A	0.12
Cda Life Money Market S-29	0.7	1.8	7.3	7.0	8.0	10.5	N/A	0.17
Cdn Gen Life Ins Money Mkt C	0.6	1.8	7.2	–	–	–	N/A	–
Crown Life Pen Short Term	0.7	2.2	9.3	8.9	9.3	–	N/A	0.17
Dynamic Money Market Fund	0.7	2.0	8.0	8.1	–	–	N/A	0.11
Elliott & Page Money Fund	0.8	2.2	9.4	9.7	–	–	N/A	0.17
Everest Short Term Asset Fd	0.6	1.6	7.8	–	–	–	N/A	–
Ficadre Monetaire	0.6	1.8	7.0	7.8	–	–	N/A	0.21
Global Strategy World Money	-0.1	1.6	–	–	–	–	N/A	–
Guardian Short Term Money Fund	0.8	2.0	8.7	8.6	9.1	10.8	N/A	0.12
Guardian US Money Market Fd	0.5	1.6	–	–	–	–	N/A	–
Industrial Cash Management Fd	0.7	2.0	8.1	8.5	–	–	N/A	0.11
MER Money Market Fund	0.2	0.6	4.0	6.6	7.6	–	N/A	0.20
MONY T-Bill Fund	0.5	1.6	6.9	–	–	–	N/A	–
Montreal Trust Money Mkt fd	0.7	2.1	–	–	–	–	N/A	–
Mtl Trust RSP Money Market	0.7	2.1	–	–	–	–	N/A	–
Mutual Money Market Fund	0.6	1.8	7.7	7.5	–	–	N/A	0.13
NFM Intl Money Mkt & Income	0.3	-0.4	–	–	–	–	N/A	–
Ordre Ingenieurs Revenu Var	0.7	2.0	8.1	8.6	9.3	11.1	N/A	0.17
PH&N Money Market Fund	0.7	2.0	8.3	–	–	–	N/A	–
Prudential Money Market Fund	0.7	2.1	8.8	–	–	–	N/A	–
RoyFund Money Market Fd	0.6	1.9	7.8	–	–	–	N/A	–
Royal Trust Cdn MMF	0.7	1.9	–	–	–	–	N/A	–
Sceptre Money Market Fund	0.7	2.0	–	–	–	–	N/A	–

Fund	3 mo.	6 mo.	1 yr.	3 yr.	5 yr.	10 yr.	%	St.D.
Sentinel Cda Money Market Fd	0.7	2.2	9.7	–	–	–	N/A	–
Spectrum Cash Reserve Fund	0.7	1.9	8.0	–	–	–	N/A	–
Spectrum Savings Fund	0.7	1.9	–	–	–	–	N/A	–
St-Laurent Placmt-Monetaire	0.7	1.8	–	–	–	–	N/A	–
St-Laurent Reer-Epargne-Plus	0.7	1.5	8.3	–	–	–	N/A	–
Talvest Money Fund	0.8	2.4	9.5	–	–	–	N/A	–
Trimark Interest Fund	0.7	2.1	8.6	–	–	–	N/A	–
Trust General Money Market	0.1	1.0	11.2	–	–	–	N/A	–
United Cdn Money Market Fund	0.8	2.2	–	–	–	–	N/A	–
United US$ Money Market Fund	0.6	1.8	–	–	–	–	N/A	–
Universal Sector Currency Fd	0.2	0.8	–	–	–	–	N/A	–
Viking Money Market Fund	0.7	2.1	8.4	8.9	–	–	N/A	0.09
Waltaine Instant MMF	1.3	2.7	–	–	–	–	N/A	–
HIGHEST IN GROUP	1.3	2.7	11.2	9.7	9.3	11.3		
LOWEST IN GROUP	-0.1	-0.4	4.0	6.6	7.6	10.5		
AVERAGE OF GROUP	0.6	1.8	8.1	8.3	8.8	10.9		
MARKET INDICES								
91 Day Canada T Bill	0.7	2.2	8.7	8.6	9.3	11.1		0.10
Consumer Price Index	0.6	1.5	4.1	4.3	4.3	6.9		0.23
MYW Weighted 50 Mid-Term Index	1.3	1.8	8.6	11.0	12.7	–		2.25
Standard & Poor's 500 Index	2.8	4.7	-15.3	12.2	14.2	17.2		5.04
TSE Total Return Index	6.2	4.7	-5.2	11.5	10.5	16.0